T0306130

FORESTLAND INVESTMENT

Forestland investment has surged in the past few decades as a result of land ownership change in the forestry industry. Timberland investment and management organizations and real estate investment trusts have bought up land and resources that were divested by vertically integrated forest products companies. This book provides a seminal coverage of this seismic shift in the industry, exploring the philosophy, driving factors, valuation, theory, research, implementation, practice, and effects of forestland investment. Across 15 chapters the book reviews the history of forestland investment; discusses the optimal forest rotation; explains timberland appraisal; examines the return drivers of forestland; analyzes timberland index construction methods and results; prices timberland assets; reviews financial and real options; investigates real option values in forestland management; evaluates timber harvest contracts; examines new opportunities in the emerging woody bioenergy market; and eventually offers prospects on forestland investment in the future. It also discusses how forest carbon can be used as a nature-based climate solution. This book is essential reading for forestry business students and scholars, as well as practitioners and policymakers in the industry.

Bin Mei is Professor of the Practice in Natural Resource Finance at Duke University, Durham, NC, where he teaches and conducts research in the area of natural resource investment and nature-based climate solutions. Prior to that, he was Hargreaves Professor of Forest Finance at the University of Georgia, Athens, GA. He is editor of the *Journal of Forest Business Research* and associate editor of the *Canadian Journal of Forest Research*.

Michael L. Clutter was Chief Analytics Officer at F&W Forestry, Albany, GA. In addition to his many years of experience in the forestry industry, Michael used to be the Dean and Hargreaves Distinguished Professor of Forest Finance at the University of Georgia's Warnell School of Forestry and Natural Resources. He passed away unexpectedly on December 24, 2022.

FORESTLAND INVESTMENT

Valuation and Analysis

Bin Mei and Michael L. Clutter

Routledge
Taylor & Francis Group

LONDON AND NEW YORK

First published 2023
by Routledge
4 Park Square, Milton Park, Abingdon, Oxon OX14 4RN

and by Routledge
605 Third Avenue, New York, NY 10158

Routledge is an imprint of the Taylor & Francis Group, an informa business

British Library Cataloguing-in-Publication Data
A catalogue record for this book is available from the British Library

ISBN: 978-1-032-43310-3 (hbk)
ISBN: 978-1-032-43309-7 (pbk)
ISBN: 978-1-003-36673-7 (ebk)

DOI: 10.4324/9781003366737

Typeset in Bembo
by Deanta Global Publishing Services, Chennai, India

CONTENTS

FIGURES

TABLES

BOXES

PREFACE

Over the past two decades, the authors of this book have been teaching (or used to teach) graduate-level Timberland Accounting and Taxation, and Forest Finance Decision Making classes at the University of Georgia. For these two classes, we used a variety of different sources, such as journal papers, USDA technical reports, and book chapters, for the lack of a textbook in this field. Over time, we have accumulated enough materials in this niche area and feel that they could be put together into a book. Here it comes. The book covers a number of topics pertinent to forestland investment in the United States, including timberland accounting and taxation, timberland appraisals, timberland investment return indices, portfolio diversification potential of timberland asset, option values embedded in timberland management, valuation of timberland transactions, and forest carbon.

Whenever possible, we use case studies, which can be easily adapted to real-world practices. We hope that this book can help you comprehend timberland as an asset class and that topics covered here can assist your career development.

All errors remain our own.

ACKNOWLEDGMENT

The authors thank Dr. David Newman at the State University of New York College of Environmental Science and Forestry and Dr. Fred Cubbage at North Carolina State University for their valuable comments on the early draft of the book.

1

INTRODUCTION TO FORESTLAND INVESTMENT

Highlights

- The United States, in particular the southern region of the country, has rich forest resources and active timber markets.
- Timberland ownership has shifted from vertically integrated forest products companies to timberland investment management organizations (TIMOs) (on behalf of investors) and real estate investment trusts (REITs).
- Double taxation and undervaluation of timberland under the US generally accepted accounting principles, among others, are the major drivers of the ownership change.
- Many consolidations in the timber industry have taken place. In additional to TIMOs and REITs, there are joint ventures between REITs and investors.
- Topics covered in the book are reviewed.

Timber and wood products markets

The United States has abundant forestland resources. About one-third of the county's land area, or 751 million acres, consists of forestlands. Among them, 514 million acres with an estimated market value of $460 billion are considered as commercial timberlands, which are mainly used to produce timber (Newell and Eves 2009; Smith et al. 2009). Of all timberlands, about 360 million acres are privately held (Mendell 2015). The United States is also one of the most productive countries in forest resources in the planet. The US share of global wood products output ranged from 17% to 28% over the period 1998–2013 (FAO 2021; Prestemon et al. 2015). The contribution of the forest sector to the national economy often

DOI: 10.4324/9781003366737-1

goes beyond itself and extends to many other sectors of the economy through indirect and induced effects (Li et al. 2019).

The US South, in particular, holds about 41% of the US timberland and is the world's largest wood producer (Brandeis and Hodges 2015). Timber production of the 13 southern states remained around 60% of the US total or 10% of the world's total in recent years (Brandeis and Hodges 2015; Prestemon et al. 2015). The total contribution of the forest sector to the South's gross regional product reached nearly 2% in 2011 (Brandeis and Hodges 2015). About 90% of southern timberland is privately owned, and pine plantations cover 33% of the total 205 million areas of timberland in the region (Hartsell and Conner 2013). Regarding the output, pine (softwood) products represent more than 60% of the total harvest (Wear et al. 2007). In summary, the forest industry is a significant contributor to the whole economy, especially in the US South.

Shift of timberland ownership

In the early twentieth century, most industrial timberlands in the United States were owned by vertically integrated forest products companies with both timberland holdings and manufacturing facilities (Table 1.1). By vertical integration, forest products companies acquire the ability to ensure a certain portion of internal timber supply, thus alleviating their dependence on the open markets for timber, the crucial raw material for manufacturing. However, in the past several decades, forest products firms have been divesting their timberlands and outsourcing the business of growing and harvesting timber.

Drivers for the shift of timberland ownership can be summarized as follows: (1) shift in production from diversification to specialization to exploit the "returns to scale" rather than "returns to scope"; (2) reduced insurance value of timberland due to expanding and reliable timber supplies; (3) fall in raw material costs caused by new technologies; (4) worldwide centrifugal force on manufacturing based on comparative advantages resulting from globalization; (5) double taxation for forest products companies structured as "C-Corps" (Box 1.1); (6) significant

TABLE 1.1 Top forest industry timberland owners in the early 2000s

Forestry company	Million acres
International Paper	11.7
Plum Creek	7.9
Weyerhaeuser	5.9
Temple-Inland	2.2
Boise Cascade	2.0
Mead	2.0
Rayonier	2.0
Bowater	1.8

Note: Data come from companies' websites and/or 10-K filings.

undervaluation of timberland assets under the generally accepted accounting principles (GAAP), where book values reflect historical acquisition costs rather than current fair market values; and (7) competing demand from timberland investment management organizations (TIMOs) and real estate investment trusts (REITs) (Mei 2019; Wear et al. 2007). Moreover, recent unprecedented mergers and acquisitions in the forest products industry (Mei and Sun 2008) have left substantial amounts of debt on the acquirers' balance sheets. As a value adding strategy, these acquirers liquidated their undervalued timberland assets and used the proceeds to lower their debt levels (Mei et al. 2009). As a consequence of the interaction of these forces, timberland business has been separated into a new segment.

BOX 1.1 TAXES ON C-CORPS VS. REITS

Suppose a timber company has realized $100 million of taxable income (or earnings before taxes) from timberland sales in one year. Under the C-Corp structure, the timber company has to pay 40% income tax, or $40 million, at the corporate level first. Then, if the timber company decides to use the rest $60 million to pay out dividends to its shareholders, shareholders have to pay income tax again at the individual level. Assuming an average of 20% capital gain tax rate for shareholders, on an after-tax basis, $100 million of income ends up at $100 \times (1 - 0.4) \times (1 - 0.2) = $48 million at the shareholder's level.

In contrast, under the REIT structure, the timber company has to distribute at least 90% of income at the corporate level directly to shareholders. If the timber company distributes 100% income to shareholders, then shareholders only have to pay income tax once, or $20 million, at the individual level. With the same 20% capital gain tax rate for shareholders, on an after-tax basis, $100 million of income ends up at $100 \times (1 - 0.2) = $80 million at the shareholder's level. Therefore, a REIT is more tax efficient than a C-Corp from the shareholder's perspective. This is particularly true when timberland properties have been held for a long time period, which is generally the case in the timberland sector, with the fair market value upon sales far exceeding the cost basis under the US GAAP.

While forest products companies have been the primary sellers of timberlands, institutional timberland investors have been unprecedentedly active buyers over the past 30 years. According to a recent survey on top corporate and public pension funds, endowments, and foundations, institutional commitments to the US timberland assets have increased tenfold since the early 1990s, and the growth in such investments remains strong with pension funds, endowments, and foundations being the most common form of institutional investors (Corriero et al. 2003). One major motivation in timberland investments dates back to the implementation of the Employee Retirement Income Security Act (ERISA) in 1974, which required pension fund managers to diversify into non-financial assets to minimize the risk of large losses. Thereafter, institutional investors began to consider a wide range of assets, including timberland (e.g., Binkley et al. 1996; Conroy and Miles 1989). During the same time period, several forest products firms chose to focus on timberland investment and elected to be REITs for favorable tax treatment (Baral and Mei 2022). Since REITs are required to maintain a dividend payout ratio of at least 90%, income tax at the corporate level is virtually eliminated.

As a result of the interaction between timberland sellers and buyers, over 40 million acres of timberland nationwide have changed hands in the past decade, more than 70% of which were transacted in the South (Clutter et al. 2005). Since this first foray into timberland as an alternative asset class, institutional timberland investors have developed rapidly. At the end of the 1980s, timberland assets managed by TIMOs totaled only $1 billion; in recent years, this number exceeded $40 billion (Hood et al. 2015; Zinkhan 2008). In addition, public timber REITs controlled another $35 billion of timberlands.

In the first few chapters of his book, Zhang (2021) presents a most complete history and economics of industrial and especially institutional timberland investment. It is through corporate annual reports and many interviews conducted with key players in the timber sector in the past decade that makes the work possible. Each story is unique in certain aspects and collectively they paint a clear picture of the motivation, synergy, corporate strategy, competition, financing structure, organizational arrangement, and broad impact of industrial and institutional timberland investments in the forest sector. We do not intend to repeat those anecdotes but interested readers can refer to that book and the literature therein.

Timberland investment vehicles

Prior to the 1980s, timberlands were mostly investments of farmers and large vertically integrated forest products companies, which were perceived as not actively involved in timber management (Zinkhan and Cubbage 2003). Since the early 1980s when institutional investors initially expressed their interests in timberlands, forest products firms have responded by restructuring their business segments and securitizing the illiquid timberland assets. For instance, International Paper established a master limited partnership (MLP), i.e., The IP Timberlands, Georgia-Pacific created letter stocks for its timberland assets,[1] i.e., The Timber Co., and Plum Creek (PCL) converted itself from a MLP to a REIT to retain institutional investors of The Timber Co. after it was sold to PCL. In addition, securitizations of timberland assets lowered the entry barrier and enhanced liquidity by allowing individual investors to get into the business with only a modest allocation of capital.

In 2015, Plum Creek partnered with some institutional investors and created a new investment vehicle, a long-term joint venture. The deal is known as "Twin Creeks," where Plum Creek manages day-to-day timberland operations and Silver Creek Capital Management serves as fiduciary. The initial equity of $560 million consisted of 25% of Plum Creek's timberland contribution and 75% of investor's cash (to buy Plum Creek's timberland). Twin Creeks started with 260,000 acres of southern timberland valued at $2,150 per acre with expectations to grow to $1 billion in value through acquisitions. In 2020, CatchMark formed the $1.3 billion TexMark Timber Treasury (Triple T) joint venture with several other private equity investors. However, it ended up as a failure with a huge loss in three years between 2018 and 2021 (Box 1.2).

BOX 1.2 CATCHMARK AND THE TRIPLE T JOINT VENTURE

CatchMark is a small timber REIT with a market cap of $500 million that focuses on timberland investment mainly in the US South. In 2018, CatchMark formed a five-year (extendable to seven to ten years contingent upon specific approvals) joint venture with some other investors in purchasing 1.1 million acres of timberland in east Texas with a price of about $1.4 billion, or $1,264 per acre. Within Triple T, CatchMark was the general manager as well as a co-investor with $200 contribution. The co-investment realigned the interests between the manager and the investors, and thus alleviated the agency problem. Other sources of funds include $726 million preferred equity from BTG Pactual Timberland Investment Group, Highland Capital Management, Medley Management, and British Columbia Investment Management Corporation, and $600 million debt.

As the general manager, CatchMark charges about $11 million management fee annually, whereas Triple T pays out 10.25% – 12.25% preferred dividends plus a complete return of preferred equity contribution before any distribution to CatchMark's common equity stake. The joint venture has several problems. First, the timberland acquired was harvested extensively by the previous owner and the property was under buyer-friendly wood supply agreements. All of these limited the profitability from timber in the short to medium run. Second, sales for higher and better uses were not as expected by CatchMark, which dampened the returns. Third, CatchMark had already been highly leveraged with a debt ratio of 60% beforehand. The debt ratio further increased to over 70% after the establishment of the joint venture. The obligations from the substantial amount of debt had been a significant use of free cash flows. Finally, the preferred dividend yield is way higher than the prevailing interest rate of 3%–4% at that time, implying an inferior capital structure and a higher weighted average cost of capital than its peers.

By the hypothetical liquidation at book value method, CatchMark would have realized a loss of about $200 million (or its entire investment in the joint venture) between 2018 and 2020, if CatchMark had sold the property. On January 21, 2020, Jerry Barag stepped down as the chief executive officer after about six and a half years in the role. In July 2021, the joint venture sold 0.3 million acres, or about one-third of its land base, for $497 million, or $1,656 per acre, after amending the wood supply agreement with Georgia-Pacific. The proceeds were used to reduce debt and pay out preferred dividend. However, due to the distribution waterfall of the joint venture, CartchMark did not receive a penny from the transaction despite an appreciation of 31.0% per acre and a total gain of $78.8 million.

Data source: CatchMark's website and/or its 10-K filings.

Although restructuring activities like MLPs and letter stocks once generated positive reaction by the financial markets, these kinds of timberland investment entities proved to be short-lived (Zinkhan et al. 1992). The fate of joint ventures remains to be seen. In contrast, TIMOs and REITs have gradually gained popularity in timberland investment, especially in large-scale transactions. TIMOs do not own timberlands but manage them on behalf of investors. In particular, a separate account is used if there is one major investor in a single portfolio, whereas a pooled fund allows multiple investors to participate in a relatively large, diversified portfolio of timberlands. Compared to public-equity timberland investment, private placement has higher requirements of minimum capital commitments ($50–$75 million for a separate account and $1 million for a comingled fund), but less pressure from dividend payouts. Also, securitizations have introduced systematic risk into public-equity timberland assets.

As of 2021, there were more than 30 TIMOs and four public timber REITs (Table 1.2). Major TIMOs included Manulife Investment Management (previously known as Hancock Timber Resource Group), The Forestland Group, Resource Management Service, Forest Investment Associates, Molpus Woodlands Group, Lyme Timber, BTG Pactual, Campbell Global, Wagner Forest Management, Rohatyn Group, and Timberland Investment Resources. The four public timber REITs are Weyerhaeuser (WY), Rayonier (RYN), PotlachDeltic (PCH), and CatchMark (CTT). Together, TIMOs and timber REITs accounted for more than 60% of the investable timberland universe in the United States, or about 12% of private US timberlands (TMS 2022). There are some other types of timberland ownership that are of significant sizes, including family-owned forest products companies (e.g., Sierra Pacific Industries, 2.3 million acres; Green Diamond Resource Company, 2.2 million acres; and Roseburg Forest Products, 0.6 million acres), privately held conglomerate companies (e.g., J.D. Irving, 1.3 million acres;

TABLE 1.2. Private- and public-equity timberland market of 2022

TIMOs (private equity)	Million acres	REITs (public equity)	Million acres
Manulife Investment Management	3.6	Weyerhaeuser	11.0
The Forestland Group	2.3	Rayonier	2.3
Resource Management Service	2.3	PotlachDeltic	1.8
Forest Investment Associates	2.0	CatchMark	0.4
Molpus Woodlands Group	1.7		
Lyme Timber	1.5		
BTG Pactual	1.5		
Campbell Global	1.2		
Wagner Forest Management	1.0		
Rohatyn Group	0.9		
Timberland Investment Resources	0.8		

Note: TIMOs for timberland investment management organizations and REITs for real estate investment trusts. Manulife Investment Management used to be Hancock Timber Resource Group. Campbell Global was acquired by JP Morgan Asset Management in 2021. CatchMark will be acquired by PotlachDeltic in the second half of 2022. Data source: Companies websites and/or 10-K filings.

and J.M. Huber, 0.8 million acres), and private owners (e.g., Seven Islands Land Company, 0.8 million acres; and Four Rivers Land & Timber, 0.6 million acres).

In recent years, the US timberland market has been reshuffled considerably. Hancock Timberland Resource Group and Molpus Woodlands Group bought Forest Capital Partners in 2012, BTG Pactual acquired RMK Timberland in 2013, Wells Timberland REIT went public as CTT in 2014, Weyerhaeuser acquired Plum Creek in 2016, Rayonier acquired Pope Resources in 2020, Potlach acquired Deltic Timber in 2021, and PotatchDeltic will complete the acquisition of CatchMark in the second half of 2022.[2] Looking forward, consolidation waves in the timber industry will continue. Mergers and acquisitions are expected, joint ventures between public timber REITs and institutional investors may increase, initial public offerings of TIMOs may be possible, and direct ownership may surge in its share.

Topics covered in the book

We will start with the Faustmann rotation (Faustmann 1995) in Chapter 2. The rotation decision is crucial in timberland investment and management. The optimal rotation is the one that maximizes the net present value from a stand of trees. It is directly linked to the income approach in timberland appraisals, and the Faustmann framework is extendable to include ecosystem services into the decision-making. Thus, a sound understanding of the Faustmann model not only helps investors project future returns, but also facilitates the government to design forest-related policies and laws. In Chapter 3, we discuss timberland appraisals. Given the illiquid nature of timberland assets, appraisals must be used to assign a value to a property. In addition to the income approach, the comparable sales approach and the cost approach are also widely used. We will illustrate how these approaches work in complement to each other through an example redacted from a real-world case.

In Chapter 4, we examine the return drivers of timberland investment via a southern pine plantation. The interactions among timber price change, biological growth, and land value appreciation are broken down into percentage contributions to the total investment returns. This analysis can help us recognize the unique features of timberland assets. In Chapter 5, we explain property and income taxes of timberland, which are an important part of the business. Annual property tax is based on assessed (appraised) values, where landowners often face biased values toward higher and better uses (e.g., residential or commercial development). This often creates a cash flow burden on landowners. However, there are many incentive programs that can effectively reduce property tax if the land is primarily in forest uses. For federal income tax, timber depletion is a critical concept. In general, depletion is a cost recovery method applied to natural resources. For timber depletion, it requires the establishment of three accounts (i.e., land, merchantable timber, and pre-merchantable timber) at the time of the acquisition and a dynamic bookkeeping thereafter. We show how depletion works using a fully regulated forest as an example.

In Chapter 6, we introduce the mean-variance efficient portfolio theory and some asset pricing models. This is to prepare readers for their applications to timberland assets in the following two chapters. Those who have a background in financial management can skim over or even skip this chapter. In Chapter 7, we describe different methods in constructing timberland indices and then compare the results. Here, we differentiate between private- and public-equity timberland investments by considering appraisal smoothing, liquidity, financial leverage, non-timber business segments, and geographic locations, and we illustrate how to control for these differences to make apples-to-apples comparison. In Chapter 8, we provide a review of financial analyses of timberland assets, summarize some common themes, and offer an outlook of future research in this niche.

In Chapter 9, we present the fundamentals of financial and real options. Again, readers with the relevant background can skim over or skip this chapter. In Chapter 10, we examine various embedded real options in timberland management. For example, mature trees can be easily stored on the stump with some trivial cost when timber price is low; after a clear cut, a landowner can delay the regeneration or choose genetically improved seedlings for the next cycle. All such managerial flexibilities should be considered in the evaluation of a timberland investment opportunity. In Chapter 11, we apply the option pricing models to timber harvest contracts. After divesting their timberlands, forest products companies like International Paper and Georgia-Pacific often negotiate timber harvest contracts with landowners, TIMOs, and REITs. This type of contract is often off the balance sheet, albeit their values can be significant and need to be mutually understood by both parties involved.

Forests not only provide fiber and fuel for humans, but also fix the majority of the total terrestrial carbon. In Chapter 12, we investigate the benefit and cost of forest carbon using a hypothetical southern pine plantation in the state of Georgia. Specifically, we study how carbon additionality can be achieved and at what price. In Chapter 13, we further examine the economic feasibility of co-firing wood pellets with coal in reducing CO_2 emission. Facing the price uncertainty, the fuel adoption decision is inspected by a regime-switching model under the real options framework. In Chapter 14, we do a case study on the merger between the largest two timber REITs, Weyerhaeuser and Plum Creek, in 2015. We use both the comparable company analysis and the discounted cash flow approach on the target company to derive its value range. Then we make some comments on the merger and its impact on the timber industry.

Questions

1. Why did vertically integrated forestry companies divest their timberlands?
2. List some pros and cons of joint ventures between public timber REITs and investors.

Notes

1 Letter stocks are not registered with the Securities and Exchange Commission (SEC), and hence they cannot be sold publicly in the marketplace. Letter stocks are sold directly by the issuer to the investor.
2 Prior to the merger, Plum Creek was a public timber REIT with 6.6 million acres of timberland; Pope Resources is a public timber company structured as a limited partnership with 0.2 million acres of timberland; and Deltic Timber is a public timber company structured as a C-Corp with 0.5 million acres of timberland.

Bibliography

Baral, S., and B. Mei. 2022. Development and performance of timber REITs in the United States: A review and some prospects. *Can. J. For. Res.* 52(1):1–10.

Binkley, C.S., C.F. Raper, and C.L. Washburn. 1996. Institutional ownership of US timberland: History, rationale, and implications for forest management. *J. For.* 94(9):21–28.

Brandeis, C., and D.G. Hodges. 2015. Forest sector and primary forest products industry contributions to the economies of the Southern states: 2011 update. *J. For.* 113(2):205–209.

Clutter, M.L., B. Mendell, D. Newman, D. Wear, and J. Greis. 2005. Strategic factors driving timberland ownership changes in the US South. *U.S. For. Serv.* Southern Research Station, Research Triangle Park, NC. 15.

Conroy, R., and M. Miles. 1989. Commercial forestland in the pension portfolio: The biological beta. *Financ. Anal. J.* 45(5):46–54.

Healey, T., T. Corriero, and R. Rosenov. 2005. Timber as an institutional investment. *J. Altern. Invest.* 8(3):60-74.

FAO. 2021. *FAO yearbook of forest products*. Food and Agriculture Organization of the United Nations, Rome.

Faustmann, M. 1995. Calculation of the value of which forest land and immature stands possess for forestry (Orriginally published in German Journal of Forest Research in 1849). *J. For. Econ.* 1(1):7–44.

Hartsell, A.J., and R.C. Conner. 2013. Forest area and conditions: A 2010 update of chapter 16 of the southern forest resource assessment. *Gen. Tech. Rep. SRS-174*:32.

Hood, H.B., T. Harris, J. Siry, S. Baldwin, and J. Smith. 2015. *US timberland markets: Transactions, values & market research 2000 to mid-2015*. Timber Mart-South, Athens, GA, 411p.

Li, Y., B. Mei, and T. Linhares-Juvenal. 2019. The economic contribution of the world's forest sector. *For. Policy Econ.* 100:236–253.

Mei, B. 2019. Timberland investments in the United States: A review and prospects. *For. Policy Econ.* 109:1–7.

Mei, B., A.J. Cascio, C. Sun, and M.L. Clutter. 2009. Mergers and acquisitions in the U.S. forest products industry: Motives, financing, and impacts. In *Joint ventures, mergers and acquisitions, and capital flow*, Tobin, J.B., and L.R. Parker (eds.), Nova Science Publishers, Inc., Hauppauge, NY, 143–168.

Mei, B., and C. Sun. 2008. Event analysis of the impact of mergers and acquisitions on the financial performance of the U.S. forest products industry. *For. Policy Econ.* 10(5):286–294.

Mendell, B. 2015. *Splashing in the bathtub: Putting the proposed merger of Plum Creek and Weyerhaeuser into context*. Forisk Consulting.

Newell, G., and C. Eves. 2009. The role of US timberland in real estate portfolios. *J. Real Estate Port. Manag.* 15(1):95–106.

Prestemon, J.P., D.N. Wear, and M.O. Foster. 2015. The global position of the U.S. forest products industry. *Tech. Rep. SRS-204*:24.

Smith, W.B., P.D. Miles, C.H. Perry, and S.A. Pugh. 2009. Forest resources of the United States 2007: A technical document supporting the Forest Service 2010 RPA assessment. *U.S. For. Serv. Gen. Tech. Rep. WO-78*:349.

TMS. 2022. *Timber mart-south market news quarterly*. TimberMart-South, Athens, GA.

Wear, D.N., D.R. Carter, and J. Prestemon. 2007. The US South's timber sector in 2005: A prospective analysis of recent change. *Gen. Tech. Rep. SRS-99*:30.

Zhang, D. 2021. *From backwoods to boardrooms: The rise of insititutional investment in Timberland*. Oregon State University Press, Corvallis, OR.

Zinkhan, F.C. 2008. History of modern timberland investments. In *International forest investment: An executive education conference*. Center for Forest Business, Athens, GA, Munich, Germany, 1–19.

Zinkhan, F.C., and F.W. Cubbage. 2003. Financial analysis of timber investments. In *Forests in a market economy*, Sills, E.O., and K.L. Abt (eds.), Kluwer Academic Publishers, Dordrecht, 77–95.

Zinkhan, F.C., W.R. Sizemore, G.H. Mason, and T.J. Ebner. 1992. *Timberland investments: A portfolio perspective*. Timber Press, Portland, OR, 208p.

2

OPTIMAL FOREST ROTATION

Highlights

- Capital budgeting techniques can be used to identify the optimal forest rotation.
- The Faustmann rotation occurs when the expected marginal revenue from delaying harvest for a year equals the marginal cost defined as investing the proceeds from an immediate sell of the standing timber and the land at the hurdle rate for a year.
- Silvicultural treatments and choices can be evaluated by the traditional capital budgeting methods but based on incremental cash flows.
- The Faustmann framework can be adapted to analyze uneven-aged forest management.
- The optimal rotation is directly linked to the income approach in timberland appraisals.
- An illustration on how to use the optimal rotation on the valuation of pre-merchantable timber is shown at the end of the chapter.

Forest investment involves long-term engagement. In the US South, a typical rotation length for a southern pine plantation ranges from 20 to 30 years, whereas in other regions of the country the rotation length for hardwood species may exceed 100 years. During such a long time horizon, economic conditions may change dramatically, making the evaluation of forestry projects a challenging task. In addition, silvicultural technologies and forest management techniques have developed rapidly in the past several decades. Whether to adopt and how to evaluate these forestry advancements from a landowner's standpoint remains a key concern. In this chapter, we review and apply a number of capital budgeting techniques to forest management problems.

DOI: 10.4324/9781003366737-2

A brief review of capital budgeting

In finance, we emphasize the time value of money. That is, $1 today is different from $1 tomorrow because one can either invest it for a future return or consume it for some current utility. The expected rate of return is a measure of the opportunity cost and known as cost of capital, required rate of return, hurdle rate, interest rate, or discount rate.[1] When evaluating investment opportunities, we need to lay out all the cash flows along the time line and then do discounting or compounding to make cash flows occurring at different times comparable. In capital budgeting, the rule of thumb is to discount all benefits (cash inflows) and costs (cash outflows) back to the present (year zero) and then sum them up. The result is called the net present value (NPV) and the technique is known as the discounted cash flow (DCF). All projects with positive NPVs are wealth enhancing and should be accepted.

In addition to the NPV, there are some other criteria that are widely used in practice. The first one is the internal rate of return (IRR). By definition, the IRR is the discount rate that makes the NPV zero. Whenever a project has an IRR higher than the hurdle rate, it implies a positive NPV and the project should be accepted. The second one is the benefit-cost ratio, which is defined as the present value of all future benefits over that of all costs. A benefit-cost ratio larger than one is equivalent to an NPV greater than zero or an IRR greater than the hurdle rate, and, therefore, a project with a benefit-cost ratio higher than one should be accepted.[2] The third one is the payback period, or the amount of time needed for future cash inflows to cover the initial investment cost. The shorter the payback period, the higher the profitability or the lower the risk of the project. The same as the benefit-cost ratio, both discounted and non-discount cash flows are used in the calculation in the real world, although the one with discounting is preferred.

Optimal harvest decision for a single rotation

Suppose that a landowner has some bare land, wants to plant trees on it today, and expects some revenue in the future. Denote C as the total initial site establishment cost, R as total future timber revenues from the final harvest, and T as the harvest year, the cash flows along the timeline for a single rotation are shown in Figure 2.1.

With a discount rate r, the profit function $\pi(T)$, i.e., the NPV, from this investment can be calculated as

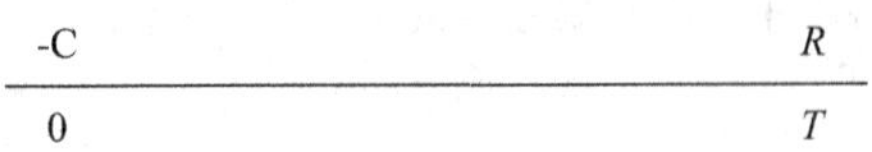

FIGURE 2.1 Cash flows with the timeline for a single rotation

$$\pi(T) = \frac{R}{(1+r)^T} - C. \tag{2.1}$$

The revenue has two contributors: One is yield from tree growth, $G(T)$, which is a function of age T, and the other is stumpage price P the landowner receives. That is, $R = G(T) \cdot P$. If we do the substitution and express the NPV using continuous-time compounding (i.e., e^{-rT} replaces $(1+r)^{-T}$ as the discounting factor), then Equation 2.1 can be rewritten as

$$\pi(T) = G(T) \cdot P \cdot e^{-rT} - C. \tag{2.2}$$

The landowner's harvest problem can be formally stated as to maximize the NPV by choosing the optimal cut time, which can be found in any classic forest economics textbook (e.g., Amacher et al. 2009; Klemperer et al. 2022; Wagner 2011; Zhang and Pearse 2011):

$$\max_{T} \ \pi(T) = G(T) \cdot P \cdot e^{-rT} - C. \tag{2.3}$$

This is very similar to the production problem in microeconomics except that revenue and cost occur at different times. For a maximum to exist, the first order derivative of the objective function with respect to the decision variable should be zero and the second order derivative should be negative.

The first order condition for this maximization problem is[3]

$$\frac{d\pi(T)}{dT} = 0. \tag{2.4}$$

Using the chain rule in calculus, Equation 2.4 is equivalent to

$$G'(T) \cdot P \cdot e^{-rT} - r \cdot G(T) \cdot P \cdot e^{-rT} = 0 \tag{2.5}$$

where $G'(T) = dG(T)/dT$. Term e^{-rT} is positive and can be cancelled out. Moving the second term to the right side of Equation 2.4, we can get

$$G'(T) \cdot P = r \cdot G(T) \cdot P. \tag{2.6}$$

The left side of Equation 2.6 indicates marginal value of growth (marginal revenue) and right side indicates the opportunity cost (marginal cost) as measured by interest on timber proceeds one forgoes by delaying harvest for one more time period. Therefore, over time, the landowner has to compare marginal revenue with marginal cost. Whenever marginal revenue is larger than marginal cost, he should wait because the total profit is expected to grow. In contrast, if marginal revenue is less than marginal cost, he should have already harvested the trees because the total profit is expected to decline. It is only when marginal revenue equals marginal cost that the NPV is maximized.

If price is constant in the short run, P can be cancelled out in Equation 2.6. Dividing both sides by $G(T)$ leads to

$$\frac{G'(T)}{G(T)} = r \tag{2.7}$$

where the left side measures instant tree growth rate and the right side is the required rate of return. Equation 2.7 means that when the growth rate is higher than the hurdle rate, the landowner should let the trees grow to realize the higher gain, whereas when growth rate falls below the hurdle rate, he should cut the trees right now and invest the proceeds to get a better return. Another conclusion that can be drawn from the first order condition is that the initial planting cost is sunk and does not affect the optimal harvest decision for a single rotation.

BOX 2.1 A NUMERICAL EXAMPLE OF THE OPTIMAL HARVEST RULE

Suppose the current stand has a value of $2,000 per acre. Over a year, the stand value is expected to grow to $2,150 per acre. Given a hurdle rate is 6%, the best decision is to wait for another year because the marginal revenue, 2,150 – 2,000 = $150, outweighs the marginal cost, 2,000 × 6% = $120. If the hurdle rate is higher at 8%, then the marginal cost will be 2,000 × 8% = $160, which is higher than the marginal revenue of $150. Hence, the best decision is to harvest the trees right now.

Alternatively, we could use percentage growth rate and compare it with the hurdle rate. In the first scenario, the expected growth rate is 150 / 2000 = 7.5%, which is higher than the hurdle rate of 6%, so we should wait; in the second scenario, the expected growth rate of 7.5% is lower than the hurdle rate of 8%, so we should harvest.

Faustmann model

Consider a case where the best use for the landowner's land is timber production, and he will replant the site immediately after the clear cut with the goal of maximizing the profit. The cash flows along with the timeline are shown in Figure 2.2. The NPV for this infinite number of rotations defines the land expectation value

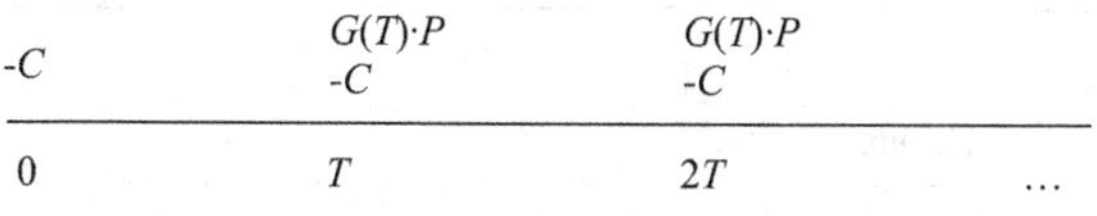

-C	$G(T){\cdot}P$ -C	$G(T){\cdot}P$ -C	
0	T	$2T$	...

FIGURE 2.2   Cash flows with the timeline for multiple rotations

(LEV), an important concept in forestry. LEV is also known as bare land value or soil expectation value and can be calculated as

$$LEV = \frac{G(T) \cdot P \cdot e^{-rT} - C}{1 - e^{-rT}}. \tag{2.8}$$

The landowner's harvest problem can be formally described as to maximize LEV by choosing the optimal rotation length:

$$\max_{T} LEV(T) = \frac{G(T) \cdot P \cdot e^{-rT} - C}{1 - e^{-rT}}. \tag{2.9}$$

The first order condition for this maximization problem can be expressed as

$$G'(T) \cdot P = r \cdot G(T) \cdot P + r \left[\frac{G(T) \cdot P \cdot e^{-rT} - C}{1 - e^{-rT}} \right] \tag{2.10}$$

or

$$G'(T) \cdot P = r \cdot G(T) \cdot P + r \cdot LEV. \tag{2.11}$$

Compared with Equation 2.6, the only difference is the extra term $r \cdot LEV$ on the right side, which indicates land rent. In other words, marginal cost has another component that measures opportunity cost from future rotations after the first one. This optimal harvest rule is called the Faustmann rotation (Faustmann 1995). It defines the optimal rotation as the time when marginal value of growth (marginal revenue) equals the rent on standing timber and bare dirt (marginal cost).

A Faustmann rotation example is shown in Table 2.1. The growth and yield data are projected for a southern pine plantation in southern Georgia. Key economic variables include a discount rate of 6%, a planting cost $180/acre, and stumpage prices of $10/ton for pulpwood, $16/ton for chip-n-saw, and $32 for sawtimber, all in real terms. At age 18, the expected marginal gain from holding for another year is $(74.6 - 74.4) \times 10 + (42.8 - 36.4) \times 16 + (1.3 - 0.7) \times 32 =$

TABLE 2.1 Optimal rotation for a southern pine plantation

	Yield (tons/acre)				Marginal	Marginal
Age	Pulpwood	Chip-n-saw	Sawtimber	LEV	revenue	cost
18	74.4	36.4	0.7	450.31	123.60	107.95
19	74.6	42.8	1.3	458.03	121.20	115.83
20	74.4	49.1	2.0	460.47	127.40	123.24
21	73.7	55.3	3.1	462.20	130.20	130.99
22	72.8	61.2	4.5	461.90	129.40	138.79
23	71.5	66.7	6.2	458.57	136.40	146.35
24	70.1	71.7	8.4	455.30	137.60	154.34
25	68.5	76.1	11.0	450.22		

Note: LEV for land expectation value.

-ΔC	ΔR	
0	T	...

FIGURE 2.3 Incremental cash flows with marginal investment

$123.60/acre and the marginal cost of waiting is (74.4 × 10 + 36.4 × 16 + 0.7 × 32 + 450.31) × 0.06 = $107.95/acre. Thus, waiting should be the best decision at age 18. The landowner keeps doing the comparison until, at age 21, the expected marginal gain of $130.20/acre is lower than the marginal cost of $130.99/acre, and he should harvest the trees. Accordingly, the optimal rotation is identified as of age 21 where the LEV is maximized at $462.20/acre.

Marginal analysis

With the development of forestry technologies, landowners have more options for their silvicultural regimes, e.g., second-generation pine seedlings vs. improved seedlings. One key concern is how to weigh the incremental cost up front against the incremental gain in the future. The cash flows on an incremental basis are depicted in Figure 2.3. The net impact can be measured by $\Delta NPV = -\Delta C + \Delta R \cdot e^{-rT}$ or $\Delta LEV = \dfrac{\Delta R \cdot e^{-rT} - \Delta C}{1 - e^{-rT}}$. If future gain in timber revenues can be predicted, then the break-even cost for using improved seedlings can be backed out by setting $\Delta NPV = 0$ or $\Delta LEV = 0$. Alternatively, for given incremental costs and revenues, landowners may calculate the marginal IRR with $\Delta NPV = 0$ or $\Delta LEV = 0$, compare it with their hurdle rates, and then make their own decisions. Of course, in the above analysis, optimal rotation age is assumed to be fixed. If this condition is relaxed, one can still calculate marginal IRR and break-even points using ΔLEV (Clutter et al. 2006).

Uneven-aged forest management

Unlike even-aged forest, trees of different ages coexist in an uneven-aged forest. There are no clear cuts but rather selective harvests. In other words, stands have no beginning or end. From the management standpoint, trees come from natural regeneration, which saves replanting cost, but a selection harvest usually incurs more cost than a clear cut.

An uneven-aged forest with trees of all ages is rare. Typically, trees are grouped in patches of similar age, but these patches are too small to be considered as even-aged. For example, an uneven-aged forest can be categorized into three size classes according to the size distribution. Once the initial condition (e.g., number of trees in each size class) is identified, a stand can be converted to a desired steady state, where harvest equals regeneration every n years, n being the harvest cycle. Assuming the first harvest takes place today, the present value of this series of harvests or the forest value (FV) is

$$FV = H + \frac{H}{e^m - 1} \tag{2.12}$$

where H is the harvest revenue every n years. If the value of current inventory is S, then the land expectation value of the uneven-aged forest (LEV_U) can be calculated as

$$LEV_U = FV - S. \tag{2.13}$$

Uneven-aged forest management can be modeled as a linear programming problem and multiple objectives can also be factored into the model. The following example is adapted from Buongiorno and Gilless (2003).

BOX 2.2 AN EXAMPLE OF UNEVEN-AGED FOREST MANAGEMENT

Suppose a sugar maple forest has three size (or age) classes. Size class 1 has the smallest trees while size class 3 has the largest trees. The growth of the forest every five years can be modeled as

$$y_{1,t+1} = 0.92y_{1,t} - 0.29y_{2,t} - 0.96y_{3,t} + 109$$

$$y_{2,t+1} = 0.04y_{1,t} + 0.9y_{2,t}$$

$$y_{3,t+1} = \qquad 0.02y_{2,t} + 0.9y_{3,t}$$

where y_1, y_2, and y_3 are the number of trees in each size class, and t indicates time. The first term in the first equation means that 92% of size 1 trees will remain in the same size class and the rest of the terms describe a natural forest regeneration process. The second equation means that 4% of size 1 trees will migrate into size class 2 and 90% of size 2 trees will remain in the same size class. The third equation means that 2% size 2 trees will migrate into size class 3 and 90% of size 3 trees will remain in the same size class. Given an initial state and a long enough time period (e.g., 100 years) without any disturbance, the forest itself may achieve a steady state, in which the number of trees in each size class does not change over time.

Next, we introduce periodic harvests into the forest management. The goal is to find the optimal harvest rule every five years so that the forest sustains a steady state, and the LEV is maximized. The respective initial number of trees for each size class is 840, 234, and 14 per hectare, and the respective economic value per tree for each size class is $0.30, $8.00, and $20.00. With the harvest decision h_1, h_2 and h_3 for each size class, the optimization problem can be stated under a linear programming framework as

$$\underset{h_1,h_2,h_3}{\text{Max }} LEV_U = FV - S$$

$$s.t. \quad FV = H + \frac{H}{e^{rn} - 1}$$

$$H = 0.3h_{1,t} + 8h_{2,t} + 20h_{3,t}$$

$$S = 0.3y_{1,t} + 8y_{2,t} + 20y_{3,t}$$

$$y_{1,t+1} = 0.92(y_{1,t} - h_1) - 0.29(y_{2,t} - h_2) - 0.96(y_{3,t} - h_3) + 106$$

$$y_{2,t+1} = 0.04(y_{1,t} - h_1) + 0.9(y_{2,t} - h_2)$$

$$y_{3,t+1} = \qquad\qquad 0.02(y_{2,t} - h_2) + 0.9(y_{3,t} - h_3)$$

$$y_{i,t+1} = y_{i,t}, \text{ for } i = 1, 2, \text{ or } 3.$$

where $y_{i,t} - h_{i,t}$ replaces $y_{i,t}$ in the forest growth function and the standing inventory value S is calculated at the steady state. With a computer software (e.g., Excel Solver), the optimal solution can be solved as $h_1 = 0, h_2 = 54.5, h_3 = 0, y_1 = 1362.5, y_2 = 54.5, y_3 = 0$, and LEV_U is maximized at $1,169 per hectare.

Note that in the above optimization, all large trees are harvested, leaving none on the ground. If tree diversity is a concern, that is, if we would like to maintain a certain number of large trees, we can add a lower bound to y_3 and run Solver again. With this extra constraint, LEV_U is lowered. The change in LEV_U is the opportunity cost of reserving tree diversity.

TABLE 2.2 A numerical example of holding value for a southern pine plantation

Age	Yield	Timber value	Forest value	Forest value growth %	DCF optimal harvest value	DCF annual cost	Land cost	Timber holding value	Forest holding value
10	6.79	135.80	385.80		487.19	21.90	87.60	377.68	627.68
11	9.63	192.60	442.60	14.07	506.67	20.28	81.11	405.29	655.29
12	12.72	254.40	504.40	13.40	526.94	18.59	74.35	434.00	684.00
13	15.93	318.60	568.60	12.23	548.02	16.83	67.33	463.86	713.86
14	19.13	382.60	632.60	10.82	569.94	15.01	60.02	494.91	744.91
15	22.25	445.00	695.00	9.47	592.74	13.11	52.42	527.21	777.21
16	25.23	504.60	754.60	8.22	616.45	11.13	44.52	560.80	810.80
17	28.03	560.60	810.60	7.09	641.10	9.07	36.30	595.73	845.73
18	30.66	613.20	863.20	6.18	666.75	6.94	27.75	632.06	882.06
19	33.11	662.20	912.20	5.39	693.42	4.72	18.86	669.84	919.84
20	35.38	707.60	957.60	4.70	721.15	2.40	9.62	709.13	959.13
21	37.50	750.00	1000.00	4.17	750.00	0	0	750.00	1000.00
22	39.48	789.60	1039.60	3.71					

Note: DCF for discounted cash flow.

Valuation of pre-merchantable timber

While timberland appraisal is the topic of the next chapter, we illustrate here how the optimal rotation is used to derive the holding value premium for pre-merchantable timber. The general steps can be summarized as follows:

1. Identify the optimal rotation (financial maturity).
2. From the optimal harvest year, discount the maximized forest (standing timber + land) value back year by year to age 1, subtract land value and management costs (e.g., administrative cost and property tax). This forms the upper bound of the pre-merch timber value.
3. Compound the establishment cost from age 1 to the cutoff age of pre-merch timber. This forms part of the lower bound of the pre-merch timber value. The other part of the lower bound consists of liquidation value, the value that can be realized by selling the timber at current market price.
4. The difference between the upper and the lower bounds defines the holding premium. Several methods can be used to determine the allocation of this premium (see Mayo and Straka 2005).

The portion of the holding value premium that can be eventually realized varies case by case but depends on a number of factors, including market conditions (seller's vs. buyer's market), bargaining power of market participants, investor's holding strategies, etc.

A numerical example is given in Table 2.2. Key parameters are $20/cord for pulpwood stumpage, $250/acre for bare land, $2.5/acre for annual cost, and 4% for discount rate. Financial maturity is reached at age 21. Timber holding value and timber value define the upper and lower bounds of pre-merchantable timber value (Figure 2.4).

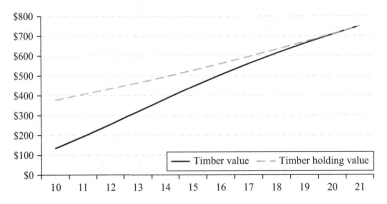

FIGURE 2.4   Illustration of upper and lower bounds of per acre pre-merchantable timber value over age

Questions

1. Explain marginal cost and marginal benefit in determining the optimal rotation of an even-aged stand.
2. In making a fertilization decision, does initial establishment cost matter? What financial criteria should we use in this case?

Notes

1 In this book, we use all these terms interchangeably.
2 Another way to calculate benefit-cost ratio is to use the cash flows directly without discounting. This way is less recommended because it ignores the time value of money.
3 The second order condition is guaranteed by the concavity nature of tree growth and yield function.

Bibliography

Amacher, G., M. Ollikainen, and E. Koskela. 2009. *Economics of forest resources.* MIT Press, Cambridge, MA, 397p.

Buongiorno, J., and J.K. Gilless. 2003. *Decision methods for forest resource management.* Academic Press, San Diego, CA, 439p.

Clutter, M.L., M. Kane, B. Borders, P. Bettinger, and J. Siry. 2006. *A method for calculating the internal rate of return on marginal silviculture investments.* Technical Report 2006–3:11.

Faustmann, M. 1995. Calculation of the value of which forest land and immature stands possess for forestry (Originally published in German Journal of Forest Research in 1849). *J. For. Econ.* 1(1):7–44.

Klemperer, W.D., S.H. Bullard, S.C. Grado, M.K. Measells, and T.J. Straka. 2022. *Forest resource economics and finance.* Stephen F. Austin University Press, Nacogdoches, TX.

Mayo, J.H., and T.J. Straka. 2005. The holding value premium in standing timber valuation. *Appraisal J.* 73(1):98–106.

Wagner, J. 2011. *Forestry economics: A managerial approach.* Routledge, New York.

Zhang, D., and P.H. Pearse. 2011. *Forest economics.* UBC Press, Vancouver, 390p.

3
TIMBERLAND APPRAISAL

Highlights

- The contents in a typical timberland appraisal report are presented and explained.
- The application of the three widely used timberland appraisal approaches (income, comparable sales, and cost approaches) are illustrated using a redacted case from the real world.
- Value reconciliation is briefly discussed.

Timberland being a real, illiquid asset, the recognition of its value depends primarily on appraisals. Therefore, understanding timberland appraisals is crucial for all stakeholders in this business segment: investors need appraisals to form expected returns; managers need appraisals to charge management fees; state and local governments need appraisals to levy property taxes. There are three commonly used methods in timberland appraisals: the income or discounted cash flow approach, the comparable sales approach, and the cost approach. For mature stands, comparable sales usually provide adequate information for the valuation. For young stands, the valuation is often more challenging and counts more on the income and the cost approaches. In a typical timberland appraisal, all three approaches are used, and the resulting values are reconciled to get a final value of the subject.

Appraisers belong to a profession required by law and professional standards to act in a manner that is independent, impartial, and objective. In the United States, appraisers are governed by the Uniform Standards of Professional Appraisal Practice. However, it is worth emphasizing that appraisals are about opinions but not facts. The eventual price of a timberland transaction (the fact) may deviate from the appraised value (the opinion) due to some unobservable or unrevealed

DOI: 10.4324/9781003366737-3

factors. In this chapter, we first briefly review the elements of a timberland appraisal report and then focus on the three appraisal approaches.

Elements of a timberland appraisal report

A timberland appraisal report usually begins with a transmittal letter from the appraiser to the client, describing what is done on a property, what is the final opinion of the value, and what the appraisal contains. Then, it comes to the main body of the report, which generally contains (1) the introduction, (2) the data, and (3) the analysis. Lastly, a bibliography section and addenda may be added at the end. A sample table of contents for a timberland appraisal report is shown in Box 3.1.

BOX 3.1 A SAMPLE TABLE OF CONTENTS FOR A TIMBERLAND APPRAISAL REPORT

Table of Contents

Letter of Transmittal
Section I: Introduction
       Summary of salient facts
       Property valuation summary
       Certification
       Assumptions and limited conditions
       Scope of appraisal
       Appraisal overview items
Section II: Factual data
       Regional and neighborhood analysis
       Regional map
       Property data
Section III: Analysis
       Higher and better use
       Property valuation
           Income approach to value
           Comparable sales approach to value
           Cost approach to value
Bibliography
Addenda

An important subsection of the introduction section is assumptions and limited conditions. The appraisal report is constrained by those assumptions and limiting

conditions and represents the appraiser's personal, impartial, and unbiased professional analyses, opinions, and conclusions. For example, if no title report of the
subject property is provided, the appraiser will not render a title opinion and will
assume the title to be clear, unencumbered, and in fee simple. Also, it is often
necessary to rely on data supplied by others in regard to comparable sales and the
subject property. Such information is usually assumed to be reliable, although it is
not always guaranteed (Cubbage et al. 2013).

In the subsection of regional and neighborhood analysis of Section II, the followings are discussed in detail: the geographic location of the subject property,
the urban-rural classification of the region, the population, the infrastructure
(e.g., highways and local roads), the forest products industry, the timberland ownership structure (e.g., public vs. private and industrial vs. nonindustrial), the local
timber market, the primary land uses, the potential for higher and better uses, and
the regional economy. A regional map is often included for illustrations.

In the subsection of property data of Section II, the site information is presented in depth. The content of this subsection varies case by case but generally
contains the following: the total size and number of individual tracts, the location, the access to the property (public roads, paved roads, graded roads, etc.), the
physiographic features, the property utility (electricity, water, sewage, etc.), the
improvements (roads, gates, bridges, etc.), the land use history, the zoning and
other regulations, the environmental issues, the timber inventory, timber rights,
and so on. Photographs of the subject property are often embedded in the text
descriptions.

Section III is the key component of the appraisal report: the valuation. It usually involves all the three appraisal methods and a valuation reconciliation at the
end. Discussion on higher and better uses, if there is any, is also presented in this
section.

To show how each appraisal method works, we will use an example redacted
from a real-world appraisal (Williams 2016). The subject property is a 30,000-acre
forestland consisting of 127 individual tracts that are managed and used primarily
for timber production and recreation. The property is located in the upper coastal
plain region of South Carolina. The effective date of the appraisal is December
31, 2015.

The income approach

In the income approach, all anticipated future benefits from the ownership of
timberland are converted into a value estimate. In general, a discounted cash flow
analysis with a ten-year projection window is used to estimate the present value
of the subject property. Specifically, net income to the subject property for each of
the next ten years as well as a residual or terminal value at the end of the projection period are forecasted. These values are then discounted to a present value at
a market-based discount rate.

Incomes derived from timberland typically come from timber sales, hunting leases, and residual land and timber, whereas expenses originate from property tax, management cost, timber sale administration cost, and reforestation cost. The discount rate is derived from comparable sales in the same manner as is done on the subject property. Given the sale prices of the comparable sales, the internal rates of return can be reverse-engineered. Alternatively, the discount rate can be generated based on certain asset pricing models (e.g., Cascio and Clutter 2008; Yao and Mei 2015; Yao et al. 2014).

Table 3.1 shows the valuation of the subject property by the income approach. There is a ten-year projection of cash flows plus a residual value with all values in real terms. The first panel is about revenue. Timber revenues (R) are generated by combining stumpage prices (P) with harvest schedules (harvests and thinnings) on the property (G), i.e., $R = PG$. Determination of stumpage prices is discussed in the cost approach. The harvest schedules involve the forecast of growth and yield and the optimal rotation. Stand level data is often grouped into strata based on species, age, stand origin, land classification, average dominant tree height, number of trees per acre, and basal area per acre. Accordingly, future harvests are estimated at the strata level.

Hunting lease, another important non-timber revenue source in the United States, is projected to be $234,463 per year based on the market condition at that time. The residual values for hunting lease, timber, and land (present value of respective future cash flows discounted back to year ten) are calculated to be $496,855, $37,839,977, and $35,680.980. These forecasts rest upon a few key assumptions, including bare land value, land value appreciation rate, harvest schedules beyond year ten, etc.

The next panel is about cost. Based on the most recent bill, annual property tax and management expense are estimated to be $92,337 and $180,000, respectively, within the ten-year projection window. Timber sale commission varies by year according to the services received (4% of the gross timber sale revenues for clear-cuts and 8% for thinnings) and is also projected for the next ten years. Like revenue, the residual value for each cost component reflects the present value of all future cash outflows discounted back to year ten. Then, net operating cash flow is calculated as total revenue minus total cost. After the capital expenditure (the reforestation cost with an estimate of $225 per acre) is taken out from net operating cash flow, we have net cash flow, which can be discounted back to year 0. With a 5.5% discount rate backed out from comparable sales, the value of the property (present value of all future cash flows) turns out to be $56,269,781, or $1,876 per acre, from the income approach.

The comparable sales approach

In the comparable sales approach, recent transactions are analyzed, and their sale prices are adjusted to reflect the subject's characteristics and current market

TABLE 3.1 Valuation of a 30,000-acre timberland property in South Carolina by the income approach

Year	1	2	3	4	5	6	7	8	9	10	Residual value
Revenue											
Harvest	1,420,986	1,590,068	1,684,092	1,785,140	1,893,792	2,010,682	2,136,495	2,271,979	2,417,944	2,575,270	
Thinning	237,727	100,626	100,541	106,576	28,988	62,896	684,249	264,418	258,300	285,148	
Hunting lease	234,463	234,463	234,463	234,463	234,463	234,463	234,463	234,463	234,463	234,463	496,855
Residual timber											37,839,977
Residual land											35,680,980
Total revenue	1,893,175	1,925,156	2,019,096	2,126,178	2,157,242	2,308,040	3,055,207	2,770,860	2,910,706	3,094,880	74,017,812
Cost											
Property tax	92,337	92,337	92,337	92,337	92,337	92,337	92,337	92,337	92,337	92,337	195,674
Management expense	180,000	180,000	180,000	180,000	180,000	180,000	180,000	180,000	180,000	180,000	381,443
Timber sale commission	75,858	71,653	75,407	79,932	78,071	85,459	140,200	112,033	117,382	125,823	394,792
Total cost	348,195	343,990	347,744	352,269	350,408	357,796	412,537	384,370	389,719	398,160	971,908
Net operating cash flow	1,544,981	1,581,166	1,671,352	1,773,909	1,806,834	1,950,244	2,642,670	2,386,490	2,520,988	2,696,721	73,045,904
Capital expense											
Reforestation	167,202	209,372	209,372	209,372	209,372	209,372	209,372	209,372	209,372	209,372	
Net cash flow	1,377,779	1,371,794	1,461,980	1,564,537	1,597,462	1,740,872	2,433,298	2,177,118	2,311,616	2,487,349	73,045,904
Discount rate	5.50%										
Present value	56,269,781										
Value per acre	1,876										

TABLE 3.2 Comparable sales of the subject property

	Sale #1		Sale #2	Sale #3
State	NC, SC, GA, TN		FL	NC
Date	Nov. 2015		Sept. 2015	Feb. 2015
Grantor	Timberland Investment Resources		Plum Creek	Timbervest
Grantee	CatchMark		Hancock	Weyerhaeuser
Size (acres)	14,573		97,710	9,144
Total sale price ($)	29,476,000		120,210,000	20,500,000
Unit price ($/acre)	2,023		1,230	2,242

Note: NC for North Carolina, SC for South Carolina, GA for Georgia, and FL for Florida.

conditions. Then, these transactions serve as the basis for estimating the value of the subject property. Although no precedent sale is exactly the same as the subject, each sale contains some usable land and timber price data. Hence, the key component is comparable sales is to make those adjustments.

Three selected comparable sales of the subject property are listed in Table 3.2 and are used for a demonstration. In practice, appraisers usually have more than three comparable sales, but the logic is all the same. These three comparable sales differ quantitatively from the subject property in total size, acreages of each land type, merchantable timber volumes, and pre-merchantable timber acreages. They also differ qualitatively in access, location, and other physical and economic characteristics. Each of the subject's components is analyzed for both quantitative and qualitative adjustments before a final market value is reconciled for the subject.

Land mix adjustment

The per acre price of each land class in a comparable sale is multiplied by the land class acreage of the subject, resulting in a total value for each land type. These values are first summed and then divided by the total acreage of the subject, resulting in a per acre price, which represents the composition of the subject's land classes. These calculations are summarized in Table 3.3. Should all three comparable sales have the same land composition as the subject, their respective sale price per acre would be $1,191, $831, and $883. The last line of Table 3.3 shows the net adjustment for land mix.

After the quantitative adjustments above, timberland sales are next analyzed for differences in the following qualitative elements: property rights conveyed, financing terms, conditions of sale, immediate post-purchase expenditures, market conditions, physical characteristics, economic characteristics, land uses, and non-realty components of value. For simplicity, we shall omit such adjustments here.

Timber price adjustment

Adjustments to the merchantable timber component are similar to those to the land. Yet, unlike the land mix adjustment, qualitative adjustments are made first

TABLE 3.3 Land mix adjustment in the comparable sales approach

	Sale #1	Sale #2	Sale #3
Subject acreage			
Old field	48	48	48
Upland timberland	24,584	24,584	24,584
Lowland timberland	797	797	797
Bottomland timberland	2,078	2,078	2,078
Slope timberland	1,751	1,751	1,751
Non-forest	743	743	743
Total subject acreage	30,000	30,000	30,000
Sale price ($/acre)			
Old field	1,310	915	940
Upland timberland	1,310	915	940
Lowland timberland	1,310	915	940
Bottomland timberland	524	366	564
Slope timberland	524	366	564
Non-forest	524	366	564
Total sale value ($)			
Old field	62,225	43,463	44,650
Upland timberland	32,204,385	22,493,903	23,108,490
Lowland timberland	1,044,070	729,255	749,180
Bottomland timberland	1,088,872	760,548	1,171,992
Slope timberland	917,262	640,683	987,282
Non-forest	389,332	271,938	419,052
Total adjusted land value ($)	35,706,146	24,939,789	26,480,646
Adjusted land value ($/acre)	1,190	831	883
Original land value ($/acre)	1,191	690	914
Land mix adjustment ($/acre)	−1	141	−31

because they may be applied to individual timber products but not to overall per acre timber values. For instance, pine pulpwood prices may increase over time, while prices of other products remain stable. Then, the pine pulpwood price needs to be adjusted to reflect the price at the effective date.

Timber price adjustments are often benchmarked against the price trends, evidenced by some widely used data published by a third party such as TimberMart-South (TMS 2022). The adjustments account for both temporal and geographical differences, and the process is described in Table 3.4. For example, comparable sale #2 is located in Florida and the transaction date is a quarter earlier than the effective date. According to TimberMart-South data, pine pulpwood in South Carolina in 2015Q4 is 11.59 − 12.26 = −$0.67/ton lower than that in Florida in 2015Q3. Expressed in percentage, it is −0.67 / 12.26 = −5.46%. Given an actual pine pulpwood price of $12.50/ton from the sale, the implied price is 12.50 ⋆ (1 − 5.46%) = $11.82/ton after the adjustments for date and location. That is, had comparable sale #2 happened at the effective date (instead of a quarter ago) and in South Carolina (instead of Florida), the pine pulpwood price would likely be $11.82/ton. Prices for other timber products are similarly adjusted.

TABLE 3.4 Timber price adjustment in the comparable sales approach

	Subject	Sale #1	Sale #2	Sale #3
TMS price for sale date and location				
State	SC	NC, SC, GA, TN	FL	NC
Date	Dec. 2015	Nov. 2015	Sept. 2015	Feb. 2015
Product				
Pine pulpwood	11.59	12.26	16.30	13.19
Pine chip-n-saw	19.60	19.41	23.43	19.34
Pine sawtimber	27.01	27.36	30.30	24.03
Hardwood pulpwood	9.10	9.75	7.09	7.63
Hardwood sawtimber	28.09	29.41	24.34	29.19
TMS price difference between subject and sale				
Pine pulpwood		−0.67	−4.71	−1.60
Pine chip-n-saw		0.19	−3.83	0.26
Pine sawtimber		−0.35	−3.29	2.98
Hardwood pulpwood		−0.65	2.01	1.47
Hardwood sawtimber		−1.32	3.75	−1.10
TMS price percentage difference				
Pine pulpwood		−5.46%	−28.90%	−12.13%
Pine chip-n-saw		0.98%	−16.35%	1.34%
Pine sawtimber		−1.28%	−10.86%	12.40%
Hardwood pulpwood		−6.67%	28.35%	19.27%
Hardwood sawtimber		−4.49%	15.41%	−3.77%
Original sale price				
Pine pulpwood		12.50	16.25	15.00
Pine chip-n-saw		19.50	25.50	20.00
Pine sawtimber		28.00	33.50	26.00
Hardwood pulpwood		9.00	7.50	5.00
Hardwood sawtimber		24.00	20.00	25.00
Adjusted price				
Pine pulpwood		11.82	11.55	13.18
Pine chip-n-saw		19.69	21.33	20.27
Pine sawtimber		27.64	29.86	29.22
Hardwood pulpwood		8.40	9.63	5.96
Hardwood sawtimber		22.92	23.08	24.06

Note: TMS for TimberMart-South. NC for North Carolina, SC for South Carolina, GA for Georgia, and FL for Florida. Timber price is in $/ton.

By applying the adjusted timber prices and the subject's timber volume on the comparable sales, we can further adjust for timber product mix. The upper portion of Table 3.5 shows the original sale volume and price information by timber product. Timber value per acre is calculated as total timber value (sum of values by timber product) divided by total acreage. The original timber values per acre for the three comparable sales are $678, $417, and $1,155, respectively. The lower portion of Table 3.5 shows the adjusted volume and price information and the adjusted timber values per acre for the three comparable sales are $937, $997, and $965, respectively. That is, if the three sales took place at the effective date and

TABLE 3.5 Timber product mix adjustment in the comparable sales approach

	Subject	Sale #1	Sale #2	Sale #3
Original sale information				
Sale timber volume (tons)				
Pine pulpwood	461,575	117,047	955,086	153,304
Pine chip-n-saw	260,544	215,853	126,657	108,385
Pine sawtimber	482,606	103,075	137,837	190,145
Hardwood pulpwood	325,511	55,457	2,034,262	56,972
Hardwood sawtimber	63,595	34,277	107,347	34,453
Sale timber price ($/ton)				
Pine pulpwood		12.50	16.25	15.00
Pine chip-n-saw		19.50	25.50	20.00
Pine sawtimber		28.00	33.50	26.00
Hardwood pulpwood		9.00	7.50	5.00
Hardwood sawtimber		24.00	20.00	25.00
Sale total timber value ($)		9,880,082	40,771,346	10,557,215
Sale total acreage		14,573	97,710	9,144
Sale timber value ($/acre)		678	417	1,155
Adjusted sale information				
Subject timber volume (tons)				
Pine pulpwood		461,575	461,575	461,575
Pine chip-n-saw		260,544	260,544	260,544
Pine sawtimber		482,606	482,606	482,606
Hardwood pulpwood		325,511	325,511	325,511
Hardwood sawtimber		63,595	63,595	63,595
Adjusted timber price ($/ton)				
Pine pulpwood		11.82	11.55	13.18
Pine chip-n-saw		19.69	21.33	20.27
Pine sawtimber		27.64	29.86	29.22
Hardwood pulpwood		8.40	9.63	5.96
Hardwood sawtimber		22.92	23.08	24.06
Adjusted total timber value ($)		28,116,861	29,904,184	28,939,569
Subject total acreage		30,000	30,000	30,000
Adjusted timber value ($/acre)		937	997	965
Timber mix adjustment ($/acre)		259	580	−190

in the same location as the subject, and furthermore if the three comparable sales had the same timber mix as the subject, then the adjusted timber values per acre reflect current market conditions. The last line of Table 3.5 shows the net adjustment for timber mix.

Pre-merchantable timber adjustment

Pre-merchantable timber value by age class can be adjusted in a similar manner. This is done by using a blended percentage adjustment based on pine pulpwood and chip-n-saw as in the merchantable timber adjustment process. Respective weights on pulpwood and chip-n-saw adjustments are 95% and 5%, which approximate a typical age 15 (cutoff age) product mix in a pre-merchantable stand.

TABLE 3.6 Adjustment to age 8 class pre-merchantable timber in the comparable sales approach

Product	Merchantable timber price adjustment	Weight	Weighted
Pine pulpwood	−17.50%	95%	−16.63%
Pine chip-n-saw	−5.20%	5%	−0.26%
Weighted adjustment rate			−16.89%
Original value of age 8 class ($/acre)			611
Value adjustment ($/acre)			−103
Adjusted value of age 8 class ($/acre)			508

TABLE 3.7 Pre-merchantable timber mix adjustment in the comparable sales approach

	Sale #1	Sale #2	Sale #3
Adjusted pre-merchantable timber value ($/acre)	111	101	122
Original sale pre-merchantable timber value ($/acre)	154	124	173
Pre-merchantable timber mix adjustment ($/acre)	−43	−23	−51

A sample calculation using the age 8 class for sale #1 is illustrated in Table 3.6. The weighted adjustment rate (−16.89%) is multiplied by the original value of age 8 class ($610.84 per acre) to get the price adjustment (−$103.14 per acre). Thus, the adjusted value of age 8 class is 610.84 − 103.14 = $507.70 per acre.

These adjusted values are multiplied by the corresponding age class acreage of the subject. The sum of these products is then divided by the subject's total acreage to get a pre-merchantable timber value per acre that represents the subject's pre-merchantable timber mix and the sales' adjusted pre-merchantable timber prices. The difference between this price and the original price is the pre-merchantable timber adjustment that is applied to each comparable sale (Table 3.7).

Value reconciliation

Table 3.8 summarizes all the adjustments made to the comparable sales. For example, the original sale price ($2,023/acre) of sale #1 is adjusted down by land (−$1/acre), up by merchantable timber ($259/acre), and down by pre-merchantable timber (−$43/acre) to get the adjusted price ($2,238/acre). This adjusted price times the subject's acreage (30,000) gives the indicated value of the subject ($67,140,000).

The indicated value from comparable sales ranges from $1,928/acre to $2,238/acre and averages $2,045/acre. However, sale #1 is rated "superior" to the subject, sale #2 is rated "inferior" to the subject, and sale #3 is rated "similar" to the subject based on some qualitative assessment. So a higher weight is assigned to sale #3. While the specific weights are a subjective choice of the appraiser, we use 15%, 15%, and 70% on the three sales for illustration. The resulting weighted

TABLE 3.8 Summary of adjustments in the comparable sales approach

	Sale #1	Sale #2	Sale #3
Size (acres)	14,573	97,710	9,144
Total sale price ($)	29,476,000	120,210,000	20,500,000
Unit price ($/acre)	2,023	1,230	2,242
Adjustment ($/acre)			
Land	−1	141	−31
Merchantable timber	259	580	−190
Pre-merchantable timber	−43	−23	−51
Adjusted price ($/acre)	2,238	1,928	1,970
Subject acreage	30,000	30,000	30,000
Indicated subject value ($)	67,140,000	57,840,000	59,100,000
Breakdown of price ($/acre)			
Land	1,190	831	883
Merchantable timber	937	997	965
Pre-merchantable timber	111	101	122

average price is $2,004/acre, and the reconciled value for the subject is 2,004 × 30,000 = $60,117,000 from the comparable sales approach.

The cost approach

In the cost approach, the values of the individual components of the subject property are estimated and then summed up, resulting in a total value indication of the subject property. In commercial and residential appraisals, this involves adding up the estimated land value and depreciated improvement values (e.g., buildings, structures, fixtures, etc.). In timberland appraisals, the land and timber values are estimated and summed in a similar manner. The major difference is that forests appreciate with biological growth in most cases, while most building improvements depreciate over time.

For timberland, the major components include bare land, merchantable timber, and pre-merchantable timber. Bare land values are derived from composite land and timber sales by subtracting timber values from the overall sale prices. Like in the comparable sales approach, recent transactions are analyzed for necessary adjustments to the bare land values to accommodate differences between the sales and the subject property.

Bare land valuation

For bare land, adjustments are made for financial terms of the sale, conditions of the sale, land class mix, market conditions, access, location, and size. For example, cash transactions often have lower sale prices than leveraged buyouts due to

TABLE 3.9 Adjustments to bare land value in the cost approach

	Sale #1	Sale #2	Sale #3
Size (acres)	14,573	97,710	9,144
Total sale price ($)	29,476,000	120,210,000	20,500,000
Unit price ($/acre)	2,023	1,230	2,242
Value component			
Timber	12,122,415	52,826,937	12,141,953
Raw land value ($)	17,353,585	67,383,063	8,358,047
Land price ($/acre)	1,191	690	914
Adjustments			
Land mix	−1	141	−31
Indicated land price ($/acre)	1,190	831	883

the simplicity in the deal structure; and larger size tracts have lower sale prices than smaller size tracts due to less competition in the auctions (TMS 2022). After the adjustments, many of which are very similar to those in the comparable sales approach, the indicated values of the subject's bare land from comparable sales are derived. While we omit the detailed discussion, Table 3.9 summarizes the adjustments to bare land value. In this special case, the only adjustment is to land mix, as what we have done in the comparable sales approach.

Given the rating of the three comparable sales relative to the subject and the subjective weights (0.15, 0.15, and 0.70), the final reconciled land price is $921/acre, and the indicated total land value is 921 × 30,000 = $27,630,000.

Merchantable timber valuation

Merchantable timber values are estimated by applying market stumpage prices to the reported timber volumes. The timber valuation is normally based on recent two-year sales located within the subject region, which can be acquired from a timber price reporting service such as TimberMart-South. The data are then analyzed for geographic locations with the help of a geographic information system software. In our case, the data indicate two general timber regions, with region 1 accounting for about 40% and region 2 accounting for about 60%.

Within each region, sales are analyzed for stumpage prices. For each product, a temporal weighted average is often calculated using a higher weight on the short-term average price and a lower weight on the long-term average price. For example, pine pulpwood prices in region 1 averaged $12.90/ton in the last 12 months and $12.30/ton in the last two years. With a weight of 75% for the short term and 25% for the long term, the temporal weighted average is calculated to be $12.75/ton. The same procedure can be repeated for other timber products across the two regions and the results are shown in Table 3.10. Multiplying the unit price by the

TABLE 3.10 Weighted average timber price and merchantable timber value in the cost approach

| | Weight or total | Pine | | | Hardwood | |
		Pulpwood	Chip-n-saw	Sawtimber	Pulpwood	Sawtimber
Price ($/ton)						
Region 1	40%	12.75	20.50	27.50	8.25	23.75
Region 2	60%	10.75	18.25	28.25	8.50	22.75
Average		11.55	19.15	27.95	8.40	23.15
Volume (tons)		461,575	260,544	482,606	325,511	63,595
Total value ($)	28,015,932	5,331,185	4,989,408	13,488,838	2,734,288	1,472,213
Share of total value	100%	19%	18%	48%	10%	5%

corresponding product volume leads to a merchantable timber value. Summing up the values across timber products results in a total merchantable timber value of $28,015,932 (Table 3.10).

Pre-merchantable timber valuation

Pre-merchantable timber values are estimated by applying commonly accepted valuation methods appropriate for the subject property. In addition to the holding value premium method discussed in the previous chapter, there are three other widely used valuation methods on pre-merchantable timber: (1) the straight line without a base value method, (2) the straight line with a base value method, and (3) the compound annual growth rate method (Box 3.2).

BOX 3.2 THREE WIDELY USED VALUATION METHODS ON PRE-MERCHANTABLE TIMBER

Assume a loblolly pine plantation reaches its first merchantability at age 15. At that time, pulpwood will be worth $10/ton. Productivity is 4 tons per acre per year. Then, at age 15, total merchantable timber value will be 4 × 15 × 10 = $600/acre.

(1) The straight line without a base value method (i.e., age 0 class has no value). The constant annual value change rate will be (600 − 0) / 15 = $40/ acre, and therefore age 1 class will be worth 0 + 1 × 40 = $40/ac, age 2 class will be worth 0 + 2 × 40 = $80/ac, and so on.

(2) The straight line with a base value method. If a base value of $200/acre is used, which reflects part or all of the initial establishment cost, then age 0 class is worth $200/acre and the constant annual value change rate is (600 − 200) / 15 = $26.67/acre. Then, age 1 class will be worth 200 + 26.67 = $226.67/acre, age 2 class will be worth 200 + 2 × 26.67 = $253.34, and so on.

(3) The compound annual growth rate method. If a base value of $200/acre is used, then the compound annual growth rate is calculated as $(600 / 200)^{1/15} - 1 = 7.6\%$. So age 1 class will be worth 200 × (1 + 7.6%) = $215.20/ acre, age 2 class will be worth $200 \times (1 + 7.6\%)^2 = \$231.56$/acre, and so on.

In this appraisal, pine trees less than 15 years old are considered pre-merchantable and their values are determined by the straight line with a base method. Like in the comparable sales approach, pulpwood and chip-n-saw prices are applied to the age 15 volume of each product to get an age 15 value. Moreover, a base value of $225/ acre, which is representative of that regional market, is used. Pre-merchantable

TABLE 3.11 Valuation summary of the cost approach

Component	Total value ($)	Price ($/acre)
Land	27,630,000	921
Merchantable timber	28,015,932	934
Pre-merchantable timber	3,277,452	109
Subject's total	58,923,384	1,964

TABLE 3.12 Final reconciled value of the subject

Approach	Total value ($)	Price ($/acre)
Income	56,269,781	1,876
Comparable sales	60,117,000	2,004
Cost	58,923,384	1,964
Reconciled value	58,436,722	1,948

timber valuation is initially conducted at the strata level and then aggregated. The total value of pre-merchantable timber of the subject is calculated to be $3,277,452.

With each component evaluated, their values are summed to a total property value (Table 3.11). By the cost approach, the subject's total value is $58,923,384 or $1,964/acre.

Final reconciliation of value

As is well known, the income approach is very sensitive to changes in the discount rate and estimates of future cash flows. Hence, the income approach generally generates a wider range of the estimated value. For example, when the discount rate is changed from 4.50% to 6.50%, the subject's value ranges between $51,719,985 and $61,298,843, which encompasses the values from the other two approaches. Overall, the income approach reasonably supports the results from the other two approaches in our sample appraisal.

A potential issue affecting the reliability of the comparable sales approach is about the similarity between the comparable sales and the subject. Unless a sale occurs in the same timber market as the subject and close to the appraisal's effective date, the value reflected by a comparable sale may represent a different timber market than the subject's. Using timber price trends reported by a third party, the comparable sales used in our sample appraisal are appropriately adjusted to reflect the subject's current market conditions. The resulting timber values are similar to those from the cost approach. Thus, the comparable sales approach is believed to produce a reliable indication of the subject's market value.

The cost approach is an easily understood and accepted method that has been historically used in the timberland market in the US Southeast. One concern is about summing price indications from two separate markets (timber and land) to reflect a composite timberland property value. In our sample appraisal, the cost approach is based on transactions of combined timber and land properties. Therefore, the sum of the parts issue is circumvented. The cost approach indicates a value that is marginally below that indicated by the comparable sales approach and the difference could be attributable to the normal market volatility. In summary, the cost approach conducted here is well supported and indicates a reliable value for the subject property.

Using an equal weight on each valuation approach, the final reconciled value of the subject is $58,436,772 or $1,948/acre (Table 3.12). In other situations, however, one valuation approach could receive a higher weight than others and a simple arithmetic average may not be appropriate. Again, appraisals are more about opinions.

Questions

1. What are the three commonly used methods in timberland appraisals?
2. What factors are the income approach mostly sensitive to?
3. What adjustments are needed in the comparable sales approach?
4. What are the value components in the cost approach?
5. Explain the straight line with a base value method in valuing pre-merchantable timber.

Bibliography

Cascio, A.J., and M.L. Clutter. 2008. Risk and required return assessments of equity timberland investments in the United States. *For. Prod. J.* 58(10):61–70.

Cubbage, F.W., R. Davis, G. Frey, and D.C. Behr. 2013. *Financial and economic evaluation guidelines for community forestry projects in Latin America.* Program on Forests (PROFOR), Washington, DC, 57.

TMS. 2022. *TimberMart-South.* Norris Foundation, Athens, GA.

Williams, J.D. 2016. *Summary report of an appraisal.* Timberland Appraisal Services, Ellijay, GA, 119.

Yao, W., and B. Mei. 2015. Assessing forestry-related assets with the intertemporal capital asset pricing model. *For. Policy Econ.* 50:192–199.

Yao, W., B. Mei, and M.L. Clutter. 2014. Pricing timberland assets in the United States by the arbitrage pricing theory. *For. Sci.* 60(5):943–952.

4

RETURN DRIVERS OF TIMBERLAND INVESTMENT

Highlights

- Broadly speaking, timberland has three return drivers: biological growth, timber price change, and land value appreciation.
- Biological growth is independent of the financial market and can buffer the impact of negative changes in timber prices.
- Land value change is relatively small compared to the other two return drivers, but land value usually appreciates with inflation.
- For loblolly pine plantations, the expected annual nominal return is about 7%, as revealed by Monte Carlo simulations.

Timberland assets exhibit several unique characteristics that are attractive to investors. In this chapter, we examine the three return drivers of timberland investments—timber price change, land value appreciation, and biological growth, in two settings. Timberland returns are analyzed via a hypothetical loblolly pine plantation bought at age 10 and sold at age 25. Results reveal that timber price had a negative contribution to the total returns. With declining timber prices, annualized average returns dropped from 14.31% for 1982–1997 by 52% to 6.88% for 1995–2010. Looking forward, timberland investment returns were simulated by Monte Carlo simulations with both random and mean-reverting timber prices. Expected mean returns with random timber prices were found to be 8.35%–10.16%, while those with mean-reverting timber prices were 7.25%–8.56%. Returns with random timber prices were more volatile. Despite different time periods under investigation and timber price assumptions in the simulations, biological growth was the dominant contributor to the total returns. However,

DOI: 10.4324/9781003366737-4

timber price assumptions affect values of timber cut contracts, timberland liquidation values, and default risks of leveraged timberland investments.

Return drivers

Returns from timberland investments have three primary drivers—timber price change, land value appreciation, and biological growth. Biological growth, per se, combines two dynamic components: the physical growth in volume and weight, and the value growth from a lower-priced to a higher-priced product. Caulfield (1998) examined the interaction of the three return drivers using a hypothetical loblolly pine (*Pinus taeda*) plantation acquired at age 10 and sold at age 25 in southern Georgia from 1982 to 1997, and found that the percentage contribution of each return driver to the annualized average return of 14.31% to be 33%, 6%, and 61%, respectively. It has now been widely accepted that biological growth is independent of business cycles and market fluctuations and, consequently, dampens the volatility of timberland investment returns during economic recessions.

Over the past several decades, substantial changes in timberland ownership have occurred in the United States. Coupled with changes in the overall economic conditions, the timber market in the US South has been unprecedentedly volatile. Take southern Georgia as an example; timber prices in recent years have tumbled by about 40% from the peak levels in the late 1990s (Figure 4.1), and bare land values followed that trend with some lags (Figure 4.2). Since the bare land value is typically much smaller than the total stumpage value at the final harvest, stumpage prices have been a major concern of timberland investors.[1] However, research has been inconclusive on whether stumpage price is random or mean-reverting (Binkley et al. 2001; Haight and Holmes 1991).

Given those changes in the timber market, it is necessary to examine the three return drivers of timberland investments and the total returns in the

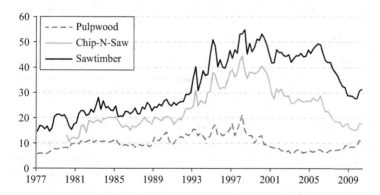

FIGURE 4.1   Nominal pine stumpage prices in $ per ton in southern Georgia, 1977Q1–2010Q4. Data source: TimberMart-South

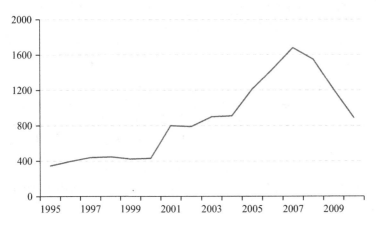

FIGURE 4.2 Nominal bare land values in $ per acre (tracts of less than 5,000 acres) in the US South. Data source: TimberMart-South

same context as in Caulfield (1998). Comparison of the results can provide some insights into the financial performance of past timberland investments. However, history may not repeat itself. Looking ahead, a frequently asked question is: what will the returns look like if one invests today? One way to address this question is to apply Monte Carlo simulations to a hypothetical forest plantation. Hence, this chapter highlights three major contributions. Foremost, we use the most recently available data and compare the results from timberland investments for two different time periods. Next, in addition to risks in timber prices, we include risks in tree growth & yield and bare land values as well in projecting future timberland investment returns. Finally, implications of the simulated results are demonstrated by three applications, namely, the valuation of a long-term timber cut contract, the liquidation value of a timberland property, and the default risk of a leveraged timberland investment.[2] All these applications have realistic meanings. First, having sold most of their lands, forest products firms still attempt to maintain some control over the wood supply. One vehicle that has been widely used is the long-term timber harvest contract, although the valuation of such contracts remains challenging (Shaffer 1984). Second, recent development in woody biomass utilization has driven pulpwood prices up (TMS 2022). Landowners now have the option to shorten the rotation length, produce more small-size timber, liquid their properties earlier, and recover their initial investment costs sooner. Third, leveraged timberland investments are not uncommon in practice. One big concern of stakeholders in the timber business is how to assess the default risk.

Analysis of return drivers

Data

Two return indices are commonly used in the timberland investment literature. One is the National Council of Real Estate Investment Fiduciaries (NCREIF) Timberland Index (NCREIF 2020), which approximates private-equity timberland returns achieved by major TIMOs. The other is the timber firm index, which approximates public-equity timberland returns achieved by a group of publicly traded timber firms (Mei and Clutter 2010). However, both indices are based on broadly diversified timberland portfolios in terms of geographic locations, species, and age classes. Therefore, they do not represent investment returns of non-industrial private forest landowners managing small tracts of land. In this chapter, this issue is examined by a hypothetical, even-aged forest plantation via the simulation technique.

Data on the three key variables, i.e., biological growth & yield, stumpage price, and bare land value, are needed for the analysis. Biological growth & yield were simulated with a hypothetical loblolly pine plantation in southern Georgia. Growing trees are assumed to be clear fell at age 25 regardless of market conditions. Other key factors in the simulation include a site index of 60 (base age 25), 700 trees planted per acre, a first-year survival rate of 85%, no pre-commercial thinning, and no fertilization. Annual management costs, annual taxes, and hunting lease income are assumed to be $4.00/acre, $5.00/acre, and $8.00/acre, respectively. Consistent with Caulfield (1998), second quarter stumpage prices are used for each year and the price data are obtained from TimberMart-South (TMS 2022).

For bare land values, two broad markets should be considered, i.e., tracts less than 5,000 acres vs. tracts larger than 5,000 acres (Humphries 2011). Smaller tracts are usually managed by individual investors and regarded as the consumer market, whereas larger tracts are usually managed by institutional investors and regarded as the commercial/institutional market. Over the past decade, bare land values between these two segments differed but followed similar trends (Humphries 2011). Since this chapter focuses on timberland investment returns for small forest landowners, bare land values for small tracts are used. The whole series for 1995–2010 is combined from Thomas (2000), Williams (2003), and Humphries (2011), where bare land values are derived from more than 800 verified transactions in Georgia. For the valuation purpose, the discount rate is set at 6% (Cascio and Clutter 2008), and the exercise prices in the timber harvest contract are assumed to be $12/ton for pulpwood, $28/ton for chip-n-saw, and $42/ton for sawtimber, respectively. All values are in nominal terms for a direct comparison with the results reported by Caulfield (1998) as well as other widely used return indices of timberland investments.

Static analysis

The general relationship between tree growth and age for an even-aged loblolly pine plantation is characterized by the sigmoid curve in Figure 4.3 (Clutter et al. 1983). Within a rotation, three growth stages can be defined: emerging growth stage, established growth stage, and mature growth stage. Emerging growth stage refers to the period after seedlings are planted but before merchantable timber can be produced. In this stage, trees are small but biological growth rate is increasing rapidly. While trees become merchantable, the stand transits into the established growth stage. The growth rate peaks in this stage but declines thereafter. Eventually, as trees mature, the stand enters into the mature growth stage, when trees continue to grow but at a much slower rate. With biological growth, trees grow in size and volume, and they increase in value. For instance, smaller and lower-value trees are used to produce pulpwood for pulp and paper or oriented strand board (OSB), whereas larger and higher-value trees are used to produce sawtimber for large dimension lumber or veneer logs for plywood. Historically, sawtimber price has been two to three times higher than pulpwood price (Figure 4.1), and there exists a positive correlation between biological growth and timberland investment returns. Following Caulfield (1998), our analysis focuses on the "established growth strategy"—purchasing a pine plantation at the established growth stage and selling it in 15 years. With this investment strategy, more emphasis is put on pulpwood and chip-n-saw production.

Stumpage value is calculated as the sum of the values in three products each year. Total value equals stumpage value plus bare land value, and it is adjusted for annual management cost, property tax, and hunting lease revenue. Annual value

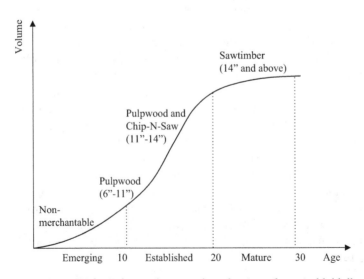

FIGURE 4.3 Biological growth, age and production of a typical loblolly pine plantation

change is calculated as the percentage change in total values. Annual return is calculated as the geometric mean return from the inception.

Dynamic analysis via Monte Carlo simulation

In finance, the efficient market hypothesis asserts that competition in financial markets creates an equilibrium in which it is extremely difficult to achieve excess returns over the market on a risk adjusted basis. That is, asset prices impound all relevant information and move almost randomly in response to new information (Fama 1970). Ever since the proposition of the efficient market hypothesis, a large number of empirical studies have been conducted to test the hypothesis, but they have led to conflicting findings (Fama 1991). Nonetheless, most agree that capital markets are efficient in the weak and semi-strong forms but not in the strong form (Copeland et al. 2005).[3] An implication of market efficiency is that asset prices evolve almost randomly over time. As for the US timber market, mixed evidence of market efficiency has been found as well (Prestemon 2003). Therefore, we consider two alternative timber price assumptions, a random walk model vs. a mean-reverting process.

A random walk is a mathematical formulization of a trajectory that consists of taking successive random steps. It is a widely used model under the efficient market hypothesis. The geometric Brownian motion model is one of the most commonly used stochastic processes in financial economics theory and practice. It has several appealing properties. Arguments for using a geometric Brownian motion to model security or commodity prices include (Hull 2009): (1) The expected returns from a geometric Brownian motion are independent of the prices, which follows the efficient market hypothesis; (2) A geometric Brownian motion assumes positive values only, which is appropriate for prices; (3) A geometric Brownian motion mimics well the paths of stock or commodity prices in the real world; and (4) Analytical solutions with a geometric Brownian motion are relatively easy. Nevertheless, a geometric Brownian motion has some constraints as well. First, a geometric Brownian motion assumes the volatility of stock or commodity prices to be constant, whereas, in reality, the volatility changes through time. Second, a geometric Brownian motion assumes returns to be normally distributed, whereas, in reality, this is usually not true (Wilmott 2006). In this chapter, random timber prices are approximated by a geometric Brownian motion

$$dP_t = \alpha P_t dt + \sigma P_t dw_t \tag{4.1}$$

where P_t is pine stumpage price, α and σ are the constant drift and volatility parameters, and dw_t is the increment of a Wiener process defined as $dw_t = \varepsilon_t \sqrt{dt}$, with ε_t being standard normal. By letting $r_t = d\ln(P_t) = \ln(P_t) - \ln(P_{t-1})$ be the continuously compounded return in the tth time interval, it was proven that $\hat{a} = \bar{r}/\Delta + s^2/2\Delta$ and $\hat{\sigma} = s/\sqrt{\Delta}$, where $\bar{r}$ and s are the sample mean and standard deviation of the series r_t and Δ is the equally spaced time interval measured in years (Tsay 2005).

Suspecting that commodity prices should reflect their long-run marginal costs of production, some researchers asserted that a mean-reversion process should depict better the time path of many commodity prices (Schwartz 1997). Mean-reverting timber prices in this chapter were approximated by a modified Ornstein-Uhlenbeck process

$$dP_t = \eta(\bar{P} - P_t)dt + \delta P dw_t \tag{4.2}$$

where $\bar{P}$ is the long-run equilibrium level the prices tend to revert to, η is the speed of reversion, and δ and dw_t are similarly defined as in a geometric Brownian motion. A mean-reverting process differs from a geometric Brownian motion in the drift parameter—the drift is positive when current price is below the equilibrium level $\bar{P}$ and negative when current price rises above $\bar{P}$. In other words, the long-run equilibrium level pulls prices in its direction in spite of short-term fluctuations. Similar to the geometric Brownian motion, the modified Ornstein-Uhlenbeck process is subject to the same constraints in the assumptions of return volatility and normality.

A discrete time approximation of the modified Ornstein-Uhlenbeck process is $P_t - P_{t-1} = \eta \bar{P}\Delta t - \eta \Delta t P_{t-1} + \delta P_{t-1}\sqrt{\Delta t}\varepsilon_t$. Dividing both sides by P_{t-1} leads to

$$(P_t - P_{t-1})/P_{t-1} = c(1) + c(2)/P_{t-1} + e_t \tag{4.3}$$

where $c(1) \equiv -\eta \Delta t$, $c(2) \equiv \eta \bar{P}\Delta t$, and $e_t \equiv \delta\sqrt{\Delta t}\varepsilon_t$ (Insley and Rollins 2005). The relevant parameters can be backed out by running a regression on Equation 4.3.

With both stochastic processes, dP_t was simulated first, and then future timber prices were generated by $P_{t+1} = P_t + dP$ repetitively for 2011–2025. For each year, dP_t was simulated 5,000 times in @Risk (Palisade Corporation 2021). The randomness in timber prices was captured by the increment of the Wiener process dw_t. To prevent prices for the three timber products from evolving in opposite directions in the simulation, they were further constrained to be positively correlated using their historical correlation matrix (Table 4.1). In addition, the uncertainty in land

TABLE 4.1 Historical price correlations among the three timber products (1977Q1–2010Q4)

	Pulpwood	Chip-n-saw	Sawtimber
Pulpwood	1		
Chip-n-saw	0.85	1	
Sawtimber	0.42	0.58	1

values and tree growth & yield was mimicked by triangular distributions with the most likely values being the expected values and the maximum and minimum values being 10% up and below the expected values. Therefore, stumpage values, total values, and returns were all calculated 5,000 times with the Monte Carlo simulation.

Applications of the simulation technique

Valuing a timber harvest contract

Suppose a landowner and a forest products firm have entered into a contract in which the firm has the right but not the obligation to cut the landowner's trees at predetermined stumpage prices on the expiration date. That is, the forest products firm will execute the option if stumpage prices in the open market exceed the predetermined prices at the predefined time, just like executing a European call option.[4] The expected present value of the realized intrinsic values from exercising the option determines the value of such a timber harvest contract.

Projecting liquidation values of a timberland property

Future timberland liquidation values have two components, timber and land sales. With Monte Carlo simulation, uncertainty in tree growth & yield, stumpage prices, and bare land values are considered simultaneously. Therefore, in addition to the mean, the 5th and the 95th percentiles of the projected future timberland liquidation values offer a better understanding of the profitability of a southern pine plantation in the short term. Moreover, the value at risk (VaR) from the simulation reflects the risk of loss from the timberland investment.

Assessing default risks of a leveraged timberland investment

To generate annual cash flows, an investor is assumed to purchase 15 acres of timberland with loblolly pine aged 10 to 24 years in 2010. In the next 15 years, the investor will clear cut the age-25 acre and sell both the timber and the land. With a certain debt level, a given interest rate and a required coverage ratio,[5] the possibility when the simulated annual cash flow is less than the interest payment times the coverage ratio measures the default risk on a leveraged timberland investment.

Results

Results from the static analysis

Columns 3–5 of Table 4.2 report the biological growth & yield of a hypothetical loblolly pine plantation generated by SiMS,[6] columns 6–8 report stumpage prices of three products in southern Georgia for 1995–2010, and column 10 reports bare land values. Using these data, it was found that the percentage contribution

TABLE 4.2 Interaction of timber price change, land appreciation, and biological growth on nominal investment returns on a hypothetical loblolly pine plantation in southern Georgia

(1)	(2)	(3)	(4)	(5)	(6)	(7)	(8)	(9)	(10)	(11)	(12)	(13)
		Volume (tons/acre)			Annual prices ($/ton)							
Year	Age	Pulp-wood	Chip-n-saw	Saw-timber	Pulp-wood	Chip-n-saw	Saw-timber	Stumpage value ($)	Land value ($/acre)	Total value ($)	Annual value change (%)	Annual return from inception (%)
1995	10	53.3	2.5	0.0	17.26	37.05	48.40	1,012.5	345	1,368.5		
1996	11	61.2	5.1	0.0	13.47	31.74	39.73	986.2	395	1,397.8	2.14	2.14
1997	12	67.7	8.6	0.0	13.08	36.15	47.08	1,196.0	438	1,659.2	18.70	10.11
1998	13	73.0	12.9	0.0	15.38	38.70	54.87	1,622.0	446	2,113.1	27.36	15.58
1999	14	77.1	18.1	0.0	10.04	37.44	48.00	1,452.1	422	1,912.3	-9.50	8.72
2000	15	80.2	23.8	0.0	9.51	39.10	51.60	1,693.7	430	2,170.3	13.49	9.66
2001	16	82.5	30.2	0.0	8.21	27.50	41.87	1,507.6	800	2,356.7	8.59	9.48
2002	17	83.9	36.9	0.0	6.91	28.96	44.67	1,648.1	790	2,486.1	5.49	8.90
2003	18	84.7	44.0	0.0	6.15	25.87	43.51	1,658.5	900	2,607.9	4.90	8.39
2004	19	84.8	51.3	0.3	6.18	26.42	44.25	1,892.0	910	2,857.8	9.58	8.53
2005	20	84.5	58.7	0.5	6.49	27.94	47.31	2,211.8	1,210	3,487.0	22.02	9.80
2006	21	83.7	66.3	0.8	6.65	25.54	45.62	2,286.1	1,440	3,799.6	8.96	9.73
2007	22	82.6	73.9	1.2	7.10	19.78	39.59	2,095.7	1,680	3,860.6	1.61	9.03
2008	23	81.1	81.4	1.7	7.23	16.64	32.55	1,996.2	1,550	3,639.2	-5.74	7.81
2009	24	79.4	88.6	2.6	8.61	15.60	28.78	2,140.6	1,210	3,469.3	-4.67	6.87
2010	25	77.5	95.8	3.6	10.83	17.86	31.43	2,663.5	890	3,711.7	6.99	6.88

TABLE 4.3 Percentage contributions of the three return drivers of timberland investments

Year	Total value ($/acre)	Biological growth ($/acre)	Timber price changes ($/acre)	Land price changes ($/acre)	Stumpage value ($/acre)
1995	1,368.5	1,024.5	–	345	1,024.5
2010	3,711.7	5,315.0	–	890	2,822.7
Change	2,343.2	4,290.5	−2,492.3	545	1,798.1
Contribution (%)	100%	183%	−106%	23%	–

of timber price had become negative, and correspondingly the annualized average return from inception decreased to 6.88% for 1995–2010, or a 52% drop from 14.31% for 1982–1997 (Table 4.2). The breakdown of each return driver's contribution is illustrated in Table 4.3. The change in total values between 2010 and 1995 was 3,711.7 − 1,368.5 = $2,343.2, resulting from the interaction of the three timberland return drivers over the 15-year investment horizon. To derive the percentage contribution of each return driver, the change in total values was further broken down into three categories.

The contribution of land appreciation is simply the net change of land values over 15 years, or 890 − 345 = $545. The combined contribution of timber price change and biological growth is the net change in stumpage values, or 2,663.5 − 1,012.5 = $1,651.0. Were timber prices fixed at the 1995 level, the stumpage value in 2010 would have been 77.5 × 17.26 + 95.8 × 37.5 + 3.6 × 48.5 = $5,104.75. Then, the net change of stumpage values over the 15 years, or 5,104.75 − 1,012.5 = $4,092.25, should be owed purely to biological growth and the rest, or 1,651.0 − 4,092.25 = −$2,441.25, should be owed to timber price change. In percentage, biological growth dominated and contributed 183% to the total returns, land appreciation contributed another 23%, but timber price change contributed negatively since timber price has been tumbling over the last 15 years. Combining Figure 4.1 and Table 4.2, it is not hard to conclude that the significant changes in timberland investment returns and the percentage contribution of each return driver were caused by the stochastic behavior of timber prices (Figure 4.4). Caulfield's (1998) corresponds to the rapid growth phase of timber prices while ours concurs with the overall declining phase.

BOX 4.1 SOME FURTHER DISCUSSION ON THE RETURN DRIVER ANALYSIS

The baseline model can be expanded in a number of ways. In what follows, we examine them one by one, changing one factor at a time. First, we change the 15-year holding period to between ages 15 and 30. As such, the initial purchase cost increases, whereas the proceeds from the future disposition also increase as more chip-n-saw and sawtimber products are produced at final harvest. The net effect is a lower annual return given the overall declining timber prices. More generally, when investing in mature forests, the contribution of biological growth shrinks because trees have passed the inflection point (the fastest growth rate) in Figure 4.3, whereas timber price change and land value appreciation play more crucial roles.

Second, we update the baseline analysis by using timber prices in the most recent 15 years. Since timber prices have been flat during this time period, the contribution of timber price is close to zero (as compared to a negative contribution in the base case). Thus, the annual return becomes higher.

Third, we consider payments that investors receive for providing ecosystem services (e.g., carbon sequestration). While the incremental cash inflows result in a higher annual return, the size of the return enhancement depends on the assumptions regarding the payments.

Last, we consider higher and better use (e.g., residential or commercial development) opportunities. In such a scenario, land value appreciation dominates the other two return drivers and contributes most to the total return. Depending on the land uses, the annual return can be significantly improved.

Results from the dynamic analysis

Parameter estimates for the two stochastic processes (Equations 4.1 and 4.2) are summarized in Table 4.4. If timber prices were random, the annual growth rate ranged 2.6%–4.2% and the volatility ranged 16.6%–21% for the three timber products. If timber prices were mean reverting, the reverting speed was highest for pulpwood at 0.25 and lowest for sawtimber at 0.15.

The corresponding half-life, the time for the expected value P_t to reach the middle between the current value P_0 and the long run mean $\overline{P}$, was about 11 months for pulpwood and 18 months for sawtimber. The long-term equilibrium levels were estimated \$10.06/ton for pulpwood, \$23.10/ton for chip-n-saw and \$33.32/ton for sawtimber, respectively. The volatility parameters were of similar size to those estimated for the geometric Brownian motion. Based on previous studies (Caulfield 1998; Zinkhan 1988), the expected mean bare land values for 2011-2025 were assumed to perfectly hedge against the expected inflation at an average rate of 2% per year (Federal Reserve Bank of Cleveland 2011).

Under the same framework for the static analysis, Monte Carlo simulation with random future timber prices suggested that, 15 years from 2010, the annualized

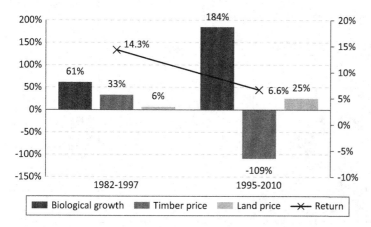

FIGURE 4.4   Comparison of percentage contributions of the three return drivers of timberland investments and annualized average nominal returns for two different periods

TABLE 4.4   Parameter estimates for random and mean-reverting nominal pine stumpage prices

	Pulpwood	Chip-n-saw	Sawtimber
Geometric Brownian motion			
α	0.0424	0.0256	0.0362
σ	0.2096	0.1742	0.1655
Modified Ornstein-Uhlenbeck process			
η	0.2543	0.1888	0.1499
$\bar{P}$	10.06	23.10	33.32
δ	0.2067	0.1718	0.1630

average future return ranged from 2.81% to 15.09% at the 90% confidence interval, with a mean of 8.35% and a standard deviation of 3.71% (Figure 4.5). With mean-reverting timber prices, in contrast, the annualized average future return had a narrower range from 4.93% to 9.83% at the 90% confidence interval, with a mean of 7.25% and a standard deviation of 1.51%. Obviously, with random prices, projected future returns were more volatile with more extreme downside and upside potential. Regardless of specific timber price assumptions, biological growth dominated in terms of percentage contribution among the three return drivers, with a mean of 127% for the case with random timber prices and 84% for the case with mean-reverting prices.

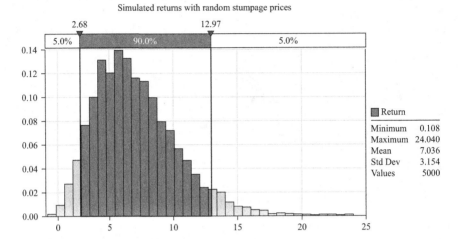

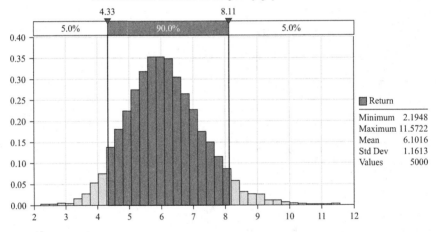

FIGURE 4.5 Monte Carlo simulation of future nominal returns of timberland investments with stochastic stumpage prices

Results for the applications

Simulated values of a timber harvest contract

Table 4.5 shows the expected proceeds, their present values and possibilities, and the values of the timber cut contract for the "base cases" over 2011–2025. Under the random price assumption, the 15-year European style call option on timber was valued at $597/acre, while under the mean-reverting price assumption the same option was valued significantly less at $62/acre. The difference was because

TABLE 4.5 Nominal values of the timber cut contract on the hypothetical loblolly pine plantation over 2011–2025

Year	Random timber prices				Mean-reverting timber prices			
	Expected proceeds ($/acre)	Present value ($/acre)	Probability	Agreement value ($/acre)	Expected proceeds ($/acre)	Present value ($/acre)	Probability	Agreement value ($/acre)
2011	95.6	90.2	0.27	24.6	84.9	80.1	0.19	15.6
2012	207.1	184.4	0.33	61.7	157.5	140.2	0.21	29.4
2013	320.5	269.1	0.37	99.5	211.0	177.1	0.20	36.2
2014	474.1	375.5	0.38	141.0	266.2	210.9	0.19	40.7
2015	608.1	454.4	0.40	181.7	305.6	228.4	0.20	45.5
2016	780.3	550.1	0.40	219.3	341.2	240.5	0.19	46.6
2017	976.1	649.2	0.40	262.2	386.6	257.1	0.19	48.9
2018	1176.6	738.2	0.41	306.2	439.9	276.0	0.19	52.5
2019	1414.7	837.4	0.42	350.4	494.5	292.7	0.20	57.6
2020	1666.9	930.8	0.42	391.4	541.0	302.1	0.19	58.1
2021	1934.6	1019.1	0.43	436.5	578.8	304.9	0.19	59.3
2022	2231.3	1108.9	0.44	483.3	613.5	304.9	0.19	58.9
2023	2530.8	1186.6	0.44	527.3	664.2	311.4	0.19	59.6
2024	2855.1	1262.8	0.45	562.8	719.8	318.4	0.19	61.9
2025	3092.8	1290.5	0.46	596.7	773.2	322.6	0.19	62.0

of the much wider range of possible cash flows from exercising the call option in 15 years under the random timber price assumption. Lastly, the value of the timber cut contract increased with the contract length, which is consistent with the option pricing theory.

Simulated liquidation values of a timberland property

Figure 4.6 shows the expected mean liquidation values along with their 5th and 95th percentiles for the hypothetical loblolly pine plantation over 2011–2025. In

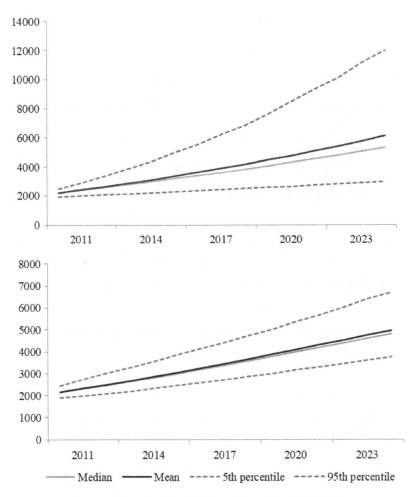

FIGURE 4.6 Projected nominal liquidation values of a timberland property over time with random and mean-reverting stumpage prices

the near term, a slight difference in the projected liquidation values was observed with different timber price assumptions, while, in the long term, a wider range of projected liquidation values was evident with random timber prices. In both cases, there was an overall increasing trend of the liquidation value. At the 5th percentile, the annual incremental rate averaged 3.17% with random timber prices and 5.49% with mean-reverting timber prices. Alternatively, the VaR of the investment's net present value (NPV) reveals the risk of loss. With an initial investment of $1,519 and a discount rate of 6%, the VaR at the 5% level for the NPV of the hypothetical loblolly pine plantation at age 15, 20, and 25 were −$283, −$415, and −$568 with random timber prices, and −$178, −$156, and −$214 with mean-reverting prices.

Simulated default risks of a leveraged timberland investment

The same hypothetical loblolly pine plantation was used to show the impact of different timber price assumptions on the default risk. The initial investment required $38,048, land plus standing timber.[7] With a 60% debt level, this meant $22,829 in debt and $15,219 in equity. Given an interest rate of 8%, no amortization on the principal and a coverage ratio of 1.5, the critical value would be $2,739/year. The possibility when the annual cash flow fell below that showed the default risk.

The default risk of such an investment is plotted in Figure 4.7. With random timber prices, the mean default risk was 9.3% with a standard deviation of 3.2%.

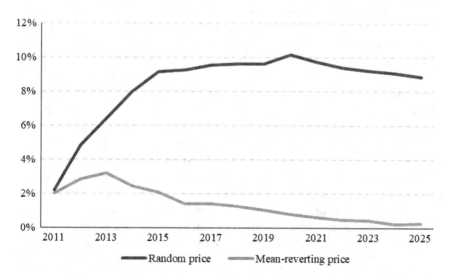

FIGURE 4.7 Default risks over time for a leveraged timberland investment with different stumpage price assumptions

With mean-reverting timber prices, the mean default risk was lower at 1.7% with a smaller standard deviation of 0.6%. The difference is rooted in the fact that there was a greater variability of timber prices and thus future cash flows with random timber prices. As the uncertainty in future cash flows increased, the default risk increased as well. Combined with previous results, it can be interpreted that random timber prices imply not only higher expected returns with higher uncertainty, but also higher default risks if financial leverage is used. Therefore, timber price assumptions influence both investors' and lenders' perspectives on the financial performance of timberland investments.

Sensitivity Analysis

The dynamic simulation formed the "base case." To consider more scenarios, sensitivity analysis was conducted. First, we changed the starting stumpage values to the estimated long-term means given the fact that current stumpage prices are below their long-term trends. Second, we assumed bare land values to appreciate at an average rate of 5.3% as observed in the historical data. Together, these might represent more normal market conditions and thus were referred to as the "normal case." Then, the expected timberland investment returns averaged at 10.16% with random stumpage prices and 8.56% with mean-reverting stumpage prices. Correspondingly, the percentage contribution of biological growth averaged at 57.5% and 63.6%, respectively.

Next, based on the "normal case," we examined the impact of changes in the volatility parameter on the simulated results. Specifically, we decreased the volatility parameters of the two stumpage price models by 20%. The simulated means of future returns remain almost unchanged; however, their volatilities decreased. This was consistent with our expectation in that less volatile stumpage prices led to less volatile stumpage values, which, in turn, led to less volatile returns. Since timber price change is only one driver to total timberland investment returns, the changes in return volatilities were less than proportional. In both scenarios, biological growth still dominated with a mean percentage contribution greater than 50%.

One key parameter in evaluating timber cut contract is the discount rate (Petrasek and Perez-Garcia 2010; Shaffer 1984). When the discount rate was raised (reduced) to 8% (4%), the value of the 15-year harvest contract decreased (increased) to $468/acre ($825/acre) with random timber prices and $44/acre ($77/acre) with mean-reverting prices. The results were consistent with the discounted cash flow rule that present values decrease with the discount rate. However, as the contract length shortened, the impact of the discount rate on the values of the timber cut contract became less significant.

Discussion and conclusions

Timberland assets have several unique features that are attractive to investors. This chapter examined the three return drivers of timberland investments—timber price change, land value appreciation, and biological growth, in two settings. Examination of a hypothetical loblolly pine plantation invested in the past 15 years revealed that timber price has nothing but a negative contribution to timberland investment returns. With declining timber prices, annualized average returns dropped by 52% to 6.88% for 1995–2010. In comparison, the NCREIF Timberland Index has shown a similar trend for the same time period—the annualized return averaged lower at 7.82%. As another measure of timberland investment returns, the John Hancock Timber Index reported an annualized average return of 8.38% for 1995–2010 (Hancock Timber Resource Group 2010). The difference could be owed to species mix, age distributions, and HBU explorations.

Looking forward, investment returns on a loblolly pine plantation over 2011–2025 were simulated by Monte Carlo simulations with both random and mean-reverting timber prices. Expected mean returns were expected to be 8.35%–10.16% with random timber prices and 7.25%–8.56% with mean-reverting timber prices. Meanwhile, future returns were found to be more volatile with random timber prices. Despite the time periods under investigation and timber price assumptions in the simulation, biological growth dominated the other two return drivers contributing the most to total returns of timberland investments. It is this unique feature that differentiates the timberland asset from other investment assets such as real estate, commodities, stocks and bonds. Because biological growth is independent of macroeconomic and capital market factors, investors can use the timberland asset for portfolio diversification.

In spite of the importance of biological growth as a return driver of timberland investments, different assumptions of timber prices implied different risks and valuations of timberland businesses. The difference became more dramatic as the investment time horizon expanded. This resulted from the fact that possible realizations of random timber prices remained unbounded, whereas those of mean-reverting timber prices moved toward their long-run equilibrium levels. Since investments in southern pine plantations usually take more than a decade, investors should carefully justify their assumptions of timber prices before evaluating their risks and returns, especially when financial leverage is used.

It is worth noting that returns from timberland investments can be improved by using a variety of structuring and management options, e.g., cooperating with consulting foresters, adopting improved seedlings, applying intensive silvicultural treatments, or seeking HBU opportunities. In addition, the 15-year management regime puts more emphasis on pulpwood and chip-n-saw production, and therefore ignores timber management flexibility. In fact, timberland investors may choose to have a longer rotation age so that more higher-value products can be produced. In other words, timberland investors can preserve value and gain from capital appreciation during weak market cycles, while raising harvest levels and gaining from cash yields during strong market cycles. Hence, long term investors can obtain better returns by exploring these embedded options in timberland investments. Finally, the origins of departure for each stochastic process matter. The higher the starting values of timber prices, the higher the simulated returns of timberland investments.

Questions

1. Explain how the three return drivers affect total timberland investment returns.
2. In the last decade, stumpage prices have been flat. What is its impact on long-term timber harvest contract?
3. What is the impact on the returns of an investment horizon between age 15 and 30?

Notes

1 Here, we exclude higher and better use (HBU) opportunities. If a timberland property has HBUs, the land value can be significantly higher.
2 The event in which debt borrowers are unable to make the required payments on their debt obligations.
3 The weak form efficient market hypothesis claims that asset prices reflect all historical information; the semi-strong form efficient market hypothesis claims that asset prices reflect all publicly available information and that asset prices respond rapidly and fully to new public information; and the strong form efficient market hypothesis claims that asset prices instantly reflect to all information, including insider information (Fama 1970).
4 Generally speaking, there are two styles of options in finance, European vs. American options. A European option can be exercised only at the expiry date, whereas an American option can be exercised any time before the expiry date. The buyer (holder) of a European call option has the right, but not the obligation, to buy an agreed quantity of a particular commodity or financial instrument from the seller at the expiry date at the strike price, and the seller (writer) is obligated to sell the commodity or financial instrument should the buyer so decide. The buyer pays a fee (called a premium) for this right.
5 Coverage ratio is the ratio of cash available for debt servicing to interest, principal, and lease payments. It is a popular benchmark used to measure an entity's ability to generate sufficient cash flow to make its scheduled debt payments.
6 SiMS is a simulator for managed timber stands developed by Forestech International, LLC.
7 Including 15 acres of land priced at $890/acre, 1,160 tons of pulpwood priced at $10.83/ton, 602 tons of chip–n–saw priced at $17.86/ton, and 7 tons of sawtimber priced at $31.43/ton.

Bibliography

Binkley, C.S., C.I. Washburn, and M.E. Aronow. 2001. *Stochastic simulation in timberland investment. Research Note R-01-2.* Hancock Timber Resource Group, Boston, MA. 6 .

Cascio, A.J., and M.L. Clutter. 2008. Risk and required return assessments of equity timberland investments in the United States. *For. Prod. J.* 58(10):61–70.

Caulfield, J.P. 1998. Timberland return drivers and investing styles for an asset that has come of age. *Real Estate Financ.* 14(4):65–78.

Clutter, J.L., J.C. Fortson, L.V. Pienaar, G.H. Brister, and R.L. Bailey. 1983. *Timber management: A quantitative approach.* Wiley, New York.

Copeland, T.E., J.F. Weston, and K. Shastri. 2005. *Financial theory and corporate policy.* Pearson Addison Wesley, Boston, MA, 1000p.

Fama, E.F. 1970. Efficient capital markets: A review of theory and empirical work. *J. Financ.* 25(2):383–417.

Fama, E.F. 1991. Efficient capital markets: II. *J. Financ.* 46(5):1575–1617.

Federal Reserve Bank of Cleveland. 2011. *Cleveland fed estimates of inflation expectations.* https://www.clevelandfed.org/. Last accessed August 20, 2022.

Haight, R.G., and T.P. Holmes. 1991. Stochastic price models and optimal tree cutting: Results for Loblolly pine. *Natural Res. Model.* 5(4):424–443.

Hancock Timber Resource Group. 2010. *Historical returns for Timberland. Research Note N-10-13.* Hancock Timber Resource Group, Boston, MA 10.

Hull, J.C. 2009. *Options, futures, and other derivatives.* Pearson Prentice Hall, Upper Saddle River, NJ, 822p.

Humphries, W.R. 2011. Southern timberland market - A windshield assessment. *Timber Mart-South Market News Quarterly* 16(3):12–17.

Insley, M., and K. Rollins. 2005. On solving the multirotational timber harvesting problem with stochastic prices: A linear complementarity formulation. *Am. J. Agri. Econ.* 87(3):735–755.

Mei, B., and M.L. Clutter. 2010. Evaluating the financial performance of timberland investments in the United States. *For. Sci.* 56(5):421–428.

NCREIF. 2020. *National council of real estate investment fiduciaries.* https://www.ncreif.org/. Last accessed August 20, 2022.

Palisade Corporation. 2021. *@RISK risk analysis and simulation add-in for excel: A software package, version 7.6.* Palisade Corporation, Newfield, NY.

Petrasek, S., and J.M. Perez-Garcia. 2010. Valuation of timber harvest contracts as American call options with modified least-squares Monte Carlo algorithm. *For. Sci.* 56(5):494–504.

Prestemon, J.P. 2003. Evaluation of U.S. southern pine stumpage market informational efficiency. *Can. J. For. Res.* 33(4):561–572.

Schwartz, E.S. 1997. The stochastic behavior of commodity prices: Implications for valuation and hedging. *J. Financ.* 52(3):923–973.

Shaffer, R.M. 1984. Valuation of certain long-term timber cutting contracts. *For. Sci.* 30(3):774–787.

Thomas, M. 2000. Bare timberland prices in the South rose in the '90s. *Timber Mart-South Market News Quarterly* 5(2):6–7.

TMS. 2022. *TimberMart-South.* Norris Foundation, Athens, GA.

Tsay, R.S. 2005. *Analysis of financial time series,* 2nd ed. John Wiley & Sons, Hoboken, NJ, 640p.

Williams, J. 2003. Bare timberland values. *Timber Mart-South Market News Quarterly* 8(1):13–14.

Wilmott, P. 2006. *Paul Wilmott on quantitative finance.* John Wiley & Sons Ltd, West Sussex, 363p.

Zinkhan, F.C. 1988. Forestry projects, modern portfolio theory, and discount rate selection. *South. J. Appl. For.* 12(2):132–135.

5

PROPERTY AND INCOME
TAX OF TIMBERLAND

Highlights

- Property tax on forestland can be biased toward development uses without any enrollment in tax reduction incentive programs.
- Preferential Agricultural Assessment, Conservation Use Valuation Assessment, Forest Land Protection Act, and Qualified Timberland Property are common programs that can reduce property tax on forestland.
- Timber depletion is an accrual accounting technique used to allocate the cost of harvesting timber.
- Timber depletion is an important deduction item that reduces federal income tax on timber sales.

Property tax is a major source of revenue for state and local governments. For total property tax collected in Georgia, about 61% is spent on the school system, about 38% is spent on county governments, and less than 1% is spent on the state government. Each county is different in how property is assessed and taxed (Li 2018). In this chapter, we use Georgia as an example and discuss its timberland property tax and incentive programs to reduce property tax. Timber depletion is an accrual accounting technique used to allocate the cost of harvesting timber. Unlike depreciation of equipment and property, which gauges the deduction in value due to aging, depletion is the actual physical depletion of forest resources. There are both tax depletion and financial (normalized) depletion. The former is used to calculate timber tax, whereas the latter is used in financial statement reporting.

DOI: 10.4324/9781003366737-5

Forestland property tax

In Georgia, forest landowners are taxed on both land and timber. Assessed value of land is based on the fair market value (FMV)[1] of the bare land, which considers all future potential higher and better uses. Then, timber is taxed again when it is harvested. Therefore, there is a concern of double taxation because timber value has already been incorporated into the bare land value calculation. Compared with neighboring states (NC, SC, AL, and MS), Georgia has a higher timberland property tax on a per acre basis.

In determining property tax rate, also known as millage rate[2], county-level budget and tax digest are used. Using the Greene County as an example, the annual budget development process starts about nine months prior to the beginning of the fiscal year. Officials at the department level submit operating and capital budget requests for review by the mayor. By the end of April, the mayor will submit a recommended budget to the Commission, which will review and make necessary adjustments before it is adopted in June.

Once the budget is finalized, it serves as the numerator for the millage rate. The denominator is the tax digest, which is the total value of all assessments within a county. In Georgia, the assessed value is 40% of the FMV. In recent years, the average millage rate across 159 counties in Georgia is about 25, or 2.5%. Reversely, given the tax rate and the assessed value of a property, the property tax can be calculated. For instance, if a bare land in Georgia is valued at $500/ac, its assessed value will be 500 × 40% = $200/acre. Given a tax rate of 2.5%, the property tax will be $200 × 2.5% = $5/acre.

Because property tax is based on FMV, which is biased toward development values, property taxes on timberland around metropolitan areas were made higher because of the urban sprawl. To relieve the tax burden of forest landowners, several tax reduction incentives have been created since the 1980s (Izlar et al. 2020), which will be discussed next.

In 1983, Preferential Agricultural Assessment (PAA) came into use by qualified landowners. PAA is a ten-year covenant targeting lands for the commercial production of agriculture products, including timber. It reduces the assessed value to 30% of FMV, resembling a 25% tax saving. PAA sets a 2000-acre limit per landowner, including all land and up to $100,000 agriculture processing and storage buildings but excluding residential buildings. Breach of the covenant, however, incurs penalties. Although PAA is able to ease taxes, the effect is limited because the assessed value is still closely related to FMV, which is influenced by development potential.

In 1991, Conservation Use Valuation Assessment (CUVA) was adopted. Like PAA, CUVA is a ten-year covenant targeting agricultural lands managed primarily for subsistence and commercial production of agricultural products. But lands managed for conservation and restoration purposes (e.g., carbon sequestration, mitigation and conservation banking, ecosystem products and services, and wildlife habitat) are also qualified. With CUVA, the assessed value is made of 65% current use value and 35% FMV, and thus reduces timberland property tax by 50% to 75%. CUVA has the same 2,000-acre limit per landowner but allows for early out under certain circumstances.

In 2008, the Forest Land Protection Act (FLPA) was passed. FLPA is a 15-year covenant targeting forestlands solely in Georgia. Like CUVA, assessed value leans heavily toward current use value and thus significantly reduces tax. It requires a minimum of 200 acres of contiguous land but allows partial conveyance, and breach of the partial conveyance does not affect the entire original tract. FLPA also allows for early out under certain circumstances. Figure 5.1 shows that the acreage under CUVA and FLPA has been growing, whereas that under PAA has been declining since 2000.

In 2018, the Georgia General Assembly passed House Resolution 51, Forest Land Conservation and Timberland Properties Amendment, and its enabling legislation, House Bill 85. The amendment became law in 2019. Qualifying forestland owners started applications in the tax year 2020. The legislation created a separate class of real property for ad valorem tax purposes—Qualified Timberland Property (QTP). This law can improve uniformity of timberland valuation for ad valorem tax purposes, decrease the number of tax appeals and litigation costs, and offer qualified forest landowners another option for property tax planning (Li and Izlar 2020). It is worth noting that with QTP the appraisal of forestland is vested with the state, not the county.

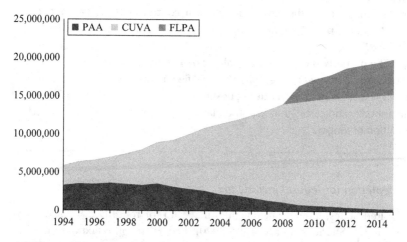

FIGURE 5.1 Acreage under each tax reduction incentive program in Georgia (1994–2015)

Note: PAA for Preferential Agricultural Assessment, CUVA for Conservation Use Valuation Assessment, and FLPA for Forest Land Protection Act. Data source: Izlar and Li (2017).

Unlike other preferential tax programs, QTP is not subject to long-term covenants or tax penalties, which relieves forest landowners' concerns about their long-term commitment to the county. Forest landowners may also benefit from enrolling in QTP if they are not qualified for other incentive programs (e.g., size limit), or if the FMV is inflated due to the erroneous inclusion of standing timber or speculative uses. Regarding the tax saving, a general rule of thumb for forest landowners is to compare the current property tax bill to 175% of the property's FLPA value. If the former is higher, it is very likely that QTP could help save property taxes on the forestlands (Li and Izlar 2020). Box 5.1 lists the requirements for QTP. Due to its less restrictive nature, not only small forest landowners, but also industrial forest landowners (e.g., TIMOs and REITs) and may benefit from enrolling in QTP.

BOX 5.1 WHAT PROPERTIES ARE ELIGIBLE FOR QTPS

According to the Georgia Code (O.C.G.A. § 48-5-604), timberland properties eligible for QTPs should meet the following requirements:

(1) Timberland property must be at least 50 contiguous acres;

(2) Production of trees must be for the purpose of making a profit;

(3) Production of trees must be the primary activity taking place on the property;

(4) Consistent efforts must be demonstrated in land management in accordance with accepted commercial forestry practices, which may include reforestation, periodic thinning, undergrowth control of unwanted vegetation, fertilization, prescribed burning, sales of timber, and maintenance of firebreaks; and

(5) The property is owned by a qualified owner, i.e., an individual or entity registered to do business in Georgia. The qualified owner needs to apply to the Georgia Department of Revenue requesting assessment under the QTP program annually and certify that the timberland is used for bona fide commercial production of timber.

Timber depletion for federal income tax

In the United States, federal tax revenues make up for roughly 20% of the size of the economy (Sherlock and Marples 2020). Federal income taxes are used to provide national programs, such as national defense; veterans and foreign affairs; social programs; physical, human, and community development; law enforcement; and interest on the national debt. The federal income tax system has several components. In terms of revenue generated, the individual income tax is the largest, followed by payroll taxes and corporate taxes. In recent years, about 50% of federal revenue came from the individual income tax, 40% came from payroll taxes, 5% came from corporate taxes, and the rest came from other sources (Sherlock and Marples 2020).

The federal individual income tax is levied on an individual's taxable income defined as adjusted gross income less deductions. The amount of tax liability is jointly determined by the taxable income and tax rates. In the United States, tax rates are progressive so that higher levels of income are taxed at higher rates. While it is every citizen's obligation to pay income tax, understanding how to calculate it, what legitimate deductions are, and how income tax can affect one's after-tax returns is crucial for financial planning and capital budgeting purposes.

Selling timber usually generates economic gains. As long as the holding period is longer than 12 months, the gain is treated as long-term capital gain for federal income tax purpose.[3] Specifically, timber income tax is calculated as

$$tax = T(R - D) = T[(p - d)Q] \qquad (5.1)$$

where T is the tax rate, R is timber revenue, D is deduction, p is stumpage price, d is depletion rate (unit), and Q is harvest volume. Both p and d are expressed as dollars per unit of volume (e.g., $/ton) and d changes with timber value and inventory over time. A numerical example is shown in Box 5.2, where a transaction of timberland consists of 6,050 tons of merchantable timber valued at $161,100, $54,900 of pre-merchantable timber, and $34,000 of land for a total of $250,000. The initial depletion rate is calculated as 161,100 / 6,050 = $26.63/ton. Should the landowner sell the timber at $30/ton right now, the taxable income per unit will be 30 − 26.63 = $3.37. If the landowner sells 1,000 tons and has a marginal tax rate of 25%, the total tax due will be 1,000 × 3.37 × 25% = $843. However, if there is no bookkeeping on the cost basis of timberland, then there is no timber depletion, and the total tax due will be 1,000 × 30 × 25% = $7,500. Therefore, the landowner's after-tax return declines substantially without timber depletion.

Suppose the landowner will harvest 8% of the inventory every year, and the biological growth (after harvest) is 6% per year, then each year he has to update the depletion rate. For example, in year 1, total harvest will be 6,050 × 8% = 484 tons and new inventory will be (6,050 − 484) × 1.06 = 5,900 tons. After the havest and growth, new value of merchantable timber will be recognized as original timber value minus harvest value (using the initial depletion rate) plus migration value from pre-merchantable timber, i.e., 161,100 − 484 × 26.63 + 8,750 = $156,961. Note that we use book values rather than market values under the generally accepted acounting principles (GAAP) adopted in the United States.[4] With new timber value and inventory, the new depletion rate equals 156,961 / 5,900 = $26.60/ton.

BOX 5.2 AN EXAMPLE OF TIMBER DEPLETION

Purchase price = $250,000

    Timber = $161,100
    Pre-merchantable timber = $54,900

Age	Value ($)
15	8,750
14	6,500
13	5,750
12	4,850
⋮	⋮

  Land = $34,000

Initial inventory = 6,050 tons
Initial depletion rate = 161,100 / 6,050 = $26.63/ton.

Similary, in year 2, total harvest will be 5,900 × 8% = 472 tons, new inventory will be (5,900 − 472) × 1.06 = 5,754 tons, and new timber value will be 156,961 − 472 × 26.60 + 6,500 = $150,906. Thus, the new depletion rate is 150,906 / 5,754 = $26.23/ton. This calculation keeps repeating untill new acquisitions occur, at which time the three timber accounts (merchantable timber account, pre-merchantable timber account, and land account) will be reconciled and the depletion dynamics will restart.

Financial depletion

Financial depletion captures the average depletion over a rotation. It is used in financial reporting by timber companies.[5] The following example illustrates the difference between tax depletion and financial depletion.

Assume we have a 20-acre, 20-age class fully regulated forest so that we harvest the age 20 acre and immediately replant that acre each year. The yield data come from SiMS (ForesTech International 2009) and is shown in Table 5.1. Suppose age 10 and below are considered as pre-merchantable timber, and the total acquisition cost of this fully regulated forest can be broken down into three components: merchantable timber, pre-merchantable timber, and land.[6] Given $8/ton pulpwood price, $11/ton chip-n-saw price, $24/ton sawtimber price, and merchantable timber volume for age 11-20, total merchantable timber sums to 1,232.5 tons and is valued at $11,793.10, and annual harvest is valued at $1,734.30 (8 × 69.2 + 11 × 92.5 + 24 × 6.8). If we assume a $200/acre for bare land, the 20-acre land is valued at $4,000.

TABLE 5.1 Growth and yield data of a loblolly pine plantation

| Age | Growth & yield (tons/ac) | | | |
	Pulpwood	Chip-n-Saw	Sawtimber	sum
1	0.0	0.0	0.0	
2	0.0	0.0	0.0	
3	0.0	0.0	0.0	
4	0.0	0.0	0.0	
5	10.6	0.0	0.0	
6	22.2	0.1	0.0	
7	33.2	1.2	0.0	
8	42.3	4.0	0.0	
9	49.4	8.4	0.0	
10	54.8	14.1	0.0	
11	58.9	20.6	0.0	79.5
12	62.2	27.5	0.0	89.7
13	64.7	34.5	0.2	99.4
14	66.6	41.7	0.4	108.7
15	67.9	48.8	0.6	117.3
16	69.1	55.8	1.0	125.9
17	70.2	64.2	1.6	136.0
18	69.9	75.4	3.1	148.4
19	69.6	84.7	4.8	159.1
20	69.2	92.5	6.8	168.5
Sum	668.3	545.7	18.5	1,232.5

Next, we have to determine the pre-merchantable timber value. Recall from Chapter 2 that there are lower and upper bounds of pre-merchantable timber values. For depletion purposes, we would like the pre-merchantable timber values to be as high as possible because this leads to higher depletion rates and thus less income taxes. For the lower bound, we simply compound the establishment cost over time at the discount rate. Assume $200/acre site establishment cost and 6% discount rate, the lower bound values are calculated in column 2 of Table 5.2.

For the upper bound, we assume that a landowner can sell the timber as well as the land based on the optimal rotation. For example, for age 10 class, if the landowner can hold the timber for ten more years, then according to Table 5.1, he expects 69.2 tons of pulpwood, 92.5 tons of chip-n-saw, and 6.8 tons of sawtimber per acre valued at $1,734.3. In addition, the maximized BLV is $495.15/acre.[7] Those optimized timber and land values are discounted by ten years, and the land component is taken out to get the upper bound of age 10 pre-merchantable timber value. Same logic applied to other age classes, and column 3 of Table 5.2 lays out the upper bound.

In this example, we use the average of the low and high values as the pre-merchantable timber value. In practice, it could be some weighted average but using the upper bound values may not pass the audit of the Internal Revenue Services.

TABLE 5.2 Determination of pre-merchantable timber value for income tax purposes

Age	Lower	Upper	Average
1	$212.00	$241.71	$226.85
2	$224.72	$285.92	$255.32
3	$238.20	$332.79	$285.49
4	$252.50	$382.46	$317.48
5	$267.65	$435.12	$351.38
6	$283.70	$490.94	$387.32
7	$300.73	$550.10	$425.41
8	$318.77	$612.82	$465.79
9	$337.90	$679.29	$508.60
10	$358.17	$749.76	$553.97
Sum	$2,794.33	$4,760.90	$3,777.62

The sum of pre-merchantable timber values across 1–10 age classes, $3,777.62, serves as the book value of the pre-merchantable timber account. For simplicity, we ignore all other transaction fees and the total sale price $19,570.72 consists of 1,232.5 tons of merchantable timber valued at $11,793.10, $3,777.62 of pre-merchantable timber, and $4,000 of land. Hence, the initial depletion rate is 11,793.10 / 1,232.5 = $9.57/ton.

In year 1, 168.5 tons of timber are harvested and original age 10 class merged into the merchantable timber account. Thus, the new balance of the merchantable timber account is 11,793.10 – 9.57 × 168.5 + 553.97 = $10,734.78, and the inventory remains at 1,232.5 tons since the forest is fully regulated. Year 1 depletion rate is 10,734.78 / 1,232.5 = $8.71/ton. Also, note that the newly replanted acre has a book value of $200, which equals the regeneration cost. Over the 20 years, the dynamics of the depletion calculation is shown in Table 5.3.

For financial depletion, total silviculture cost $5,777.62 (pre-merchantable timber value $3,777.62 plus 10-year regeneration cost $2,000) is added to the initial timber account $11,793.10 to get the total dollar amount $17,570.71 to be depleted over a 20-year period. Total cycle volume 4,602.5 equals initial inventory 1,232.5 plus cycle growth 3,370 (168.5 × 20). Thus, the financial depletion over 20 years is calculated as 17,570.71 / 4,602.5 = $3.82/ton. A comparison of tax depletion and financial depletion and their impact on profit and loss in financial reporting are shown in Table 5.4. Total timber tax at year 0 is (1,734.30 – 9.57 × 168.5) × 38% = $46.37 and net operating profit after tax (NOPAT) would be reported as $75.65. With financial depletion, timber tax is still at $46.37 but NOPAT rises to $1,044.66. Regardless, free cash flow, which is available for distribution to all stakeholders of a business after operating expenses and capital expenditures, is independent of depletion method and equals $1,487.93. In sum, using financial depletion enhances earnings before interest and taxes (EBIT) and NOPAT, but does not change free cash flows.

TABLE 5.3 Depletion dynamics for a 20-acre fully regulated forest

Year	0	1	2	3	4	5	6	7	8	9	10
Dep. $	11,793	10,735	9,776	8,905	8,113	7,391	6,732	6,129	5,577	5,070	4,603
Pre-merch.		553.97	508.60	465.79	425.41	387.32	351.38	317.48	285.49	255.32	226.85
Inventory	1,232.5	1,232.5	1,232.5	1,232.5	1,232.5	1,232.5	1,232.5	1,232.5	1,232.5	1,232.5	1,232.5
Harvest		168.5	168.5	168.5	168.5	168.5	168.5	168.5	168.5	168.5	168.5
Dep. rate	$9.57	$8.71	$7.93	$7.23	$6.58	$6.00	$5.46	$4.97	$4.52	$4.11	$3.74

Year	11	12	13	14	15	16	17	18	19	20
Dep. $	4,174	3,803	3,483	3,207	2,969	2,763	2,585	2,432	2,299	2,185
Pre-merch.	200.00	200.00	200.00	200.00	200.00	200.00	200.00	200.00	200.00	200.00
Inventory	1,232.5	1,232.5	1,232.5	1,232.5	1,232.5	1,232.5	1,232.5	1,232.5	1,232.5	1,232.5
Harvest	168.5	168.5	168.5	168.5	168.5	168.5	168.5	168.5	168.5	168.5
Dep. rate	$3.39	$3.09	$2.83	$2.60	$2.41	$2.24	$2.10	$1.97	$1.87	$1.77

TABLE 5.4 A comparison of tax depletion and financial depletion and their impact on profit and loss in financial reporting at year 0

	Tax Depletion	Financial Depletion
Tax Rate:	38%	38%
Capitalized silviculture:	0	200.00
Total silviculture		5,777.62
Timber account	11,793.10	11,793.10
Total book dollars	11,793.10	17,570.72
Initial inventory	1,232.5	1,232.5
Rotation growth	0	3,370
Total cycle volume	1,232.5	4,602.5
Depletion rate	9.57	3.82
Profit & loss effect		
Tons harvested	168.5	168.5
Timber revenue	1,734.30	1,734.30
Other revenue	0	0
Silviculture expense	0	0
Other expense	0	0
Depletion expense	1,612.28	643.27
EBIT	122.02	1,091.03
Tax	46.37	46.37
NOPAT	75.65	1,044.66
Capitalized silviculture	200.00	200.00
Free cash flow	1,487.93	1,487.93

Conclusions

Property tax on timberland is based on FMV, which considers future better uses. This represents a burden on forest landowners whose primary goal of managing the land is for timber production. To ease the pressure, several tax reduction incentive programs can be used. For federal income tax, timber depletion is a legitimate deduction item that recovers the capital expenditure on timber investment and management, and therefore reduces the tax liability. A clean bookkeeping of the timber account ensures a correct calculation of depletion rates. A misrepresentation of depletion can lead to unattended results. For example, in November 2014, Rayonier admitted that it had understated the depletion rate by including environmentally sensitive or inaccessible timber regions into their timber inventory, and therefore underestimated its depletion rate and overestimated its net income. In two days following this news, Rayonier's stock price plummeted by 20% and its long-term dividends were cut too.

Questions

1. Compare current use value and fair market value. How do they affect the property tax on timberland?

2. How is tax depletion different from financial depletion?
3. In calculating depletion rate, should we use book value or market value of timber? Why?
4. Explain the dynamics of depletion rate calculation.

Notes

1 The amount a knowledgeable buyer would pay and a willing seller would accept in a bona fide sale.
2 Millage rate is defined as the dollar amount for tax per 1,000 dollars of assessed value.
3 Tax rate on long-term capital gain is lower than on ordinary income and is capped at 20%. Tax rate on ordinary income can be as high as 39.6%.
4 By the international financial reporting standards (IFRS), market but not book values are used. Adopting GAAP or IFRS implies different tax liabilities.
5 There is no authority in the tax code about financial depletion. Each firm may use a different method in calculating it.
6 In practice, all fees (e.g., boundary survey, title transfer, consulting, etc.) that occur in the timberland transaction should be added to the total purchase cost and then allocated to the three accounts proportionally to their respective fair market value. Ignoring these fees results in lower depletion rates. Note that land value cannot be depleted.
7 The 20-year rotation is chosen as to maximize BLV given the aforementioned values of key economic variables.

Bibliography

ForesTech International. 2009. *SiMS 2009: Growth and yield simulator for southern pine.* ForesTech International, Watkinsville, GA.

Izlar, R., and Y. Li. 2017. Property tax analysis reveals Georgia is still not competitive with surrounding states. *Georgia Forestry* Winter:26–29.

Izlar, R., Y. Li, and T. Smith. 2020. *Property tax incentives for the Georgia landowners.* Harley Langdale Jr. Center for Forest Business, Athens, GA.

Li, Y. 2018. A comparative overview of current-use valuation of forests for property-tax purposes in the US South. *J. For.* 117(1):46–54.

Li, Y., and R. Izlar. 2020. *Qualified Timberland property: A new property class for Georgia forest landowners to consider.* Warnell School of Forestry and Natura Resources, Athens, GA, 6.

Sherlock, M.F., and D.J. Marples. 2020. *Overview of the federal tax system in 2020.* Congressional Research Service, Washington, DC, 22.

6

PORTFOLIO THEORY AND ASSET PRICING MODELS

Highlights

- The modern portfolio theory can be used by risk-averse investors to construct diversified portfolios that maximize their returns at acceptable levels of risk.
- The capital market line represents portfolios that optimally combine the risk-free asset and the market portfolio of risky assets.
- The slope of the capital market line is the Sharpe ratio of the market portfolio.
- The security market line is a graphical representation of the capital asset pricing model, with the X-axis being the systematic risk that is inherent to the entire market.
- Capital asset pricing model is based on the mean-variance efficiency framework and is a widely used single-factor, single-period model.
- Multifactor asset pricing models consider other variables in addition to the market portfolio.

Idiosyncratic risk means inherent factors that impact individual securities or a specific group of assets. It is also known as specific or unsystematic risk. Idiosyncratic risk can generally be mitigated in an investment portfolio through the use of diversification. By holding a portfolio of not-so-correlated assets, investors reduce extreme downside risk and enhance investment efficiency. This chapter first reviews the modern portfolio theory and then explains various asset pricing models.

Portfolio theory

Assume we have two assets: A and B, with expected annual returns 10% and 15%, and standard deviations 20% and 25%, respectively. The correlation (ρ) between

DOI: 10.4324/9781003366737-6

A and B is 0.2. If we hold 50% each, the expected portfolio return is $0.5 \times 0.1 + 0.5 \times 0.15 = 0.125$, and the expected standard deviation is $((0.5 \times 0.2)^2 + 2 \times 0.2 \times 0.2 \times 0.25 + (0.5 \times 0.25)^2)^{0.5} = 0.175$. The expected return of the portfolio is a linear function of the respective returns of A and B, but not the risk. Indeed, the expected standard deviation of the portfolio is lower than the average of those of A and B (i.e., $0.175 < 0.225$). This phenomenon is related to the concept of efficient frontier, which will be discussed later.

More generally, denote the expected returns on A and B to be $\bar{R}_A$ and $\bar{R}_B$, standard deviations to be σ_A and σ_B, weights in the portfolio to be w_A and w_B, then the expected return of the portfolio is

$$R_P = w_A \bar{R}_A + w_B \bar{R}_B \tag{6.1}$$

and the standard diveation is

$$\sigma_P = \left[\left(w_A \sigma_A \right)^2 + 2\rho w_A w_B \sigma_A \sigma_B + \left(w_B \sigma_B \right)^2 \right]^{0.5}. \tag{6.2}$$

Given that $-1 \leq \rho \leq 1$, $\sigma_P \leq \left[\left(w_A \sigma_A \right)^2 + 2w_A w_B \sigma_A \sigma_B + \left(w_B \sigma_B \right)^2 \right]^{0.5}$, i.e., $\sigma_P \leq w_A \sigma_A + w_B \sigma_B$. With a series of different weight sets (Table 6.1), we can plot the return-risk pairs of the portfolio (Figure 6.2).

The upper part of the plot (curve MB) resembles the efficient frontier (Markowitz 1952). For example, asset A is less efficient than the portfolio in the sense that for the same level of risk (20%), the portfolio can achieve a higher return. For the same reason, the lower part of the plot (MA) is not preferred. Point M is known as the minimum variance portfolio, which represents the minimum achievable risk from the two-asset portfolio. Along the efficient frontier, investors can obtain a target return based on their risk tolorance by changing the allocation.[1] The straight line AB corresponds to $\rho = 1$. That is, with a perfect

TABLE 6.1 Weights and expected returns and risks of the two-asset portfolio

w_A	w_B	R_P	σ_P
0.0	1.0	15.00%	25.00%
0.1	0.9	14.50%	22.98%
0.2	0.8	14.00%	21.17%
0.3	0.7	13.50%	19.60%
0.4	0.6	13.00%	18.36%
0.5	0.5	12.50%	17.50%
0.6	0.4	12.00%	17.09%
0.7	0.3	11.50%	17.15%
0.8	0.2	11.00%	17.69%
0.9	0.1	10.50%	18.66%
1.0	0.0	10.00%	20.00%

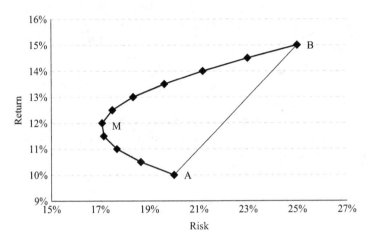

FIGURE 6.1 Efficient frontier with two assets

correlation, there is no deversification benefit by holding a portfolio of A and B. Both expected return and standard deviation of the portfolio is a linear function of assets A and B. On the flip side, as the correlation weakens, the curve bends more to the left, implying a lower risk minimum variance portfolio and a wider range of achievable risk–return relationships.

BOX 6.1 CORRELATIONS BETWEEN TIMBERLAND AND SOME SELECTED ASSETS

During 1987Q1 – 2017Q4, timberland (i.e., the NCREIF Timberland Index) had almost zero correlations with stocks (S&P 500, Dow Jones Index, and decile portfolios by market capitalization), moderate correlations with bonds (US Treasury bonds and investment-grade corporate bonds) and farmland, and low correlations with emerging markets, hedge funds, private equity, venture capital, comodities, and commercial real estate (Mei 2022). Therefore, including timberland in a mixed-asset portfolio can ehance the investment efficiency, especially for investors with a lower risk tolerance.

Graphically, as shown in Figure 6.1, it means that curve MB shifts up and point M moves to the left. That is, investors can achieve a higher return for a given risk level or a less risky minimum variance portfolio if they chose to do so. Of course, correlations are time dependent. For a different sample period, the correlation coefficients between timberland and other assets can change.

Note: NCREIF for National Council of Real Estate Investment Fiduciaries.

When there are more than two assets, the efficient frontier can be likely derrived. To be more concise, we use linear algebra for notations. Denote the expected returns of N candidate assets in a column vector R, standard deviations in a column vector S, weights in a column vector W, and correlations in a $N \times N$ matrix Ψ, then the expected return of the portfolio is

$$R_P = W'R \qquad (6.3)$$

the variance of the portfolio is

$$\Omega = diag(S)\psi\, diag(S) \qquad (6.4)$$

where the $diag(S)$ function makes a diagonal matrix with standard deviations on the diagonal and zeros everywhere else, and the variance of the portfolio is

$$\Pi = W'\Omega W. \qquad (6.5)$$

Again, the efficient frontier can be identified by changing the weights. Or stated as a linear programming problem, given a target return μ, we choose to minimize the variance of the portfolio by changing the weights (Cochrane 2005):

$$\min_{W} \Pi = W'\Omega W$$

$$s.t.\ W'R = \mu \qquad (6.6)$$

$$W'1 = 1$$

where 1 is a unit vector. The first constraint sets the target return, and the second constraint sums all weights to 100%. To solve the problem, two Lagrange multipliers 2λ and 2δ are introduced into the Lagrange equation:

$$\ell = W'\Omega W - 2\lambda(W'R - \mu) - 2\delta(W'1 - 1). \qquad (6.7)$$

For a minimum to exist, the first-order condition requires $\dfrac{\delta \ell}{\delta W} = 0$, i.e., $2\Omega W - 2\lambda R - 2\delta 1 = 0 \Leftrightarrow W = \Omega^{-1}(\lambda R + \delta 1)$. Substitute W into the two constraint equations, we get the following system of equations:

$$R'\Omega^{-1}(\lambda R + \delta 1) = \mu$$

$$1'\Omega^{-1}(\lambda R + \delta 1) = 1 \qquad (6.8)$$

In matrix forms, Equation 6.8 can be expressed as

$$\begin{bmatrix} R'\Omega^{-1}R & R'\Omega^{-1}1 \\ 1'\Omega^{-1}R & 1'\Omega^{-1}1 \end{bmatrix} \begin{bmatrix} \lambda \\ \delta \end{bmatrix} = \begin{bmatrix} \mu \\ 1 \end{bmatrix}. \tag{6.9}$$

Using the Cramer's rule, λ and δ can be solved as

$$\lambda = \frac{C\mu - B}{AC - B^2}$$

$$\delta = \frac{A - B\mu}{AC - B^2} \tag{6.10}$$

where $A = R'\Omega^{-1}R, B = R'\Omega^{-1}1$, and $C = 1'\Omega^{-1}1$. Then, λ and δ can be substituted back to the weight equation and weights can be solved. Alternatively, one can use Solver in MS Excel or statistics software R for the weights. With a series of target returns, minimum variances and associated weights can be solved iteratively. Thus, we identify the efficient frontier with more than two candidate assets.

Capital asset pricing model

Once the efficient frontier is recognized, we introduce a risk-free asset (R_f) so that investors can lend or borrow at this rate freely. Then, a tangency (market) portfolio is introduced by drawing a tangent line, known as capital market line (CML), from R_f to the efficient frontier (Figure 6.2). Now, individual investor's risk tolerance does not matter and all investors benchmark their returns based on CML instead of the efficient frontier because for the same risk, higher return can be achieved by using financial leverage. That is, all investors hold a two-asset

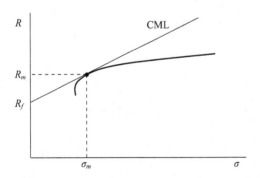

FIGURE 6.2 Tangency portfolio and capital market line (CML)

portfolio consisting of a risk-free asset and a market asset. Where an investor's expected return ends up being depends on whether the investor is a net lender (to the left of the market portfolio) or net borrower (to the right of the market portfolio). In the real world, a risk-free asset usually does not exist. We often use short-term US government bond as a proxy.

The slope, $(R_m - R_f)/\sigma_m$, of the CML is known as the Sharpe ratio (Sharpe 1994). It is often used to rank candidates of market portfolios. If an investor can shift the efficient frontier outward by carefully selecting the basis assets, then such a market portfolio is superior to the original one. For a given standard deviation, the expected return can be calculated using the Sharpe ratio. Standard deviation is unbounded and less interpretable in certain circumstances. Instead, $\beta_i = \sigma_{im}/\sigma_m^2$, is used for the horizontal axis, where σ_{im} is the covariance of asset i with the market portfolio (Figure 6.3). The resulting line is known as security market line (SML). By definition, market portfolio has a beta of one. Assets with betas higher than one are said to be risker than the market and have higher expected returns.

Beta is widely known as the systematic risk, market risk, or undiversifiable risk that is inherent to the entire market. It is the systematic risk an investor takes that is rewarded. Unsystematic risk or diversifiable risk is not compensated for because it can be cancelled out in a broad market portfolio. In equilibrium, all assets should fall onto the SML. In the real world, nonetheless, there are exceptions. Assets above the SML have superior returns after absorbing the risk. Similarly, assets below the SML have inferior returns. The SML lays the ground for the capital asset pricing model (CAPM). Using basic geometry, the gradient of the SML is $R_m - R_f$, and the expected return is $E[R_i] = R_f + \beta_i[R_m - R_f]$. In empirical CAPM analysis, regressions in the excess return form are used,

$$R_i - R_f = \alpha_i + \beta_i(R_m - R_f) + \mu_i \tag{6.11}$$

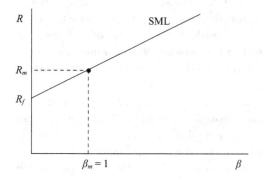

FIGURE 6.3 Security market line (SML)

where ex post returns replace ex ante ones and an intercept is added to capture abnormal performance (Jensen 1968).

Fama-French three-factor model

CAPM is a single-factor model. In addition to the market risk, other factors have been identified in empirical research. Fama and French (1993b) claimed small and value firms outperformed large and growth firms on a consistent basis. Therefore, they proposed that the size and value factors should be added to the CAPM. Specifically, the size factor represents the return difference between a portfolio of small stocks and a portfolio of large stocks (SMB as "Small minus Big"); and the value factor represents the return difference between a portfolio of high book-to-market stocks and a portfolio of low book-to-market stocks (HML as "High minus Low").[2]

The model is known as Fama-French three-factor (FF3F) model, and the expected return is expressed as follows:

$$E[R_i] - R_f = \beta_{RMRF,i}E[R_{RMRF}] + \beta_{SMB,i}E[R_{SMB}] + \beta_{HML,i}E[R_{HML}] \qquad (6.12)$$

where $R_{RMRF} = R_m - R_f$ is the same market factor as in the CAPM; $R_{SMB} = R_S - R_B$ is the size factor; and $R_{HML} = R_H - R_L$ is the value factor. By the same logic, portfolio can be formed by ranking stocks based on operating profitability, change in total assets, past returns, etc., and such factors can be included in the model. Like the CAPM, regressions in the form of excess returns are used in empirical FF3F analysis.

Arbitrage pricing theory

The APT was developed by Ross (1976) and enriched by others (Roll and Ross 1980). It requires less restrictive assumptions than the CAPM. The APT is based on the law of one price, which asserts that, in an efficient market, all identical assets should have only one price. Unlike the CAPM that uses the market risk as the single factor, the APT derives factors in a more intuitive manner (Ross et al. 2002). It assumes that asset returns are linearly related to a set of industry- and market-wide factors, which are called common factors. For example, when pricing timberland assets, the common factors could be timber prices, housing starts, industrial metal prices, inflation, and aggregate consumption.

The identification of the common factors can be achieved via factor analysis. It is a dimension reduction technique that describes the variance relationships among many variables in terms of a few unobservable random factors. Given an observable p-dimensional random vector X with a mean μ and a covariance matrix Σ, an orthogonal factor model states that X is linearly dependent on

n ($n \le p$) common factors $F' = (F_1, F_2, \dots, F_n)$, and p additional specific factors (errors) $\varepsilon' = \varepsilon_1, \varepsilon_2, \dots, \varepsilon_p$ (Johnson and Wichern 2007),

$$X_1 - \mu_1 = l_{11}F_1 + l_{12}F_2 + \cdots + l_{1n}F_n + \varepsilon_1$$

$$X_2 - \mu_2 = l_{21}F_1 + l_{22}F_2 + \cdots + l_{2n}F_n + \varepsilon_2$$

$$\vdots$$

(6.13)

$$X_p - \mu_p = l_{p1}F_1 + l_{p2}F_2 + \cdots + l_{pn}F_n + \varepsilon_p$$

In matrix notations, the relationship can be expressed as

$$X - \mu = L \, F + \varepsilon \qquad (6.14)$$

where L is a $p \times n$ matrix of factor loadings, $E[F] = 0$, $\text{cov}(F) = E[FF'] = I$, $E[\varepsilon] = 0$, $\text{cov}[\varepsilon] = E[\varepsilon\varepsilon'] = \psi = diag(\psi_1, \psi_2, \dots, \psi_p)$, and $\text{cov}(\varepsilon, F) = E[\varepsilon F'] = 0$. In other words, the p deviations $X_1 - \mu_1, X_2 - \mu_2, \dots, X_p - \mu_p$ can be expressed in terms of $n + p$ unobservable random variables $F_1, F_2, \dots, F_n, \varepsilon_1, \varepsilon_2, \dots, \varepsilon_p$.

Provided observed values $x_1, x_2, \dots, x_n$ on p correlated variables, factor analysis seeks a small number of factors that can adequately represent the data. If £ significantly deviates from a diagonal matrix, the problem is to estimate the factor loadings l_{ij} and the specific variances ψ_i. The two most widely used estimation methods are the principal component method and the maximum likelihood method. The former uses eigenvalue-eigenvector pairs (λ_i, e_i) of £ in its spectral decomposition, whereas the latter assumes joint normality of F_j and ε_j in maximizing the likelihood function. Once factor loadings are estimated, they are usually further rotated to aid interpretations. Among others, VARIMAX is a commonly used orthogonal rotation method to group variables. Thus, each variable tends to be associated with a small number of factors and each factor represents only a small number of variables (Kaiser 1958). With factor loadings and specific variances obtained, estimated values for the common factors, so-called factor scores, can be constructed and used in subsequent analyses (Johnson and Wichern 2007).

Under the APT framework, asset returns are generated by the following stochastic model

$$R_i - E[R_i] = \beta_{i1}F_1 + \beta_{i2}F_2 + \dots + \beta_{in}F_n + e_i \qquad (6.15)$$

where R_i and $E[R_i]$ are the same as defined in the CAPM and e_i is the error term. Like in the CAPM, β_i's are interpreted as risk measures for asset i corresponding to the common factors. Along with the assumption of zero arbitrage profit, the expected return can be calculated by

$$E[R_i] = R_f + \beta_{i1}\lambda_1 + \beta_{i2}\lambda_2 + \ldots + \beta_{in}\lambda_n \tag{6.16}$$

where λ's are the risk premiums associated with the n risk factors. Empirically, β's and λ's need to be estimated first.

Sensitivity coefficients β's are estimated by the regression model

$$R_{it} = \beta_{i0} + \beta_{i1}\delta_{1t} + \beta_{i2}\delta_{2t} + \cdots + \beta_{in}\delta_{nt} + \xi_{it} \tag{6.17}$$

where β_{i0} is the intercept, δ's are factor scores associated with the common factors, and ξ_{it} is the error term. After $\hat{\beta}$'s are obtained, λ's are estimated via cross-sectional regressions

$$R_{it} = \lambda_{0t} + \hat{\beta}_{i1}\lambda_{1t} + \hat{\beta}_{i2}\lambda_{2t} + \ldots + \hat{\beta}_{in}\lambda_{nt} + \eta_{it} \tag{6.18}$$

for $i = 1,2,\ldots,N$ and $t = 1,2,\ldots,T$, where λ_{0t} is the intercept, η_{it} is the error term, N is the total number of assets used to derive the common factors, and T is the sample length. That is, there is one regression across the N assets for each time period and there are T such regressions in total.

Real CAPM

The Fisher's hypothesis states that nominal interest rate equals real interest rate plus inflation (Fisher 1930). Similarly, nominal rate of return R_i for asset i or a risk-free asset can be expressed as

$$1 + R_i = (1 + r_i)(1 + \pi)^{\gamma_i} \tag{6.19}$$

where r_i is the rate of return without inflation, π is the inflation rate, and γ_i is the inflation response coefficient for asset i (Lee et al. 1988). The rate of return without inflation and inflation response coefficient are not observable but can be estimated by

$$\ln(1 + R_i) = \ln(1 + r_i) + \gamma_i \ln(1 + \pi) + e_i \tag{6.20}$$

and γ_i can be interpreted as the asset's inflation hedging ability in the following three categories: (1) complete inflation hedging with $\gamma_i = 1$; (2) superior inflation hedging with $\gamma_i > 1$; and (3) inferior inflation hedging with $\gamma_i < 1$.

However, investors not only care about hedging inflation, but also diversifying their residual risk. Therefore, a two-factor model, i.e., the CAPM in real terms, which accounts for market risk, is more appropriate for examining the marginal ability of inflation hedging (Lee et al. 1988). To get real CAPM, Equation 6.20 is first linearized using the Taylor expansion (Chen and Boness 1975):

$$R_i = r_i + \gamma_i \pi + e_i^*. \tag{6.21}$$

Then the econometric CAPM (Equation 6.11) in real terms can be written as

$$R_i - \gamma_i \pi - r_f = a_i + b_i(R_m - \gamma_m \pi - r_f) + \varepsilon_i. \tag{6.22}$$

Rearranging the terms, Equation 6.22 becomes

$$R_i - r_f = a_i + b_i(R_m - r_f) + c_i \pi + \varepsilon_i. \tag{6.23}$$

where $c_i = \gamma_i - \gamma_m b_i$.. Equation 6.23 can be viewed as an APT model under inflation (Elton et al. 1983), since c_i signifies how the return generating process relies on inflation (Lee et al. 1988). Actual inflation in Equation 6.23 can be further decomposed into expected inflation π_e and unexpected inflation π_u, which leads to (Lausti 2004)

$$R_i - r_f = a_i + b_i(R_m - r_f) + c_{i,e}\pi_e + c_{i,u}\pi_u + \varepsilon_i, \tag{6.24}$$

and can be used to test an asset's hedging ability on expected and unexpected inflation.

Intertemporal CAPM

To improve the CAPM, Merton (1973) proposed the multifactor intertemporal CAPM (ICAPM), which assumes that investors trade continuously and maximize their expected utility of lifetime consumptions. In addition to the market risk, risk of unfavorable shifts in the investment opportunity set, as approximated by changes of the so-called state variables, should be compensated for. The ICAPM being important from a theoretical standpoint, identifying state variables remains a challenge in empirical studies (Breeden 1979).

Summarizing from past studies, state variables can be categorized into: (1) macroeconomic variables; (2) financial factors; and (3) aggregate consumptions. In the first category, identified state variables include interest rate, term spread, and default spread. Interest rate is observable and time dependent, representing the stochastic nature of the investment opportunity set (e.g., Abhyankar and Gonzalez 2009; Campbell and Vuolteenaho 2004; Hui 2006). Innovation in interest rate helps predict cross-sectional returns (Brennan et al. 2004; Petkova 2006). Term spread (TERM), or yield differential between long-term and short-term bonds, is capable of tracking short-term fluctuations in the business cycle (Fama and

French 1989). Default spread (DEF), or yield differential between low-rating and high-rating bonds, reflects the macroeconomic condition. Both term spread and default spread have significant impacts on expected returns (e.g., Bali 2008; Bali and Engle 2010; Evans 1994; Petkova 2006).

In the second category, the small-minus-big (SMB) and high-minus-low (HML) factors launched by Fama and French (1993a) represent the size and value effects of stocks and can explain more cross-sectional variations of stock returns than the CAPM (e.g., Bali 2008; Bali and Engle 2010; Kothari and Shanken 1997). In the last category, the aggregate consumption rate represents a significant fraction of the true consumption and adds explanatory power to the expected returns (e.g., Bollerslev et al. 1988; Breeden 1979; Hui 2006).

Rather than using state variables directly for the empirical implementation of the ICAPM, Campbell (1996) suggests using innovations in the state variables to signify changes in the future investment opportunity set. To achieve this, Brennan et al. (2004) assume the Ornstein-Uhlenbeck process, Petkova (2006) uses a first-order vector autoregression model, and Dorfman and Park (2011) apply the Bayesian approach and the bivariate generalized autoregressive conditional heteroskedasticity (GARCH) in the mean model. All studies find significant risk premiums induced by innovations in the state variables.

Under the ICAPM, an asset's expected return is a linear function of the market excess returns and innovations in state variables. The unconditional expected excess return can be written as

$$E[R_{i,t}] - R_{f,t} = \beta_{i,m}\lambda_{m,t} + \sum_{k=1}^{K} \beta_{i,k}\lambda_{k,t} \tag{6.25}$$

where λ_m is the market risk premium, λ_k is the price of risk for innovation in state variable k, and subscript t indicates time. Using the Fama and MacBeth (1973) two-step method, beta loadings are estimated via the following time-series regression as the first step:

$$R_{i,t} - R_{f,t} = \alpha_i + \beta_{i,m}(R_{m,t} - R_{f,t}) + \sum_{k=1}^{K} \beta_{i,k}\varepsilon_{k,t} + u_{i,t} \tag{6.26}$$

where ε_k is the innovation in state variable k, and u_i is the error term.

To estimate prices of risk factors, cross-sectional regressions are used in the second step,

$$R_{i,t} - R_{f,t} = \lambda_{0,t} + \lambda_{m,t}\hat{\beta}_{i,m} + \sum_{k=1}^{K} \lambda_{k,t}\hat{\beta}_{i,k} + e_{i,t} \tag{6.27}$$

where $\lambda_{0,t}$ is the intercept, $\hat{\beta}_{i,m}$ and $\hat{\beta}_{i,k}$ are beta loadings estimated in the first step, $e_{i,t}$ is the error term. With a total number of N assets and a sample length of T, there is one regression across the N assets for each time period and there are T such regressions in total. This way, a time series for each risk premium is constructed. Then, averages are taken over the whole sample time period as

$$\bar{\lambda}_k = \sum_{t=1}^{T} \lambda_{k,t} / T$$ for each state variable. In lieu of running T cross-sectional regres-

sions, one can run a single one that uses average returns of all assets over time.

Stochastic discount factor

The single-period asset pricing models ignore the consumption decisions. In effect, investors make their consumption and portfolio choices simultaneously in an intertemporal setting. Under the framework of an exchange economy, an investor maximizes the expectation of a time-separable utility function (Lucas 1978),

$$\underset{C_t}{Max} \quad E_t \left[\sum_{i=0}^{\infty} \beta^i U(C_{t+i}) \right]$$

$$s.t. \quad \sum_{j=1}^{N} x_t^j p_t^j + C_t = W_t + \sum_{j=1}^{N} x_{t-1}^j (p_t^j + d_t^j)$$

(6.28)

where x_t^j is the amount of security j purchased at time t, p_t^j is the price of security j at time t, W_t is the individual's endowed wealth at time t, C_t is the individual's consumption at time t, d_t^j is the dividend paid by security j at time t, and β is time discount. Express C_t in terms of x_t^j, and differentiate the objective function with respect to x_t^j, then we can get the following first-order condition:

$$E_t[U'(C_t)p_t^j] = E_t[\beta U'(C_{t+1})(p_{t+1}^j + d_{t+1}^j)]$$

(6.29)

for all j. After rearranging the terms, we can get

$$E_t[(1 + R_{i,t+1})M_{t+1}] = 1$$

(6.30)

with $M_t = \dfrac{\beta U'(C_{t+1})}{U'(C_t)}$ and $R_{t+1} = \dfrac{p_{t+1}^j + d_{t+1}^j}{p_t^j} - 1$, where $R_{i,t+1}$ is the return on asset i in the economy and M_{t+1} is known as the stochastic discount factor (SDF), or intertemporal marginal rate of substitution, or pricing kernel (Campbell et al. 1997).

Hansen and Jagannathan (1991) demonstrated how to identify the SDF from a set of basis assets, i.e., the derivation of the volatility bounds. These bounds are recognized as regions of admissible mean–standard deviation pairs of the SDF. Their major assumptions are the law of one price and the absence of arbitrage opportunities. Accordingly, there are two particular solutions for the SDF: the law of one price SDF and the no-arbitrage SDF. The process of retrieving the reverse-engineered law of one price SDF is equivalent to the following constrained optimization problem,

$$\underset{M_t}{Min} \ \sigma_{M_t} = \left[\frac{1}{T-1} \sum_{t=1}^{T} (M_t - v) \right]^{1/2}$$

$$s.t. \ \frac{1}{T} \sum_{t=1}^{T} M_t = v \qquad\qquad (6.31)$$

$$\frac{1}{T} \sum_{t=1}^{T} M_t (1 + R_{i,t}) = 1$$

for a range of selected v (mean of M_t), and for all assets $i = 1, 2, \cdots, N$. Under the stronger condition of no arbitrage, another positivity constraint on M_t is needed. Therefore, the only difference between the law of one price SDF and the no-arbitrage SDF is whether M_t is allowed to be negative. Last, sample size T should be sufficiently large such that the time–series version of law of large numbers applies; that is, the sample moments on a finite record converge to their population counterparts as the sample size becomes large (Hansen and Jagannathan 1991).

Provided the existence of a risk-free asset, it can be shown that $E_t[(R_{i,t+1} - R_f)M_{t+1}] = 0$. This equation presents the basis for testing the risk-adjusted performance of a portfolio (Chen and Knez 1996). Namely, one can test whether

$$\alpha_i = E_t[\alpha_{i,t}] = E_t[(R_{i,t+1} - R_f)M_{t+1}] = 0 \qquad\qquad (6.32)$$

Ahn et al. (2003) pointed out that this measure generalizes Jensen's alpha and does not count on a specific asset pricing model.

Discussion and conclusions

Investors usually hold portfolios rather than individual assets to diversify risks. A key factor in determining portfolio allocations is the correlation between assets. The lower the correlation, the larger the diversification benefit. To evaluate the investment performance, investors need to form expectations. That is where asset pricing models are used. The expected rate of return is also linked to the discount rate in the income approach of timberland appraisals. As shown in Chapter 3, the appraised timberland value by the income approach is most sensitive to the discount rate. Therefore, the discount rate based on asset pricing models can serve as an alternative scenario on top of those reverse engineered from comparable timberland sales.

The classic CAPM is based on the mean-variance efficiency framework, and it is easy to use. However, it has the most restrictive assumptions. To improve the CAPM, other more sophisticated models have been proposed. Despite the better capability in explaining variations in cross-sectional returns, implementations of these models require advanced econometric and statistical knowledge. Applications of various asset pricing models on commercial timberlands will be covered in later chapters.

Questions

1. Explain the efficient frontier, the capital market line, and the Sharpe ratio.
2. What is systematic risk? Why does it matter?
3. Why is inflation important? How to test inflation hedging?

Notes

1 The weights can be solved with Solver in MS Excel.
2 The Fama-French factors are constructed using six value-weight portfolios formed on size and book-to-market. Details can be found at Kenneth R. French's website: http://mba.tuck.dartmouth.edu/pages/faculty/ken.french/index.html.

Bibliography

Abhyankar, A., and A. Gonzalez. 2009. News and the cross-section of expected corporate bond returns. *J. Bank. Financ.* 33(6):996–1004.
Ahn, D.-H., J. Conrad, and R.F. Dittmar. 2003. Risk adjustment and trading strategies. *Rev. Financ. Stud.* 16(2):459–485.
Bali, T.G. 2008. The intertemporal relation between expected returns and risk. *J. Financ. Econ.* 87(1):101–131.
Bali, T.G., and R.F. Engle. 2010. The intertemporal capital asset pricing model with dynamic conditional correlations. *J. Monet. Econ.* 57(4):377–390.
Bollerslev, T., R.F. Engle, and J.M. Wooldridge. 1988. A capital-asset pricing model with time-varying covariances. *J. Polit. Econ.* 96(1):116–131.
Breeden, D.T. 1979. Intertemporal asset pricing model with stochastic consumption and investment opportunities. *J. Financ. Econ.* 7(3):265–296.
Brennan, M.J., A.W. Wang, and Y.H. Xia. 2004. Estimation and test of a simple model of intertemporal capital asset pricing. *J. Financ.* 59(4):1743–1775.
Campbell, J.Y. 1996. Understanding risk and return. *J. Polit. Econ.* 104(2):298–345.

Campbell, J.Y., A.W. Lo, and A.C. MacKinlay. 1997. *The econometrics of financial markets.* Princeton University Press, Princeton, NJ, 611p.

Campbell, J.Y., and T. Vuolteenaho. 2004. Bad beta, good beta. *Am. Econ. Rev.* 94(5):1249–1275.

Chen, A.H., and A.J. Boness. 1975. Effects of uncertain inflation on investment and financing decisions of a firm. *J. Financ.* 30(2):469–483.

Chen, Z., and P.J. Knez. 1996. Portfolio performance measurement: Theory and applications. *Rev. Fin. Stud.* 9(2):511–555.

Cochrane, J.H. 2005. *Asset pricing.* Princeton University Press, Princeton, NJ.

Dorfman, J.H., and M.D. Park. 2011. Estimating the risk-return tradeoff in agribusiness stocks: Linkages with the broader stock market. *Am. J. Agr. Econ.* 93(2):426–433.

Elton, E., M. Gruber, and J. Rentzler. 1983. The arbitrage pricing model and returns on assets under uncertain inflation. *J. Financ.* 38(2):525–537.

Evans, M.D.D. 1994. Expected returns, time-varying risk, and risk premia. *J. Financ.* 49(2):655–679.

Fama, E.F., and K.R. French. 1989. Business conditions and expected returns on stocks and bonds. *J. Financ. Econ.* 25(1):23–49.

Fama, E.F., and K.R. French. 1993a. Common risk-factors in the returns on stocks and bonds. *J Financ. Econ.* 33(1):3–56.

Fama, E.F., and K.R. French. 1993b. Common risk factors in the returns on stocks and bonds. *J. Financ. Econ.* 33(1):3–56.

Fama, E.F., and J.D. MacBeth. 1973. Risk, return, and equilibrium: Empirical tests. *J. Polit. Econ.* 81(3):607–636.

Fisher, I. 1930. *The theory of interest.* The MacMillan Company, New York, 566p.

Hansen, L.P., and R. Jagannathan. 1991. Implications of security market data for models of dynamic economies. *J. Polit. Econ.* 99(2):225–262.

Hui, G. 2006. Time-varying risk premia and the cross section of stock returns. *J. Bank. Financ.* 30(7):2087–2107.

Jensen, M.C. 1968. The performance of mutual funds in the period 1945–1964. *J. Financ.* 23(2):389–416.

Johnson, R.A., and D.W. Wichern. 2007. *Applied multivariate statistical analysis* (6th ed.). Pearson Prentice Hall, Upper Saddle River, NJ.

Kaiser, H. 1958. The varimax criterion for analytic rotation in factor analysis. *Psychometrika* 23(3):187–200.

Kothari, S.P., and J. Shanken. 1997. Book-to-market, dividend yield, and expected market returns: A time-series analysis. *J. Financ. Econ.* 44(2):169–203.

Lausti, A. 2004. The inflation-hedging characteristics of forest ownership, private housing and stocks in Finland. *LTA* 4(4):427–451.

Lee, C.F., F.C. Jen, and K.C.J. Wei. 1988. The real and nominal parameters in the CAPM: A responsive coefficient approach. *Int. J. Financ.* 1(1):113–130.

Lucas, R.E., Jr. 1978. Asset prices in an exchange economy. *Econometrica* 46(6):1429–1445.

Markowitz, H. 1952. Portfolio selection. *J. Financ.* 7(1):77–91.

Mei, B. 2022. On the performance of timberland as an alternative asset. *J. For. Econ.* 37(2):169–184.

Merton, R.C. 1973. An intertemporal capital asset pricing model. *Econometrica* 41(5):867–887.

Petkova, R. 2006. Do the Fama-French factors proxy for innovations in predictive variables? *J. Financ.* 61(2):581–612.

Roll, R., and A.S. Ross. 1980. An empirical investigation of the arbitrage pricing theory. *J. Financ.* 35(5):1073–1103.

Ross, A.S. 1976. Arbitrage theory of capital asset pricing. *J. Econ. Theory* 13(3):341–360.

Ross, A.S., W.R. Westerfield, and F.J. Jaffe. 2002. *Corporate finance*. McGraw-Hill Primis. New York, NY. 946p.

Sharpe, W.F. 1994. The sharpe ratio. *J. Port. Manag.* 21(1):49–58.

7

TIMBERLAND INDEX CONSTRUCTION METHODS AND RESULT

Highlights

- TIMOs and REITs differ in management structure, financial leverage, liquidity, entry barrier, and business segments.
- NCREIF Timberland Index is appraisal based and gross of fees, while REIT return is transaction based and net of fees.
- Appraisal smoothing can result in an artificially lower volatility and should be corrected in cross-asset comparisons.
- A pure-play index can be constructed so that the index has exposure only to the timberland segments of public timber companies.

Timberland return indices and benchmarks help investors understand the comparative performance of timberland assets. This chapter compares different index construction methods of timberland investment returns and evaluates the resulting indices by various asset pricing models. In addition to various NCRIEF indices,[1] we include an unsmoothed index, which attempts to restore property market values; a transaction-based index, which tracks ex post transaction prices; and a pure-play index, which is based on unleveraged returns of public timber firms and has exposures only to the timber segment.

Background

Over the years, timberland has been recognized as an alternative asset class that has low risk and offers commensurate long-term investment returns. Unique to this asset class, timberland value appreciates while trees are growing and timber products can be stored on the stump for many years with little cost other than

DOI: 10.4324/9781003366737-7

the opportunity cost of the capital employed (Zinkhan et al. 1992).[2] As such, the biological growth that forests produce functions as a "buffer zone" for timberland investors during economic downturns. For example, even if timber prices plummet by 15% for a given year, the total timberland investment return falls by less than 15% because the positive biological growth offsets some of the negative price effect on the total timber revenue.

TIMOs and REITs have emerged as major owners of industrial timberland due to recent shifts in timberland ownership within the forest products industry. Together, TIMOs, representing private equity, control about 20 million acres of timberland, while public firms, representing public equity, control about 23 million acres of timberland (Hood et al. 2015). In addition to the five major public timber REITs, including Weyerhaeuser (WY), Plum Creek (PCL), Rayonier (RYN), Potlatch (PCH), and CatchMark (CTT), there are two publicly traded timber firms, Deltic Timber (DEL) and Pope Resources (POPE).[3]

To provide return information of public- and private-equity timberland investments, a number of indices exist. For private-equity timberland investment, the NCREIF Timberland Index (NTI) is widely acknowledged as the primary source for return information. For public-equity timberland investment, the value-weighted return of public timber firms (PUBLIC) is often used. Comparison of these two return series has been targeted by a few studies (e.g., Mei and Clutter 2010; Wan et al. 2013; Yao et al. 2014). However, there are some fundamental differences in how these return indices are constructed and reported.

First, public timber firms use a considerable amount of debt. Debt ratio for the six public timber firms varied from 7% to 35% over the period 2010–2014. Because financial leverage changes the risk-return profile of the underlying equity, the PUBLIC should not be compared with the NTI directly because the NTI is an unlevered index (NCREIF 2020). Second, liquidity of the public- and private-equity timberland markets is quite different. Shares of stocks of public timber firms can be bought and sold easily without any appreciable impact on the price, while private timber funds require a minimum commitment, usually in millions of dollars, and they require more time to execute transactions. In other words, the PUBLIC is a constant-liquidity index but the NTI is a variable-liquidity index. Third, public timber firms often have some non-timber business segments, such as wood products manufacturing, that provide substantial operating income, whereas TIMOs focus more on timberland investments. As such, the two indices essentially reflect returns on two different business models rather than the core timberland assets. Lastly, the PUBLIC is based on real transactions on security exchanges, while the NTI is based on periodic appraisals, sales and purchases, and measures the performance of a large pool of commercial timberland properties acquired in the private market for investment purposes only (NCREIF 2020).

BOX 7.1 DIFFERENCES BETWEEN REITs AND TIMOs

Historical interest rate on the long-term debt for public timber REITs ranged 3%–9% (Mei 2015b). With a lower cost than equity, the use of debt can lower the overall cost of capital. The downside of financial leverage is periodic debt obligations (interest expenses and debt repayment), which increases the financial distress risk. As timber REITs aim to maintain a steady dividend yield, they are not as highly levered as some other industries. In contrast, TIMOs usually use no debt and therefore have less pressure of generating cash flows at the early stage of their closed-end funds. In short, financial leverage changes the risk-return profile of an otherwise identical investment. Deleveraging on REIT returns is needed before comparing it to the NTI.

Another implication of the cash needs is on the acquisition and disposition strategies of REITs and TIMOs: REITs tend to acquire mature or close to mature forests to produce cash flows, while TIMOs can afford to acquire young forests and capture the rapid biological growth and long-term capital appreciation (Mei 2021). Over time, we have seen more transactions of cutover lands sold from REITs to TIMOs and mature stands sold back from TIMOs to REITs (Zhang 2021). All these may translate to the difference in the risks and returns between REITs and TIMOs.

Securitized timberland is traded by shares of stocks, whereas a comingled fund and a separate account managed by TIMOs have a respective minimum capital commitment of about $1 million and $50 million. Hence, public timber REITs are the natural option for retail investors interested in timberland, while TIMOs are more for institutional investors and wealthy families. But do not take it wrong—timber REITs have a significant portion of institutional investment too. For example, Weyerhaeuser has more than 80% of its stocks held by institutions. In recent years, open-end funds have been used by a few TIMOs (e.g., Resource Management Service and BTG Pactual) for more liquidity. However, the overall liquidity of TIMO-managed timberland assets is not comparable to that of REITs, and TIMOs should bear liquidity premium. Therefore, liquidity should be controlled for prior to the REIT and TIMO return comparison.

Timber REITs, not TIMOs, often have exposures to the wood manufacturing business. However, this trend is likely to reverse as some adventurous TIMOs (e.g., Timberland Investment Resources) started to be vertically integrated with downstream forest products manufacturing for improved diversification and profit margin. To concentrate on the timberland business segment, we need the pure-play index.

The geographic locations of timberland properties also differ between REITs and TIMOs. Those of REITs are publicly disclosed, and they can be aggregated by region and used as weights on the regional NCREIF Timberland Indices for the location adjustment. In addition, TIMOs typically charge a 2% asset management fee and a 20% carried interest (a payment for investment services that is taken out of the profits for investors). The NTI is reported gross of fees, while REIT returns are net of fees. Finally, the NTI is appraisal based and subject to smoothing, while REIT returns are transaction based.

The objective of this chapter is to expand existing benchmarks by including two alternative indices, i.e., the transaction-based timberland index (TBTI) and the pure-play timberland index based on securitized timber firms (PURE) because they measure timberland investment returns from different angles. Then, all indices are evaluated by several asset pricing models. The goal is not to simplistically assert that one index is correct or better than the others but rather to uncover some insights that lie behind each index. Given the fact that timberland investment return data are very limited in both quantity and quality, such comparisons may reveal the historical reality evidenced across all the indices as well as some weaknesses of the assumptions and methods in constructing such indices.

Past research

Research in timberland investment returns has been prolific in the past 15 years. The vast majority of these analyses use the NTI. Sun and Zhang (2001) used the CAPM and the arbitrage pricing theory in pricing forest-related assets and concluded that the NTI exhibited a low systematic risk and a positive abnormal return. Newell and Eves (2009) used the NTI to show that US timberland was a strongly performing asset class with significant portfolio diversification benefits over the period 1977–2007. Liao et al. (2009) and Clements et al. (2011) used cointegration analyses on a number of assets and argued that the NTI was cointegrated with other indices in the long run. Mei and Clutter (2010) compared the NTI with the PUBLIC and concluded that the former had significant abnormal returns over the years 1987 to 2009. Gao and Mei (2013) demonstrated that investor attention has significant impacts on the abnormal performance of the NTI. Wan et al. (2013) found that the NTI could hedge against both anticipated and unanticipated inflation. La and Mei (2015) revealed no general trends among timber REIT returns and the S&P 500, and recommended each timber REIT as a separate long-term risk diversifier. Wan et al. (2015) showed that the NTI maintained a significant allocation in the mixed portfolio under the mean-conditional-value-at-risk framework. Yao et al. (2014) applied the arbitrage pricing theory to the NTI and found that it had higher required returns as more risk factors were included. Yao and Mei (2015) claimed that the excess returns of both the NTI and the PUBLIC were declining over time based on the intertemporal capital asset pricing model.

Realizing the weakness of existing timberland indices, a few studies further tested them or explored alternative ways to gauge timberland investment returns. Mei (2015a) illustrated that the assumption of independent and identically distributed returns is violated by the NTI but not the PUBLIC. Scholtens and Spierdijk (2010) removed the appraisal smoothing in the NTI and found less evidence of improved mean-variance efficiency by including timberland assets. Mei (2015b) derived the PURE based on asset values of different business segments of public timber firms, and showed that it differed in the first two moments (mean and variance) from the NTI and that it tended to lead the NTI for about one quarter. Mei (2016) used property-level data to build the TBTI and showed that liquidity of private timberland equity varies with business cycles, and that volatility of the TBTI is twice as high as that of the NTI.

Index construction methods

NCREIF timberland index

The NTI is released on a quarterly basis and dates back to 1987Q1. It is based on data reported by data contributing members and tracks returns from a changing collection of privately held timberland properties in the United States. As of 2014Q4, the NTI consisted of over 13 million acres with a market value of about $24 billion (NCREIF 2020). The NTI includes both income return,[4] which comes from operating activities such as timber sales, and capital appreciation, which is based on appraisals. The formulas used to calculate the index are

$$IR_t = \frac{EBITDDA_t}{MV_{t-1} + 0.5(CI_t - PS_t + PP_t - EBITDDA_t)} \tag{7.1}$$

$$CR_t = \frac{MV_t - MV_{t-1} - CI_t + PS_t - PP_t}{MV_{t-1} + 0.5(CI_t - PS_t + PP_t - EBITDDA_t)} \tag{7.2}$$

where IR_t and CR_t are the income return and capital return, respectively; CI_t equals the capitalized expenditures (e.g., forest regeneration); PS_t equals the net proceeds from land sales; PP_t equals the gross costs of new land acquisitions; MV_t equals the market value of the property (Binkley et al. 2003).

Many analysts argue that the appraisal-based NTI underestimates the volatility of timberland returns and does not necessarily reveal the information of real transactions. Moreover, the NTI measures gross returns before investment advisory fees. To deal with the latter concern, the NCREIF released the timberland Comingled Fund Index (CFI) and Separate Account Index (SAI) dating back to 1988Q1.[5] The fund-level indices reflect returns at the fund level and are available net of management and advisory fees (NCREIF 2020).

Unsmoothed index

A number of statistical techniques have been proposed to solve the problem of appraisal smoothing. An in-depth comparison of these desmoothing methods is beyond the scope of this study, albeit the one outlined in Geltner (1993) is adopted to desmooth the NTI. To recover the true market values, the following transfer function is used

$$\kappa_t^* = \frac{\kappa_t - (1-a)\kappa_{t-1}}{a} \tag{7.3}$$

where κ^* is the unobservable return, κ is the observed appraisal-based return and a is an adjustment factor that accounts for seasonality and appraiser confidence. Geltner (1993) suggested that $a = 0.40$ with a reasonable range of 0.33–0.50.[6] The recovered series should be rescaled so that it preserves the mean of the original series.

Transaction-based index

The NTI is an ex ante index that is based on the expected selling price in the open market that applies to any property assuming a constant market liquidity.[7] In contrast, the transaction-based index is a measure of value changes of a given pool of properties only when they are traded. That is, the TBTI is an ex post index that is based only on actual transactions that each differ in quality and market liquidity. A typical timberland sale process can be described by a double-sided search market. In Figure 7.1, the bell curves show the frequency distributions of market participants' reservation prices, with buyers' on the left, sellers' on the right, and the horizontal axis denoting reservation prices. The total number of sellers (buyers) willing to sell (buy) at any price P is revealed by the area to the right (left) under the seller (buyer) reservation price frequency distribution. The dispersion in the distributions indicates the difference in perceptions of values and search costs of market players, whereas the overlap grants profitable trades of properties. At time t, P_1 is the highest bid price from buyers, P_2 is the lowest ask price from sellers, P_0 is the expected market clearing price, and the size of the overlap area resembles the trading volume or degree of liquidity. A transaction is likely to arise whenever there is a seller-buyer match with $P_2 \leq P_0 \leq P_1$. When market conditions change or investor/manager objectives change, reservation price distributions may shift or change shape and sellers and buyers will adjust their reservation prices accordingly. These changes may not occur in the same manner and the resulting overlap area varies over time, reflecting the variations in the trading volume for a given population of assets.

The expected sale price responds to both underlying market and firm specific movements in reservation price distributions, whereas the trading volume responds to differential movements only. The differential movements influence

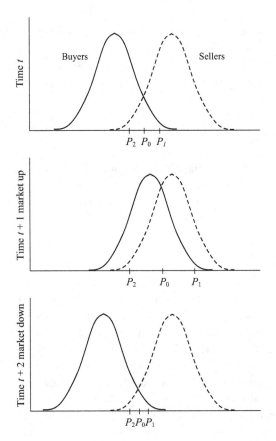

FIGURE 7.1   Evolution of buyer and seller reservation price distributions and transaction turnover

both trading price and volume, which are linked to the ease of selling a property. Thus, the TBTI reflects variable market liquidity, as illustrated in Figure 7.2, where demand shifts up further (from D to D') than supply (from S to S') in equilibrium during an economic expansion.[8] The observed trading price rises from P^{*} to P^{V} and the trading volume moves from Q^{*} to Q^{V}. Nonetheless, the constant-liquidity price ends up at P^{C}, where the new demand function D' intersects the fixed trading volume Q^{*}. The opposite is true for an economic contraction. Regardless of the direction of market moves, the observed price change (e.g., $P^{V}P^{*}$) is less than the constant-liquidity price change (e.g., $P^{C}P^{*}$) as long as the market liquidity varies pro-cyclically. Using property-level timberland transaction data and the Heckman (1979) procedure, Mei (2016) derives the TBTI.[9]

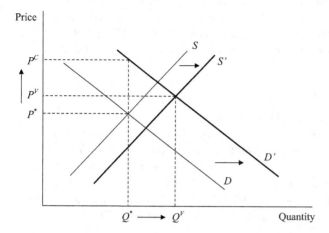

FIGURE 7.2   Constant- vs. variable-liquidity price movements in an up-market equilibrium

Pure-play index

A modified version of the Geltner-Kluger model can be employed to construct pure-play return indices, in which contemporaneous, unleveraged monthly returns of public timber firms are regressed on a set of variables that denote percentage business-segment holdings of each firm (Horrigan et al. 2009),

$$r_{i,t} = b_{1,t}x_{1,i,t} + b_{2,t}x_{2,i,t} + \cdots + b_{K,t}x_{K,i,t} + e_{i,t} \tag{7.4}$$

where $r_{i,t}$ is the deleveraged total return of firm i,[10] $x_{j,i,t}$ indicates firm i's proportion of total assets held in segment j ($j \in \{1,2,\ldots K\}$ with K representing the total number of segments and $\sum_{j}^{K} x_{j,i,t} = 1$ for all i and t), $b_{j,t}$ is segment j's market index return, and $e_{i,t}$ is the error term, all at time t ($t \in \{1,2,\ldots T\}$ with T representing the length of the observation period).

Suspecting that larger firms have smaller idiosyncratic return variances owing to larger, more diversified property holdings, generalized least squares (GLS) is typically used to estimate Equation 5.4. Using unleveraged returns of six publicly traded timber firms, i.e., WY, PCL, RYN, PCH, DEL, and POPE, in the United States over the period 2010–2014, Mei (2015b) constructs the PURE.

Other return indices and data frequency

Market return (MKT) is proxied by the value-weighted return of all CRSP firms incorporated in the United States and listed on the NYSE, AMEX, and

NASDAQ. Risk-free rate is proxied by the one-month Treasury bill rate. These combined with the Fama–French factors, the five-industry portfolio returns, and the returns on ten-year Treasury bonds all come from WRDS (WRDS 2020). The five industries consist of consumer goods, manufacturing, hi-tech, health care, and others.

Data frequency varies across timberland indices. Annual data are used considering the following facts. First, although the NTI is reported quarterly, most appraisals occur at year end. This introduces artificial variations in the fourth quarter of each year and makes the quarterly NTI less interpretable than the annual one (Cascio and Clutter 2008). Second, the TBTI can be derived only at the annual level after 2002 given the limited number of transactions within each quarter. Hence, all other higher-frequency indices are compounded into annual ones, resulting in 1988–2014 series for all NCREIF indices and the PUBLIC, 2010–2014 series for the PURE, and 2003–2014 series for the TBTI.

Results

Descriptive statistics

Summary statistics of various return indices are reported in Table 7.1. According to the length of the PURE and the TBTI, two additional subsamples are used, i.e., 2003–2014 and 2010–2014.[11]

For the sample period of 1988–2014, the NCREIF indices show significant advantages over the PUBLIC and the MKT with respect to the return-to-risk ratio. However, the advantages disappear after the unsmoothing because the UNTI has a volatility almost twice as large as that of the NTI and higher than those of the PUBLIC and the MKT. The PUBLIC and the MKT are very similar in their mean and variance. These findings are consistent with those from previous research. For the sample period of 2003–2014, both mean and variance are lower for the NCREIF indices, but not for the PUBLIC and the MKT. By the return-to-risk ratio, the NCREIF indices are still superior to the PUBLIC and the MKT. The TBTI, however, has a much lower mean and a much higher standard deviation than the NCREIF indices, leading to the lowest return-to-risk ratio among all indices. For the sample period 2010–2014, the public-equity indices have significantly higher means, resulting in similar or even higher return-to-risk ratios than the NCREIF indices. The PURE is most rewarding per unit of risk. In addition, the TBTI shows a slightly negative mean and a comparable risk to the public-equity indices.

According to the pairwise correlation coefficients, the NTI is highly correlated with other NCREIF indices but weakly correlated with public-equity indices. The TBTI has moderate positive correlations with the NCREIF indices but negative correlations with public-equity indices. The PURE has negative correlations

Timberland Index Construction Methods and Result **95**

TABLE 7.1 Descriptive statistics of various return indices

	NTI	UNTI	CFI	SAI	PUBLIC	PURE	TBTI	MKT
Individual samples								
Mean	12.58	12.58	9.59	12.61	13.09	21.69	8.32	12.38
Median	10.92	12.57	10.51	10.64	13.79	21.21	7.69	15.40
Max	37.35	63.80	25.87	34.13	39.09	33.82	23.00	36.81
Min	-5.24	-27.50	-6.32	-3.01	-39.15	9.91	-17.88	-36.74
SD	10.79	21.17	7.67	9.46	18.75	9.85	11.87	18.35
Mean/SD	1.17	0.59	1.25	1.33	0.70	2.20	0.42	0.67
2003–2014								
Mean	8.71		7.67	8.73	13.60		5.32	11.98
Median	9.61		9.65	9.51	13.24		7.69	13.66
Max	19.36		15.86	18.94	39.09		23.00	35.21
Min	-4.75		-6.32	-2.86	-39.15		-17.88	-36.74
SD	7.11		7.51	6.63	20.39		11.87	18.69
Mean/SD	1.22		1.02	1.32	0.67		0.42	0.64
2010–2014								
Mean	5.87		4.48	6.34	16.04	21.69	3.22	16.25
Median	7.75		7.42	5.89	9.75	21.21	3.04	16.34
Max	10.48		9.96	13.06	37.89	33.82	11.66	35.21
Min	-0.15		-3.44	1.67	9.17	9.91	-17.88	0.48
SD	4.85		6.20	4.83	12.36	9.85	11.27	12.55
Mean/SD	1.21		0.72	1.31	1.30	2.20	-0.01	1.29
Pairwise correlations								
NTI	1.00							
UNTI	0.79	1.00						
CFI	0.89	0.74	1.00					
SAI	0.98	0.76	0.88	1.00				
PUBLIC	0.15	0.34	0.06	0.04	1.00			
PURE	-0.52	0.13	-0.33	-0.71	0.77	1.00		
TBTI	0.58	0.45	0.56	0.59	-0.43	-0.08	1.00	
MKT	0.25	0.32	0.23	0.18	0.72	-0.13	-0.28	1.00

with other indices except for the UNTI and the PUBLIC. The evolution of these indices is plotted in Figure 7.3.

Some common themes emerge across different return indices. First, all indices capture the movement of business cycles (e.g., the Internet bubble around 2000 and the housing market meltdown around 2008). However, the private-equity timberland indices lag public-equity timberland indices by about one year. Second, appraisal smoothing tends to exist in the NTI but the UNTI tends to overstate the volatility as compared to the TBTI. Third, the PUBLIC performs

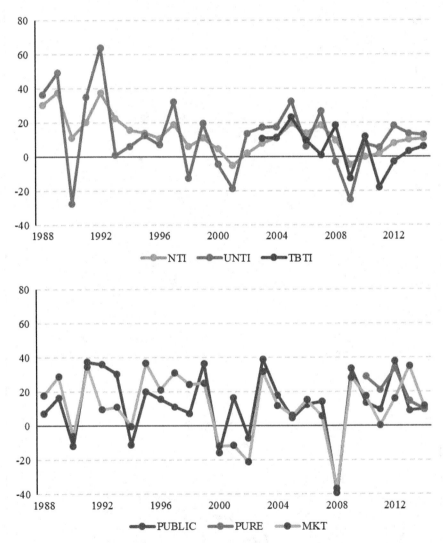

FIGURE 7.3 Evolution of various return indices (in percentage)

similar to the MKT and the PURE exhibits the lowest volatility among the three public-equity return indices.

Financial performance of timberland indices

Performance results for various timberland indices are reported in Table 7.2. According to the CAPM, timberland assets, especially private-equity timberland assets, show significant positive abnormal returns. For example, the NTI has an α of 11.64%. The magnitude of this abnormality is reduced to 9.43% after the appraisal smoothing is removed, and further reduced to 7.03% when real timberland transactions replace appraisals in deriving the return indices. Between the two types private timber funds, separate accounts outperform the commingled funds by about 3%.

In contrast, the PUBLIC has a lower abnormal return of 6.30%. Based on β estimates, timberland exhibits lower systematic risk than the market. However, the R^2 remains low for all return indices except for the PUBLIC. This is consistent with results from previous studies on private-equity timberland investment (e.g., Cascio and Clutter 2008; Mei and Clutter 2010). Specifically, the low R^2 results from the small sample size because annual data are used in the regression.

TABLE 7.2 Financial performance of various timberland return indices

	NTI	UNTI	CFI	SAI	PUBLIC	TBTI
CAPM						
α	11.64	9.43	8.97	12.13	6.30	7.03
	0.000	0.043	0.000	0.000	0.032	0.106
β	0.11	0.35	0.07	0.05	0.76	−0.19
	0.374	0.124	0.414	0.613	0.000	0.339
R^2	0.03	0.09	0.03	0.01	0.55	0.09
Fama-French three-factor						
α	11.02	7.94	8.51	11.54	5.67	5.81
	0.000	0.113	0.000	0.000	0.048	0.131
β_{RMRF}	0.16	0.41	0.12	0.11	0.72	-0.29
	0.209	0.103	0.181	0.314	0.000	0.142
β_{SMB}	−0.22	0.08	−0.23	−0.25	0.53	0.38
	0.262	0.836	0.094	0.140	0.019	0.310
β_{HML}	0.16	0.26	0.13	0.16	0.02	0.70
	0.327	0.399	0.244	0.253	0.920	0.115
R^2	0.11	0.12	0.17	0.13	0.65	0.46
Stochastic discount factor						
Performance measure	6.17	5.69	3.55	6.40	2.81	1.25
	0.003	0.162	0.016	0.000	0.435	0.585
Expected vs. actual return						
CAPM	4.71	7.75	4.26	4.06	12.78	1.09
Fama-French three-factor	5.52	9.44	4.88	4.85	13.29	2.70
Stochastic discount factor	4.99	5.51	4.75	4.76	9.19	0.94
Actual mean	12.58	12.58	9.59	12.61	13.09	5.04

Results from the Fama-French three-factor model are similar to those from the CAPM relative to both the expected returns and the precision of those estimates. Overall, the magnitude of α estimates (abnormal returns) is reduced and thus less significant, and the R^2 is improved.

The mean of the no–arbitrage stochastic discount factors is specified in the selected range of [0.9450, 1] with an increment step of 0.0025. With the five-industry portfolios plus the ten-year Treasury bonds used as the basis assets, the global minimum variance (0.7050) of the stochastic discount factors is identified at $v = 0.9500$. Under such a framework, abnormal returns are lower at 1.25–6.17%, but the performance ranking of all timberland indices remains unchanged in general. The 2.81% abnormal return of the PUBLIC is no longer significant at all standard levels of significance.

The actual and expected returns from various models are compared at the bottom of Table 7.2. In general, common asset pricing models are incapable of estimating private-equity timberland investment returns precisely. When the NTI is unsmoothed, the prediction accuracy improves but still is not as good as for the public timberland equity. In pricing timberland, the Fama-French three-factor model outperforms the CAPM and the SDF approach.

Discussion and conclusions

Timberland has attracted investor attention in recent years. Return information of timberland investments, however, remains limited. This study compares different index construction methods of timberland investment returns and evaluates the resulting indices by various asset pricing models. In addition to various NCRIEF indices, I include an unsmoothed index, which attempts to restore property market values; a transaction-based index, which tracks ex post transaction prices; and a pure-play index, which is based on unleveraged returns of public timber firms and has exposures only to the timber segment. The findings are appraisal-based timberland index has higher mean and lower volatility as compared with the transaction-based timberland index; separate accounts outperform comingled funds in private timberland market; the pure-play timberland index exhibits higher return and lower risk than the corresponding portfolio of public timber firms; and abnormal performance of timberland asset becomes less significant after controlling for the appraisal smoothing or by using real transaction data.

There are several practical implications. First, investors need to know how various timberland indices are built and on what assets to better choose the benchmark for their investments. For small, private-equity investors, the TBTI should be used because they are more exposed to idiosyncratic risk than large, more sophisticated institutional investors. Likewise, for wealthy families or sole investors investing in timberland through TIMOs via separate accounts, the SAI is a more proper benchmark albeit it is only reported at the national level. Second, for investors who prefer timberland assets but appreciate liquidity, public timber firms should be considered. Nonetheless, investors should understand the difference between business wrappers and underlying timberland assets. Securitization has introduced non-diversifiable systematic risk into public timberland equity (Sun 2013). A direct investment in public timber firms is equivalent to an investment in their business models. Should an investor be interested in pure public timberland equity, however, the pure-play strategy can be followed. The PURE represents a more comparable counterpart to other private-equity timberland indices. Of course, a thorough comparison of timberland indices is only one of many steps in an investor's decision making. Other factors, such as tax, investment horizon, governance, and transparency, among others, should be incorporated.

Third, commonly used asset pricing models, such as the CAPM, the Fama-French three-factor model and the SDF approach, fit returns on public timberland equity better than private timberland equity. This is consistent with the findings in the real estate literature where non-traded real estate assets are more difficult to be priced (e.g., Fisher et al. 2004). Finally, I have to acknowledge that the sample size of this study is limited by the data availability, especially for the PURE. The performance of various timberland indices remains to be further examined and evaluated in the future as more data are ready.

Questions

1. How is private-equity timberland investment different from public-equity timberland investment?
2. In comparing various timberland indices, what factors should be considered?
3. Explain appraisal smoothing and its impact on NCREIF Timberland Index.

Notes

1 NCREIF: National Council of Real Estate Investment Fiduciaries.
2 Capital employed includes standing timber and bare land.
3 Weyerhaeuser acquired Plum Creek on February 19, 2016.
4 Also known as cash return or EBITDDA, earnings before interest, taxes depreciation, depletion, and amortization.
5 A comingled fund is used for grouped, relatively small investors or investors that are required to invest in fund vehicles, whereas a separate account is used for a single, large investor.
6 A value of 0.33 means more smoothing and a value of 0.50 means less smoothing. A value of 0.40 implies that an appraiser puts 50% weight on the past appraised value in assessing the current value and that 55% of all properties are reappraised during the fourth calendar quarter.
7 Market liquidity means the degree to which an asset can be traded in the market without affecting its price. It measures the trade-off between the speed of the sale and the price an asset can be sold for.
8 Supply and demand functions are derived from the cumulative reservation price distributions, the area underneath the frequency (density) distributions.

9 The TBTI is an annual index ranging from 2003 to 2014 because of limited numbers of transactions for early years.

10 Deleveraged using the weighted average cost of capital equation.

11 Statistics for the UNTI are not reported for the two subsamples because the unsmoothing method is based on the full sample information.

Bibliography

Binkley, C.S., C.L. Washbrun, and M.E. Aronow. 2003. *The NCREIF timberland property index: Research notes 2003*. Hancock Timber Resource Group, Boston, MA, 10p.

Cascio, A.J., and M.L. Clutter. 2008. Risk and required return assessments of equity timberland investments in the United States. *For. Prod. J.* 58(10):61–70.

Clements, S., A.J. Ziobrowski, and M. Holder. 2011. Lumber futures and timberland investment. *J. Real Estate Res.* 33(1):49–71.

Fisher, J., D. Gatzlaff, D. Geltner, and D. Haurin. 2004. An analysis of the determinants of transaction frequency of institutional commercial real estate investment property. *Real Estate Econ.* 32(2):239–264.

Gao, L., and B. Mei. 2013. Investor attention and abnormal performance of timberland investments in the United States. *For. Policy Econ.* 28:60–65.

Geltner, D. 1993. Estimating market values for appraised values without assuming an efficient market. *J. Real Estate Res.* 8(3):325–345.

Heckman, J.J. 1979. Sample selection bias as a specification error. *Econometrica* 47(1):153–161.

Hood, H.B., T. Harris, J. Siry, S. Baldwin, and J. Smith. 2015. *US Timberland markets: Transactions, values & market research 2000 to mid-2015*. Timber Mart-South, Athens, GA. 411p.

Horrigan, H., B. Case, D. Geltner, and H. Pollakowski. 2009. REIT-based property return indices: A new way to track and trade commercial real estate. *J. Port. Manag.* 35(5):80–91.

La, L., and B. Mei. 2015. Portfolio diversification through timber real estate investment trusts: A cointegration analysis. *For. Policy Econ.* 50(0):269–274.

Liao, X., Y. Zhang, and C. Sun. 2009. Investments in timberland and softwood timber as parts of portfolio selection in the United States: A cointegration analysis and capital asset pricing model. *For. Sci.* 55(6):471–479.

Mei, B. 2015a. Illiquidity and risk of commercial timberland assets in the United States. *J. For. Econ.* 21(2):67–78.

Mei, B. 2015b. A pure-play timberland return index based on securitezed timber firms. *J. Real Estate Port. Manag.* 21(1):61–75.

Mei, B. 2016. Transaction-based timberland investment returns. *Land Econ.* 92(1):187–201.

Mei, B. 2021. From backwoods to boardrooms: The rise of institutional investment in timberland, ISBN 9780870711428, Daowei Zhang. Oregon State University Press, 2021. 280p. *For. Policy Econ.* 133:102609.

Mei, B., and M.L. Clutter. 2010. Evaluating the financial performance of timberland investments in the United States. *For. Sci.* 56(5):421–428.

NCREIF. 2020. *National council of real estate investment fiduciaries*. https://www.ncreif.org/. Last accessed August 20, 2022.

Newell, G., and C. Eves. 2009. The role of US timberland in real estate portfolios. *J. Real Estate Port. Manag.* 15(1):95–106.

Scholtens, B., and L. Spierdijk. 2010. Does money grow on trees? The diversification properties of US timberland investments. *Land Econ.* 86(3):514–529.

Sun, C. 2013. On the market risk of securitized timberlands. *J. For. Econ.* 19(2):110–127.

Sun, C., and D. Zhang. 2001. Assessing the financial performance of forestry-related investment vehicles: Capital asset pricing model vs arbitrage pricing theory. *Am. J. Agri. Econ.* 83(3):617–628.

Wan, Y., M.L. Clutter, B. Mei, and J.P. Siry. 2015. Assessing the role of US timberland assets in a mixed portfolio under the mean-conditional value at risk framework. *For. Policy Econ.* 50:118–126.

Wan, Y., B. Mei, M.L. Clutter, and J.P. Siry. 2013. Assessing the inflation hedging ability of timberland assets in the United States. *For. Sci.* 59(1):93–104.

WRDS. 2020. *Wharton research data services.* The Wharton School at the University of Pennsylvania, Philadelphia, PA.

Yao, W., and B. Mei. 2015. Assessing forestry-related assets with the intertemporal capital asset pricing model. *For. Policy Econ.* 50:192–199.

Yao, W., B. Mei, and M.L. Clutter. 2014. Pricing timberland assets in the United States by the arbitrage pricing theory. *For. Sci.* 60(5):943–952.

Zhang, D. 2021. *From backwoods to boardrooms: The rise of insititutional investment in Timberland.* Oregon State University Press, Corvallis, OR.

Zinkhan, F.C., W.R. Sizemore, G.H. Mason, and T.J. Ebner. 1992. *Timberland investments: A portfolio perspective.* Timber Press, Portland, OR. 208p.

8
FINANCIAL ANALYSIS OF TIMBERLAND

Highlights

- Timberland, especially privately placed, has been identified as a risk diversifier.
- Risk of private-equity timberland tends to increase as the investment horizon lengthens.
- Timberland returns are often not normally distributed so the conditional value at risk is a better risk metric than the standard deviation.
- Most asset pricing models can price public timber REITs well but not TIMOs.
- Timber REIT conversions have gained favor from the investors.
- Large-cap stock factor contributes most to timber REIT return and volatility.

Timberland maturing as an alternative asset class, many studies have examined its financial characteristics from various angles. This chapter summaries the literature with an emphasis on journal articles the authors of this book recently published.

Role of timberland in a mixed portfolio

A number of studies have employed the modern portfolio theory to evaluate timberland's diversification potential. Mills and Hoover (1982) used the mean-variance (M-V) optimization approach to examine the risk-return relationship of forest investments and showed that forest investment could provide diversification benefits. Zinkhan et al. (1992) and Caulfield (1998) demonstrated that adding timberland assets to a portfolio could improve the portfolio performance and provided asset allocation suggestions for institutional investors. Newell and Eves (2009) analyzed the risk-adjusted performance of US timberland assets in real estate portfolios and concluded that timberland was a strongly performing asset

DOI: 10.4324/9781003366737-8

over the period 1987–2007. Scholten and Spierdijk (2010) found that US private-equity timberland assets did not significantly improve the efficient frontier after removing the appraisal smoothing bias.

Thomson (1997) employed the multiperiod portfolio optimization approach and showed that timber (e.g., Douglas Fir and Southern Pine) had been valuable either as a single asset or as an addition to a financial portoflio. Waggle and Johnson (2009) compared timberlands, farmlands, and commercial real estates in a mixed asset portfolio with stocks and bonds, and found that timberlands entered all portfolios, whereas farmlands entered only low-risk portfolios. Overall, these studies suggest that adding timberland assets to a portfolio can improve the efficient frontier or enhance the long-term financial performance.

Under the M-V framework, variance or standard deviation (SD) of asset returns is used to measure the portfolio risk under a multivariate normal distributional assumption. When asset returns follow a normal distribution, SD can help us understand how asset returns vary around the mean value. However, investors are more concerned about potential losses or negative returns from the extreme events, such as financial crises, and, therefore, more attention has been paid to downside risks in practice. Caulfield and Meldahl (1994) used the downside risk semivariance to construct portfolios of southeastern timberland assets and found that this approach resulted in more efficient frontiers than the M-V approach. Hildebrandt and Knoke (2011) also pointed out that downside risk models could provide an important implication for risk management in forestry. Meanwhile, value at risk (VaR) has become a popular tool among portfolio managers to measure the downside risk since it is easy to calculate and interpret. VaR gives the maximum loss that will not be exceeded with a given probability over a period of time. It can help us understand the potential loss of an asset or a portfolio, but it cannot measure the risk under the scenarios of exceeding VaR. Conditional VaR (CVaR) is capable of measuring the loss greater than VaR by incorporating the left-tail distribution (Hull 2012).

Returns of financial assets such as stocks and bonds are not normally distributed (Sheikh and Qiao 2010). Timberland returns also depart from normality to some degree (Mei 2015; Petrasek et al. 2011; Zhang and Mei 2021). These asset returns generally exhibit non-normality properties, such as skewness and kurtosis in the real world. For instance, negatively skewed asset returns suggest that the left tail is longer than the right tail, implying that the probability of the occurrence of negative returns is higher than that of positive returns. Asset returns with fat tails imply that both of the extreme negative and positive returns occur more likely than those normally distributed. In a nutshell, the mean and variance alone may fail to describe the true distribution of asset returns, the M-V approach may not fully reveal the risk-return relationship, and using mean and standard deviation may not correctly construct the efficient frontier.

To address the risk metric and non-normality issues, the mean-conditional value at risk (M-CVaR) optimization method, in which the downside risk measured by

CVaR is minimized with a given target return without assuming a normal distribution, is applied by Wan et al. (2015) and Restrepo et al. (2020). Results revealed that private-equity timberland remained a risk diversifier despite its time-varying weight in the mixed-asset portfolio. Zhang and Mei (2019) showed that the M-CVaR framework could more precisely estimate the downside risk and that farmland replaced timberland as risk increased along the efficient frontier. This approach has also been used to construct hedge fund portfolios with minimum tail risks (Giamouridis and Vrontos 2007) and to demonstrate the extent to which the M-V approach underestimates the tail risks (Agarwal and Naik 2004). To better illustrate how downside risk VaR can be appropriately calculated, a set of non-normal asset returns relative to a normal distribution is drawn. In Figure 8.1, the impact of skewness and kurtosis on the downside risk VaR is illustrated. The VaR of negatively skewed or fat-tailed asset returns is underestimated compared with that of a normality assumption. In contrast, it is overestimated if asset returns are positively skewed or thin-tailed. It is intuitive that investors prefer the assets with positively skewed and thin-tailed returns because both cases expose investors to smaller probabilities of extreme negative returns.

In the field of timberland investment, Mei (2015) examined the relationship between return and risk of various timberland investment vehicles and the holding period. Results from the BDS test reject the null hypothesis of independent and identically distributed returns and results from the bootstrapping simulation indicate that the average quarterly return remains almost constant and thus independent of the holding period, but the average quarterly risk (standard deviation) varies

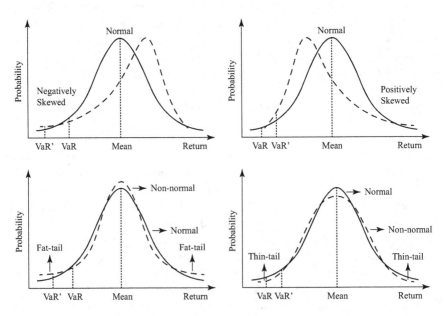

FIGURE 8.1 Impact of skewness and kurtosis on the VaR.

among different timberland investment vehicles. For private-equity timberlands, the average periodic risk increases with the holding period, whereas for public-equity timberlands, it stays relatively constant (Figure 8.2). Furthermore, Zhang and Mei (2021) demonstrated the crucial role of serial correlation in defining an asset's financial performance. They modified return, volatility, and correlation

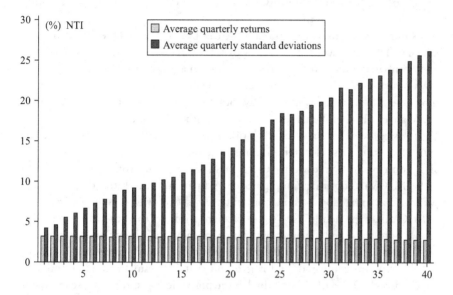

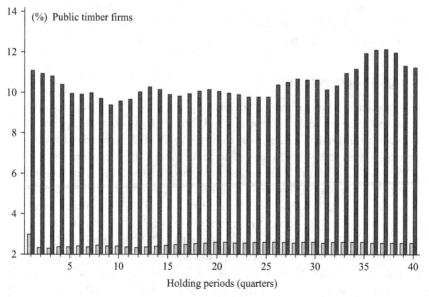

FIGURE 8.2   Average quarterly returns and standard deviations of different timberland return indices

for multiyear horizons to account for the nature of long-term investments and showed that private-equity timberland could be substituted by other liquid assets, including public-equity timberland, as the lengthening holding period substantially reduced their volatilities. Overall, there is some evidence that private-equity timberland returns as measured by various NCREIF timberland indices tend to be not independent and identically distributed, a violation of the key assumption for the modern portfolio theory.

In summary, the M-CVaR framework can better define the efficient frontier than the M-V framework. Regardless of the choice of the risk metric, private-equity timberland tends to be a risk diversifier in a mixed asset portfolio.

Washburn et al. (2012) first introduced the M-CVaR approach to assess how timberland allocations perform in a hypothetical portfolio from the risk perspective. Wan et al. (2015) further formulated both static and dynamic optimizations to assess whether the asset allocation is consistent. To better understand the downside risk, the risk decomposition is introduced to understand how portfolio risk is contributed by individual assets. First, the efficient frontier is constructed by the M-CVaR optimization approach, which minimizes the downside risk CVaR and accounts for the non-normality of asset returns. Results indicate that the M-CVaR approach leads to more efficient frontiers than the M-V approach. Second, both static and dynamic optimizations show that timberland assets maintain a significant allocation in the mixed portfolio. Third, three metrics of the portfolio risk are compared, and it is found that SD results in underestimation compared with VaR and CVaR. Finally, the portfolio risk is decomposed to identify the contributions of individual assets via backtesting under four scenarios. Both large-cap stocks and small-cap stocks are risk intensifiers, whereas treasury bills, treasury bonds, and timberland assets are risk diversifiers.

Pricing timberland assets

Using those models described in Chapter 6, past studies attempted to price timberland and form expected returns. Mei and Clutter (2010) compared private- and public-equity timberland investment using the NCREIF Timberland Index and return on a dynamic portfolio of public timber firms. Results from the CAPM and FF3F model reveal that private-equity timberland exhibits a low systematic risk and a positive abnormal return, whereas public-equity timberland fares similarly as the market. Results from the nonparametric SDF approach reveal that both private- and public-equity timberlands have high excess returns.

Expressing all returns in real terms, the real CAPM has an inflation factor in addition to the market factor. Actual inflation can be further broken down into expected and unexpected inflations, and the estimated coefficients can be tested for an asset's ability to hedge against inflations (Zhang et al. 2011). Wan et al. (2013) found that private timberland equity but not public timberland equity was able to hedge against both expected and unexpected inflations. Hedging effectiveness depends on the state of the economy. Private-equity timberland assets are effec-tive in hedging inflation during a boom and less effective during a recession. Investment horizon also plays a significant role in timberland inflation hedging. The longer people invest in the private-equity timberland assets, the stronger and more consistent the hedging ability holds.

Liao et al. (2009) and Clements et al. (2011) demonstrated the impact of cointe-gration on expected private-equity timberland returns and portfolio optimization. Liao et al. (2009) found that timberland return was largely driven by stumpage price in the long-run equilibrium. Clements et al. (2011) examined the impacts of lumber futures, capitalization rates (risk premium), and anticipated construction on timberland value using Johansen's cointegration technique. They found that in the long run, timberland values had a significant positive equilibrium relationship with lumber futures and building permits and a significant negative relationship with capitalization rates. In the short run, unexpected shocks in the three vari-ables cause a permanent change in timberland values.

Although there are overabundant sources of information, only a small portion is consumed. Information of interest is usually buried in distracting alternatives. As a result, we live in a world with a wealth of information but a poverty of attention. In theory, a framework has been proposed in which limited attention can impact asset returns; however, in practice, direct proxies of investor attention are hard to find and a variety of indirect proxies, such as extreme returns, trad-ing volume, and news and headlines, have been used (Barber and Odean 2008; Hirshleifer and Teoh 2003; Peng and Xiong 2006; Sims 2003). In the Internet era, when there are more and more electronic information sources, human beings' capability to acquire information has been improved, especially with the help of Internet search engines. With about 66% Internet search market share,[1] Google provides aggregate information acquisition statistics, which could be the best available attention proxy.

Most recently, Da et al. (2011) put forward a new and direct measure of investor attention by using the Google search frequency, known as the search volume index (SVI), and found that variations in the SVI affected both short- and long-run stock prices. Gao and Mei (2013) used the SVI of timberland related terms to test inves-tor attention on timberland asset pricing. Results reveal that investor attention to the finished wood products market, the global climate change, the emerging biomass market, and the overall manufacturing industry has significant effects on the abnormal returns of timberland investments. Similarly, Yao et al. (2016) used the orthogonalized investor sentiment index formed by Baker and Wurgler (2006) to examine the relationship between investor sentiment and returns of private-equity timberland investment. Results show that current investor sentiment is an important factor that determines the one-quarter future returns of timberland and the predicting power persists over the next one to five years. Both the short- and long-term studies obtain negative coefficients on investor sentiment, indicating that current increase in investor sentiment drives prices up and lowers future returns. In addition, significantly different return variances and insignificantly different average returns of timberland investment are obtained between low- and high-sentiment periods. This further confirms the ability of earning long-term stable returns by timberland investment.

Considering multiple factors in the economy, Yao et al. (2014) assessed the financial performance of US timberland investments by the arbitrage pricing theory. Results show that public-equity timberland assets have higher mean excess returns in general. Compared with the CAPM, a larger portion of the variations in timberland returns are explained by the arbitrage pricing theory because more causal factors are considered. Expected returns of timberland assets are found to be declining over time, which may imply an improved efficiency of the timberland market. Yao and Mei (2015) used ICAPM to assess the risk-return relationship between forestry-related assets and innovations in state variables. Market excess returns and innovations in the small-minus-big and high-minus-low factors, interest rate, term spread, default spread, and aggregate consumption explain about 80% of the variation in cross-sectional returns of 16 forestry-related assets. Beta loadings on innovations in high-minus-low, interest rate, and term spread induce significant risk premiums, and should be priced to determine the cross-sectional expected returns of the forestry-related assets. In general, average excess returns of the forestry-related assets decrease over time. Significant positive excess returns are obtained for private- and public-equity timberland assets over the period 1988–1999. Insignificant excess returns are obtained for forest products and timber products in the whole sample period of 1988–2011.

Under the ICAPM framework, Mei et al. (2020) found evidence of market segregation and one-way information flow from the timberland and farmland market to the commercial real estate market. They concluded that commercial real estate and timberland and farmland assets were driven by different market fundamentals and that lagged timberland and farmland returns could help predict current commercial real estate returns. The only exception was during market downturns when commercial real estate and timberland and farmland markets are somewhat integrated and driven by some factors that were not specified in their study. Mei (2022) compared private-equity timberland with other alternative assets, including commodities, hedge funds, private equity, venture capital, real estate, and emerging markets. Results show that timberland had superior performance than stocks and most other alternative assets. There was also evidence that alternative asset market was not integrated with conventional asset market as the risk premiums for these two asset groups differed significantly.

In summary, most classic asset pricing models in finance can price public timber REITs well and suggest that public timber REITs behave like large-cap stocks. Nevertheless, the same models have some difficulties in pricing private-equity timberland assets and suggest significant abnormal returns. The difference diminishes when unsmoothed NCREIF Timberland Index or transaction-based timberland index is used (Mei 2016). Overall, multifactor, multiperiod asset pricing models outperform CAPM in pricing timberland assets. State variables like the value factor, interest rate, and term spread help form expectations of timberland investment returns. In addition, indices that measure investor attention or sentiment have marginal prediction power after controlling for traditional asset pricing factors. Yet the persistence of these indices in making forecast remains to be seen in the future. The dynamics of timberland investment returns could be related to recent consolidation of the timber industry and improved efficiency of timberland market as more capital flows into this market.

Public timber REITs

Public timber REITs are quite different from TIMOs in a number of aspects as discussed in the last chapter. Much research has been done on public timber REITs thanks to the abundantly available financial data. Newell and Hsu Wen (2006) categorized timber REITs as specialty REITs and confirmed their risk-reduction and portfolio diversification benefits. Regarding the structural changes in the timber sector, Mendell et al. (2008) and Piao et al. (2017) examined respective short- and long-term market response to REIT conversion announcements and found significant abnormal returns. Sun (2013b) assessed the joint distribution between daily returns of timber REITs and two market indices and asserted that timber REITs had smaller volatility of tail dependence after the conversion. Sun et al. (2013) found increased volatility coupled with significant abnormal returns related to the conversion.

In addition, Sun (2013c) used GARCH and extreme value models to examine price variation and volume dynamics of timber master limited partnerships (MLPs) and REITs and found a positive return-volume relation. Compared to MLPs, REITs exhibited larger total shares and daily turnover rates. Sun (2013a) estimated the 1% level daily value-at-risk of timber REITs to be 13% for the 2008–2009 recession period. La and Mei (2015) investigated the diversification ability of securitized timberlands via cointegration analysis. They found no general trends within timber REITs or between REITs and S&P 500. Therefore, there is long-run diversification potential with each timber REIT as a unique candidate. Piao et al. (2016) compared the financial performance of timber REITs, other specialized REITs, and common REITs. They found that timber REITs had larger market capitalizations, smaller unconditional variance, and no excess returns, and that timber REITs were insensitive to recessionary shocks but more vulnerable to idiosyncratic shocks.

Lumber being derived from timberland, a relationship between lumber prices and timberland prices is expected. Prices of timber REITs are intrinsically determined by the value of timber grown and harvested. Therefore, expected lumber prices should manifest the price discovery of timber REITs. Using vector error correction and GARCH models, Clements et al. (2017) found a positive long-run equilibrium relationship between lumber futures, capitalization rates, publicly traded real estate equity, and timber REITs. Short-run results generally corroborated those of the long-run results.

Most lately, Mei and Clutter (2020) examined risk-return characteristics and information transition dynamics of public- and private-equity timberland investments. They found that timber REITs had higher systematic risk than TIMOs after controlling for the lead-lag effects and REIT returns help predict TIMO returns. Baral and Mei (2022b) examined the relationship between public timber REITs, private timberland, real estate, and financial asset returns and investigated the time-varying volatility of timber REITs. Results indicated that timber REITs were positively sensitive to large-cap stocks and bonds, and that large-cap stock factor contributed most to their volatility. Along the same line, Baral and Mei (2022a) found that large-cap stock and idiosyncratic risk factors were the major contributors of timberland and farmland REIT volatility despite some differing patterns over time.

In summary, the REIT structure for timberland management has received a positive response from the market. Among all specialized REITs, timber REITs have some risk-reduction ability but no excess returns. Lumber futures price tends to be a lead variable of timber REIT returns. Timber REITs behave more like large-cap stocks.

Discussion and conclusions

Timberland is a real asset and has many distinct features from financial assets. Overall, research found NCREIF Timberland Index, compared with timber REIT returns, has lower correlations with other asset classes, has a significant and larger abnormal return, has a lower systematic risk, has the inflation hedging ability, and has a superior return-risk ratio. The conclusions largely remain unchanged, despite some weaker evidence, even after desmoothing the index. As the investment horizon lengthens, however, the return-risk ratio of TIMO and REIT returns become more comparable.

Being a special type of real estate, timberland's financial characteristics have not been fully explored yet. Nonetheless, with a rapid progress in real estate finance in academia and timberland investment in practice, we envision a prolific period of research in timberland finance in the next few years. We share some of our prospects in timberland investments in Box 8.1.

BOX 8.1 SOME PROSPECTS IN TIMBERLAND INVESTMENTS

Timberland investments in the United States have been unprecedentedly active since the 1980s, when timberland ownership started shifting from industrial firms to institutional investors (via TIMOs) and REITs. Not echoing this trend, the top 100 forest products companies in the world have increased timberland holdings between 2007 and 2012 in order to reduce risks associated with the flow of raw materials (Korhonen et al. 2016). An example is IKEA's recent acquisition of US timberlands as part of a broad strategy to invest in the sustainable production of resources that IKEA consumes. The increased vertical integration in the global forest products industry presents both opportunities and challenges for timberland investors in the United States. Forest products companies usually have different valuation models than TIMOs or REITs in that the inclusion of the insurance value of internal wood supply often adds a premium to timberland's intrinsic value. Therefore, this provides existing landowners an incentive to exit and secure a portion of the premium. For new investors, nonetheless, this trend of vertical integration implies a higher demand of timberland and eventually a higher acquisition cost, which may reduce expected future returns.

In addition to vertical integration, there has been a trend toward timberland investments for climate change mitigation purposes (e.g., carbon offsets) at the global level. In theory, this has similar implications to timberland investors as those from vertical integration; however, in practice, the impact differs substantially by region. In the United States, attitudes toward climate change mitigation are significantly influenced by the emergence of climate change legislation at the federal level (Thompson and Hansen 2012). In other words, most organizations are taking a passive approach toward climate change mitigation projects in the United States and the development of this market will be an iterative process that requires global collaborations given the integrated nature of climate change mitigation (Thompson and Hansen 2012). For timber production itself around the world, returns and costs for major timber plantation species as well as other institutional, forestry, and policy factors that affect investments for a set of countries are compared and reported in Cubbage et al. (2014) and Cubbage et al. (2020).

Although timberland investments in the United States have attracted many research interests in recent years, many facets of timberland, a special type of real estate and an alternative asset, have not been fully explored yet. One example is the linkage between lumber prices and TIMO returns. In the US South, lumber prices have been high in the past few years with the recovery of the housing market, whereas sawtimber prices have been stagnating due to the supply overhang. The higher profit margin of wood products manufacturing has triggered many greenfield as well as brownfield investments in this region. Some TIMOs (e.g., Timberland Investment Resources) have even started investing in wood manufacturing facilities to secure a further diversification and a higher profit margin. Yet, TIMOs lack the expertise, the experience, and the proven track record in operating wood processing mills, and therefore the risk-return profiles of such integrated TIMOs remain to be seen. There is also a rising trend of direct timberland ownership and joint ventures between investors and public timber REITs, all of which further intensifies the competition in this niche market in the United States.

Questions

1. How are private-equity timberland investment returns different from those of public-equity timberland investments?
2. What are the commonly identified state variables in the multifactor models used to price timberland?
3. Give some evidence of the non-normal distribution nature of the NCREIF Timberland Index.
4. Why have some TIMOs started investing in wood manufacturing facilities? What are some challenges for such TIMOs?

Note

1 Average from 2005 to 2011 according to comScore.com.

Bibliography

Agarwal, V., and N.Y. Naik. 2004. Risks and portfolio decisions involving hedge funds. *Rev. Finan. Stud.* 17(1):63–98.

Baker, M., and J. Wurgler. 2006. Investor sentiment and the cross-section of stock returns. *J. Financ.* 61(4):1645–1680.

Baral, S., and B. Mei. 2022a. Integration of public farmland and tmberland REITs with their private equity counterparts and selected asset classes. *Agri. Financ. Rev.* 83(1):186–200.

Baral, S., and B. Mei. 2022b. The time-varying link of public timber REITs with private timberland, real estate, and financial assets. *For. Sci.* 68(5-6):464-472.

Barber, B.M., and T. Odean. 2008. All that glitters: The effect of attention and news on the buying behavior of individual and institutional investors. *Rev. Financ. Stud.* 21(2):785–818.

Caulfield, J., and R. Meldahl. 1994. Timberland investments return volatility and implications for portfolio construction. In *Proceedings of 24th annual southern forest economics workshop*. University of Georgia, New Orleans, Louisiana, 144–162.

Caulfield, J.P. 1998. A fund-based timberland investment performance measure and implications for asset allocation. *South. J. Appl. For.* 22(3):143–147.

Clements, S., A. Tidwell, and C. Jin. 2017. Futures markets and real estate public equity: Connectivity of lumber futures and timber REITs. *J. For. Econ.* 28:70–79.

Clements, S., A.J. Ziobrowski, and M. Holder. 2011. Lumber futures and timberland investment. *J. Real Estate Res.* 33(1):49–71.

Cubbage, F., B. Kanieski, R. Rubilar, A. Bussoni, V.M. Olmos, G. Balmelli, P.M. Donagh, R. Lord, C. Hernández, P. Zhang, J. Huang, J. Korhonen, R. Yao, P. Hall, R. Del La Torre, L. Diaz-Balteiro, O. Carrero, E. Monges, H.T.T. Thu, G. Frey, M. Howard, M. Chavet, S. Mochan, V.A. Hoeflich, R. Chudy, F. Maass, S. Chizmar, and R. Abt. 2020. Global timber investments, 2005 to 2017. *For. Policy Econ.* 112:102082.

Cubbage, F., P. Mac Donagh, G. Balmelli, V.M. Olmos, A. Bussoni, R. Rubilar, R. De La Torre, R. Lord, J. Huang, V.A. Hoeflich, M. Murara, B. Kanieski, P. Hall, R. Yao, P. Adams, H. Kotze, E. Monges, C.H. Perez, J. Wikle, R. Abt, R. Gonzalez, and O. Carrero. 2014. Global timber investments and trends, 2005–2011. *N. Z. J. Forest. Sci.* 44:12.

Da, Z., J. Engelberg, and P. Gao. 2011. In search of attention. *J. Financ.* 66(5):1461–1499.

Gao, L., and B. Mei. 2013. Investor attention and abnormal performance of timberland investments in the United States. *For. Policy Econ.* 28(0):60–65.

Giamouridis, D., and I.D. Vrontos. 2007. Hedge fund portfolio construction: A comparison of static and dynamic approaches. *J. Bank. Financ.* 31(1):199–217.

Hildebrandt, P., and T. Knoke. 2011. Investment decisions under uncertainty—A methodological review on forest science studies. *For. Policy Econ.* 13(1):1–15.

Hirshleifer, D., and S.H. Teoh. 2003. Limited attention, information disclosure, and financial reporting. *J Account. Econ.* 36(1–3):337–386.

Hull, J. 2012. *Options, futures, and other derivatives*. Boston: Prentice Hall, 841p.

Korhonen, J., Y. Zhang, and A. Toppinen. 2016. Examining timberland ownership and control strategies in the global forest sector. *For. Policy Econ.* 70:39–46.

La, L., and B. Mei. 2015. Portfolio diversification through timber real estate investment trusts: A cointegration analysis. *For. Policy Econ.* 50:269–274.

Liao, X., Y. Zhang, and C. Sun. 2009. Investments in timberland and softwood timber as parts of portfolio selection in the United States: A cointegration analysis and capital asset pricing model. *For. Sci.* 55(6):471–479.

Mei, B. 2015. Illiquidity and risk of commercial timberland assets in the United States. *J. For. Econ.* 21(2):67–78.

Mei, B. 2016. Transaction-based timberland investment returns. *Land Econ.* 92(1):187–201.

Mei, B. 2022. On the performance of timberland as an alternative asset. *J. For. Econ.* 37(2):169–184.

Mei, B., and M.L. Clutter. 2010. Evaluating the financial performance of timberland investments in the United States. *For. Sci.* 56(5):421–428.

Mei, B., and M.L. Clutter. 2020. Return and information transmission of public and private timberland markets in the United States. *For. Policy Econ.* 113:102092.

Mei, B., W. Wu, and W. Yao. 2020. Private-equity commercial real estate, timberland, and farmland: Market integration and information transition dynamics. *Can. J. For. Res.* 50(11):1101–1112.

Mendell, C.B., N. Mishra, and T. Sydor. 2008. Investor responses to timberlands structured as real estate investment trusts. *J. For.* 106(5):277–280.

Mills, W., Jr., and W. Hoover. 1982. Investment in forest land: Aspects of risk and diversification. *Land Econ.* 58(1):33–51.

Newell, G., and C. Eves. 2009. The role of US timberland in real estate portfolios. *J. Real Estate Port. Manag.* 15(1):95–106.

Newell, G., and P. Hsu Wen. 2006. The role of non-traditional real estate sectors in REIT portfolios. *J. Real Estate Port. Manag.* 12(2):155–166.

Peng, L., and W. Xiong. 2006. Investor attention, overconfidence and category learning. *J. Financ. Econ.* 80(3):563–602.

Petrasek, S., B. Keefer, M.E. Aronow, and C. Washburn. 2011. *Statistical distributions of timberland returns.* Hancock Timber Resource Group, Research Report, 29p.

Piao, X., B. Mei, and Y. Xue. 2016. Comparing the financial performance of timber REITs and other REITs. *For. Policy Econ.* 72:115–121.

Piao, X., B. Mei, and W. Zhang. 2017. Long-term event study of timber real estate investment trust conversions. *For. Policy Econ.* 78:1–9.

Restrepo, H., W. Zhang, and B. Mei. 2020. The time-varying role of timberland in long-term, mixed-asset portfolios under the mean conditional value-at-risk framework. *For. Policy Econ.* 113:102136.

Scholtens, B., and L. Spierdijk. 2010. Does money grow on trees? The diversification properties of US timberland investments. *Land Econ.* 86(3):514–529.

Sheikh, A., and H. Qiao. 2010. Non-normality of market returns: A framework for asset allocation decision making. *J. Altern. Invest.* 12(3):8–35.

Sims, C.A. 2003. Implications of rational inattention. *J. Monet. Econ.* 50(3):665–690.

Sun, C. 2013a. Extreme risk of public timber REITs during the global financial crisis. *J. Real Estate Port. Manag.* 19(1):73–88.

Sun, C. 2013b. On the market risk of securitized timberlands. *J. For. Econ.* 19(2):110–127.

Sun, C. 2013c. Price variation and volume dynamics of securitized timberlands. *For. Policy Econ.* 27:44–53.

Sun, C., M.M. Rahman, and I.A. Munn. 2013. Adjustment of stock prices and volatility to changes in industrial timberland ownership. *For. Policy Econ.* 26:91–101.

Thompson, D.W., and E.N. Hansen. 2012. Institutional pressures and an evolving forest carbon market. *Bus. Strateg. Environ.* 21(6):351–369.

Thomson, T. 1997. Long-term portfolio returns from timber and financial assets. *J. Real Estate Portfol. Manage.* 3(1):57–73.

Waggle, D., and D. Johnson. 2009. An analysis of the impact of timberland, farmland and commercial real estate in the asset allocation decisions of institutional investors. *Rev. Finan. Econ.* 18(2):90–96.

Wan, Y., M.L. Clutter, B. Mei, and J.P. Siry. 2015. Assessing the role of US timberland assets in a mixed portfolio under the mean-conditional value at risk framework. *For. Policy Econ.* 50:118–126.

Wan, Y., B. Mei, M.L. Clutter, and J.P. Siry. 2013. Assessing the inflation hedging ability of timberland assets in the United States. *For. Sci.* 59(1):93–104.

Washburn, C.L., B. Keefer, M.E. Aronow, and S. Petrasek. 2012. Timberland portfolio allocation and the mean-conditional value at risk. *Hancock Timberland Investor* Q1:1–6.

Yao, W., B. Cheng, and B. Mei. 2016. Investor sentiment and timberland investment returns. *For. Prod. J.* 66(3–4):147–154.

Yao, W., and B. Mei. 2015. Assessing forestry-related assets with the intertemporal capital asset pricing model. *For. Policy Econ.* 50:192–199.

Yao, W., B. Mei, and M.L. Clutter. 2014. Pricing timberland assets in the United States by the arbitrage pricing theory. *For. Sci.* 60(5):943–952.

Zhang, M., B. Mei, T.G. Harris, J.P. Siry, M.L. Clutter, and S.S. Baldwin. 2011. Can timber hedge against inflation? An analysis of timber prices in the US South. *For. Prod. J.* 61(4):276–282.

Zhang, W., and B. Mei. 2019. Assessing the risk and return of optimal portfolios of US timberland and farmland. *J. Real Estate Port. Manag.* 25(1):99–113.

Zhang, W., and B. Mei. 2021. Volatility decay and diversification role of timberland as the investment horizon lengthens. *For. Sci.* 67(5):501–513.

Zinkhan, C., W. Sizemore, G. Mason, and T. Ebner. 1992. *Timberland investments: A portfolio perspective.* Timber Press, Portland, 208p.

9

FINANCIAL AND REAL OPTIONS

Highlights

- Financial options are derivatives based on financial assets, such as stocks and bonds, while real options are based on real assets, such as real estate and commodities.
- Options offer managerial flexibilities and their values should be considered in the capital budgeting process.
- Factors that determine option values include underlying asset price, exercise price, time to maturity, volatility of asset returns, and risk-free rate.

This chapter reviews the definitions and pricing models of options at a very high level. This is to pave the road for some applications of option analysis in timberland investment and management in the next three chapters. We focus more on call options because put options can be very similarly described. The value of a put option can be derived from the put-call parity.

Definitions of options

A call (put) option gives the owner the right but not the obligation to buy (sell) an underlying asset at a predefined price within a certain time window. If the holder can exercise the option anytime prior to the expiry, the option is known as an American option. If the holder can exercise only on the expiry date, the option is known as a European option. In terms of valuation, American options have

DOI: 10.4324/9781003366737-9

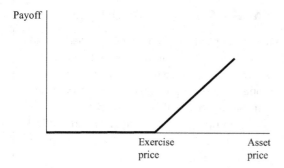

Payoff

Exercise
price

Asset
price

FIGURE 9.1   Payoff of a call option

higher values than European options, all else equal, because of more managerial
flexibility.

The payoff of a call option is illustrated in Figure 9.1. As long as the asset price
is higher than the exercise price, the holder should choose to exercise because he
can buy at a lower price and turn around to sell at the open market price for a
profit. The larger the difference between asset price and exercise price, the higher
the payoff, and this is called an in-the-money call. On the downside, however, the
payoff curve is trancated because the holder is not obligated to exercise the option
and the payoff is simply zero. In this scenario, the call is out-of-the-money. When
the asset price equals the exercise price, the holder is indifferent in exercising the
option or not, and the call is at-the-money.

For financial options, the underlying assets are typically liquid financial
assets, such as publicly traded stocks and bonds. For real options, the underlying assets are real and hard assets (e.g., properties, plants, and equipment)
not as liquid as those financial assets. Nevertheless, the logic behind is the
same. For example, an investment opportunity in a physical project is similar
to a call option in that the exercise is the lump-sum initial investment cost,
the underlying asset is the risky project with uncertain cash flows during the
designed lifespan, and the expiry is the time an investor can wait for before the
investment opportunity vanishes. When the present value of the cash flows of
the project is higher than the investment cost, the "call" is in-the-money and
can be exercised. Otherwise, the "call" is out-of-the-money, but it does not
necessarily lead to abandonment. With an upswing potential, an investor can
wait and then decide to exercise or not at a later time. Thus, the payoff of an
investment opportunity is exactly the same as that of a financial call option,
as depicted in Figure 9.1. Some forestland-related real options are briefly discussed in Box 9.1.

> ## BOX 9.1 SOME FORESTLAND-RELATED REAL OPTIONS
>
> After devesting timberland, many forest products companies have been using timber havest contracts with landowners. For example, when International Paper sold its timberland to Resource Management Service and Forest Investment Associates, it maintained wood supply agreements with the two TIMOs to insure the provision of the raw materials for manufacturing. Such contracts are like call options with forest products companies being the option holders (buyers), landowners being the option writers (sellers), and timber products being the underlying assets (Mei and Clutter 2013).
>
> From the timber management perspective, there are several real options embedded in timberland investments (Mei and Clutter 2015). For example, landowners can delay harvesting if stumpage prices are depressed. When trees are left on the stump, there are minimum costs (e.g., property tax and administration costs), but landowners may benefit from enhanced timber revenues should stumpage prices revert. The delayed harvest may also provide landowners some compensation for additional forest carbon fixed on the ground. Or landowners may enjoy some recreational benefits (e.g., hunting and fishing) from retaining mature forests. All these managerial flexibilities should be factored into a timberland investment decision.
>
> Another illustration is the choice of timber management intensity according to the performance of the timber market. When the timber market is booming, landowners can choose intensive timber mangement (e.g., applying fertilizers and herbicides) to improve the yield; when the timber market is sluggish, landowners can choose operational timber management to minimize efforts and costs. Such decisions can be switched contingent upon the market conditions. After a clear cut, landowners can explore higher and better uses (e.g., conversion to cropland), if there are any, for a better financial return (Mei et al. 2022; Zinkhan 1991), or time the market on the regenerations (Duku-Kaakyire and Nanang 2004).

Valuations of options

Five factors determine the value of an option: (1) underlying asset price (S), (2) exercise price (E), (3) volatility of the asset (σ), (4) risk-free rate (R_f), and (5) time to expiration (T). For a call option, S, σ, R_f, and T have positive impacts whereas E has a negative impact on its value, ceteris paribus. This is because the higher the asset price, the higher the gain from exercising the call, the higher the volatility, the higher the asset price can reach in the future,[1] the higher the risk-free rate (discount rate), the lower the present value of exercise cost and, hence, the higher the payoff and the longer the maturity, the more likely the asset price can rise.

Binomial tree

To price a call option, we use the strategy of a replicating portfolio, a portfolio that can mimic the payoff of a call regardless of future market conditions. To prevent arbitrage, two assets with same future cash flows ought to have the same price today. That is, the call's price today must equal that of the replicating portfolio.

Assume a stock is worth $40 today. In one year, it will be worth either $60 or $20. We aim to determine the value of a call option with an exercise price of $50. First, the payoff of the call is illustrated in the left portion of Figure 9.2. When stock price goes up, the payoff is $60 - 50 = \$10$; when stock price goes down, the call will not be exercised, resulting in $0 payoff. Then, we construct a replicating portfolio by holding (long) 0.25 shares of the stock and borrowing (short) $4 at a risk-free rate of 25%. Currently, the portfolio is valued at $0.25 \times 40 - 4 = \$6$. In a year, it is valued at either $0.25 \times 60 - 4 \times 1.25 = \$10$ or $0.25 \times 20 - 4 \times 1.25 = \$0$ (right portion of Figure 9.2). Since the call and the replicating portfolio have the same future payoff, they should have the same price today. That is, the call should be priced at $6 per contract.

The replicating portfolio strategy is also know as delta hedging. The number of stock shares is denoted as delta and calculated as

$$\Delta = \frac{C^H - C^L}{S_T^H - S_T^L} \tag{9.1}$$

where C^H and C^L are future high and low payoffs of the call option, and S_T^H and S_T^L are future high and low prices of the stock. Once Δ is determined, the amount of borrowing (short position) can be calculated as

$$D = \frac{\Delta \times S_T^L - C^L}{1 + R_f} \tag{9.2}$$

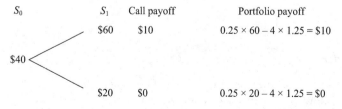

FIGURE 9.2   Pricing a call option using a replicating portfolio

Time 0 T

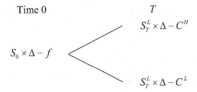

$$S_0 \times \Delta - f$$

$$S_T^L \times \Delta - C^H$$

$$S_T^L \times \Delta - C^L$$

FIGURE 9.3 Pricing a call option by constructing a risk-free portfolio

where D is the amount of debt, and R_f is the interest rate. The price of the call (f) equals the current value of the replicating portfolio, which is calculated as $f = S_0 \times \Delta - D$. Plugging those values in the previous numerical example, we can verify the results.

Using the same strategy but from another angle, we can construct a risk-free portfolio in that future payoff remains the same regardless of market conditions. Consider a portfolio consisting of a long position of Δ shares of stock and a short position of one unit of the call option (Figure 9.3), the current value of the portfolio is $S_0 \times \Delta - f$, and future values at time T are $S_T^L \times \Delta - C^H$ for the up market and $S_T^L \times \Delta - C^L$ for the down market. Being risk-free, future values should be equal so that $S_T^L \times \Delta - C^H = S_T^L \times \Delta - C^L$. Therefore, $\Delta = \dfrac{C^H - C^L}{S_T^H - S_T^L}$, same as in Eqation 9.1. By definition, the portfolio should earn a risk free return so that

$$S_0 \times \Delta - f = \frac{S_T^L \times \Delta - C^L}{\left(1 + R_f\right)^T} \quad \text{or} \quad S_0 \times \Delta - f = [S_T^L \times \Delta - C^L]e^{-R_f T} \text{ in continuous time.}$$

Substituting Δ and rearranging terms, we can get an expression for f as

$$f = e^{-R_f T}\left[pC^H + (1-p)C^L \right] \tag{9.3}$$

where $p = \dfrac{e^{R_f T} S_0 - S_T^L}{S_T^H - S_T^L}$ is known as the risk-neutral probability in the binomial tree. If we use the up and down factors so that $S_T^H = uS_0$ and $S_T^L = dS_0$, then $p = \dfrac{e^{R_f T} - d}{u - d}$. In the binomial tree approach, the volatility is linked to the up and down factors as $u = e^{\sigma\sqrt{\Delta T}}$ and $d = e^{-\sigma\sqrt{\Delta T}}$ (Hull 2009).

Black-Scholes model

Black–Scholes model is the continuous time version of the binomial tree. Suppose the stock price (S) follows a random walk as described by a Geometric Brownian motion:

$$dS = \mu S dt + \sigma S dz \tag{9.4}$$

where μ is the drift rate, dt is a small time increment as in calculus, σ is the volatility parameter of stock returns, and dz is a standardized Wiener process, which adds a random component to stock price movements. dz is continuous time analog to making random draws from a standard normal distribution. Using Ito's stochastic calculus, we can derive an expression for the price movement of a call option:

$$dC = (\frac{\partial C}{\partial S}\mu S + \frac{\partial C}{\partial t} + \frac{1}{2}\frac{\partial^2 C}{\partial S^2}\sigma^2 S^2)dt + \frac{\partial C}{\partial S}\sigma S dz \tag{9.5}$$

where $\dfrac{\partial C}{\partial S}$ refers to the partial derivative of C with respect to S.

Then, consider a riskless portfolio of selling (short position) one call and buying (long position) $\dfrac{\partial C}{\partial S}$ shares of stock, where $\dfrac{\partial C}{\partial S}$ is the hedge ratio as in the binomial model. Current value of the portfolio is

$$V = -C + \frac{\partial C}{\partial S}S \tag{9.6}$$

and the change in value is

$$dV = -dC + \frac{\partial C}{\partial S}dS. \tag{9.7}$$

Substituting the expressions for dS (Equation 9.4) and dC (Equation 9.5), the random component dz cancels out in Equation 9.7 as the two positions in the portfolio have a perfect correlation, and the new expression for change in value is

$$dV = (-\frac{\partial C}{\partial t} - \frac{1}{1}\frac{\partial^2 C}{\partial S^2}\sigma^2 S^2)dt. \tag{9.8}$$

Because the portfolio should earn the risk-free rate instantaneously, $dV = rVdt$. Doing substitutions for V (Equation 9.6) and dV (Equation 9.8), and rearranging terms, we can get the following partial differential equation:

$$\frac{\partial C}{\partial t} + rS\frac{\partial C}{\partial S} + \frac{1}{2}\sigma^2 S^2 \frac{\partial^2 C}{\partial S^2} = rC. \tag{9.9}$$

Equation 9.9 is the same as the form of a widely used partial differential equation from heat transfer in physics with a known solution, which leads to the Nobel Prize winner, the Black-Scholes model in the form of

$$C = SN(d_1) - Ee^{-R_f T}N(d_2) \tag{9.10}$$

where $N(.)$ is the standard normal cumulative distribution function, X is the exercise price, $d_1 = \dfrac{1}{\sigma\sqrt{T}}\left[\ln\left(\dfrac{S}{E}\right)+\left(R_f+\dfrac{\sigma^2}{2}\right)T\right]$, and $d_2 = d_1 - \sigma\sqrt{T}$. In practice, there are many ready-to-use Black-Scholes calculators. One just need to give the five inputs and the option value will be calculated.

A numerical example of real options

Consider a project that will last for three years. The cost of the project is $50 million. According to the market analysis, there is a 25% probability that the project will be highly successful and generate $30 million each of the three years, there is a 50% probability that the project just meet the expectation and generate $25 million each of the three years, and there is a 25% probability that the project will not succeed and only generate $5 million each of the three years. The cost of the capital is 14% and risk-free rate is 6%. The time line along with cash flows are shown in Table 9.1.

The NPV for each scenario can be calculated by using a discount rate of 14%. Then, the expected NPV of this project can be weighted by the probability of each scenario. Hence, if this is a now-or-never investment opportunity, the expected NPV is $1.08 million and should be taken. However, we ought to realize that this is a risky project in that the standard deviation of the NPV is $24.02 million and

TABLE 9.1 DCF and decision-tree analysis for the investment timing option ($ million)

Cash flows and present values

Part 1. Proceed with project today

Yr 0	Yr 1	Yr 2	Yr 3		NPV	Prob		Prob × NPV
	$33	$33	$33		$26.61	0.25		$6.65
−$50	$25	$25	$25		$8.04	0.50		$4.02
	$5	$5	$5		−$38.39	0.25		−$9.60
						1.00		
						Expected NPV		$1.08
						Std Dev		$24.02
						Coeff. of variation		22.32

Part 2. Implement in a year if optimal

Yr 0	Yr 1	Yr 2	Yr 3	Yr 4	NPV	Prob		Prob × NPV
	−$50	$33	$33	$33	$23.35	0.25		$5.84
Wait	−$50	$25	$25	$25	$7.05	0.50		$3.53
	$0	$0	$0	$0	$0	0.25		$0
						1.00		
						Expected NPV		$9.36
						Std Dev		$8.57
						Coeff. of variation		0.92

the coefficient of variation is 22.32. In other words, there is a fair chance that one can end up losing money in three years from this project.

Now, let's assume that one can afford to wait for a year to gather more information and only invest in scenarios resulting in positive NPVs. That is, in a year, one would only invest in the first two scenarios but not the third. Therefore, the cash flow for the last scenario will be all zeros, and the expected NPV (at 14%) of the project turns out to be $9.36 million, greatly enhanced from part 1. We hence can conclude that the wait option does have a positive value and should be kept alive.

It should be noted that after a year of waiting, the risk profile of the project has changed. For the first two scenarios, the investment cost should incur with certainty and the discount rate for it should be the risk-free rate. As such, the NPV of the first scenario should be $-50/1.06 + 33/1.14^2 + 33/1.14^3 + 33/1.14^4 = \$20.04$ million. With the same adjustment, the NPV of the second scenario is reduced to $3.74 million, and the expected NPV of the project is reduced to $6.88 million. The increment in the NPV ($6.88 - 1.08 = \$5.8$ million) should be owed to the waiting.

Another way to price the wait option is to mirror it to a financial call option and use the Black–Scholes model. Risk-free rate is given at 6%, time to expiry is one year, and exercise price is the initial investment cost $50 million. What we need to figure out are the current value of the risk project ("stock price") and its volatility.

To find the "stock price," we discount future profits back to year 0 (Table 9.2). Note that with the one-year wait option, all cash flows occur from year two. The expected PV is $44.80 million and that is what we use for the "stock price" in the Black–Scholes model. To find the volatility, there are two methods, the direct method and the indirect method. In the direct method, we first find the "stock value" at year one, when the timing option expires. Then, we calculate the percentage return for each scenario. With the corresponding probability, we can further calculate the mean, standard deviation, and the CoV of the return (Table 9.3). In the indirect method, we assume that "stock price" is log-normal so that the variance of the return is given by $\ln(CoV^2 + 1)/T = \ln(0.47^2 + 1)/1 = 20.0\%$.

TABLE 9.2 Estimating "stock price" of the investment timing option ($ million)

Cash flows and present values

Yr 0	Yr 1	Yr 2	Yr 3	Yr 4	PV@Yr 0	Prob	Prob × PV
		$33	$33	$33	$67.21	0.25	$16.80
Wait		$25	$25	$25	$50.91	0.50	$25.46
		$5	$5	$5	$10.18	0.25	$2.55
						1.00	
						Expected PV	$44.80
						Std Dev	$21.07
						Coeff. of variation	0.47

TABLE 9.3 Estimating the "stock return variance" of the investment timing option with the direct method ($ million)

Cash flows and present values

Part 1. PV of profits at Yr 1

Yr 0	Yr 1	Yr 2	Yr 3	Yr 4	PV@Yr 1	Prob		Prob × PV
		$33	$33	$33	$76.61	0.25		$19.15
		$25	$25	$25	$58.04	0.50		$29.02
		$5	$5	$5	$11.61	0.25		$2.90
						1.00		
						Expected PV		$51.08
						Std Dev		$24.02
						Coeff. of variation		0.47

Part 2. Implement in a year if optimal

Yr 0	Yr 1	Ret		Prob	Prob × Ret
	$76.61	71.0%		0.25	17.8%
$44.80	$58.04	29.5%		0.50	14.8%
	$11.61	−74.1%		0.25	−18.5%
				1.00	
				Expected Ret	14.0%
				Std Dev	53.6%
				Variance	28.7%

Besides the investment timing option, there are growth option (call) and abandonment option (put) too. For example, an investor can choose to invest in the same project again should the market react favorably. As such, the growth option is a call option with the exercise price being the investment cost, the time to expiry being the life span of the project, and the "stock price" and volatility similarly estimated for the investment timing option. There is also a chance that, after a certain time of testing the water, an investor can choose to liquidate the asset and take some salvage value should the market turn unfavorably. Thus, the abandonment option is like a put option with the exercise price being the salvage value and the time to expiry as the time window of water testing. Again, estimation of the "stock price" and volatility mimics those of the investment timing option using the DCF approach.

Discussion and conclusions

The NPV analysis considers only the first moment measure of cash flows. In contrast, financial and real options incorporate uncertainty (second moment measure) into the valuation. Options have many applications in the real world, both on financial and on real assets. We believe that valuations based on option analysis will play an increasingly important role in practice in the future.

Questions

1. What is the exercise price of an option?
2. What is the difference between an American and a European option? All else equal, which one should have a higher price and why?
3. What differentiates a real option from a financial option?

Note

1 Downside risk is not relevant because the payoff of a call is truncated at zero.

Bibliography

Duku-Kaakyire, A., and D.M. Nanang. 2004. Application of real options theory to forestry investment analysis. *For. Policy Econ.* 6(6):539–552.

Hull, J.C. 2009. *Options, futures, and other derivatives.* Pearson Prentice Hall, Upper Saddle River, NJ, 822p.

Mei, B., and M.L. Clutter. 2013. Valuing a timber harvest contract as a high-dimensional American call option via least-squares Monte Carlo simulation. *Natural Res. Model.* 26(1):111–129.

Mei, B., and M.L. Clutter. 2015. Evaluating timberland investment opportunities in the United States: A real options analysis. *For. Sci.* 61(2):328–335.

Mei, B., D. Wear, and Y. Li. 2022. Tree planting subsidies and land use switching between forestry and agriculture in the US South. *J. For. Econ.* (Forthcoming).

Zinkhan, F.C. 1991. Option pricing and timberland's land-use conversion option. *Land Econ.* 67(3):317–325.

10

MANAGERIAL OPTIONS IN TIMBERLAND INVESTMENT

Highlights

- Reforestation is like a call option with the site establishment cost being the exercise price and timberland as the underlying asset.
- Stumpage price uncertainty increases the investment entry threshold as compared with the static discounted cash flow analysis for risk averse investors.
- Once established, active timber management can be temporarily suspended and later reactivated contingent upon the market conditions.
- The managerial flexibility lowers the exit threshold should the timberland investment be abandoned.

In recent years, there is an increasing divergence between timberland investments and returns in the United States. On the one hand, timberland price has been chased to a higher level. On the other hand, stumpage prices have been flat or declining after the global financial crisis of 2007–2009. This seems to make timberland investments more expensive and less rewarding. In this chapter, the real options approach is applied to analyze the timberland market.

Background

With the restructuring within the forest products industry, industrial timberlands have been transferred to TIMOs and REITs. Figure 10.1 shows the trend of total acreage of timberland transacted in the United States in the past decade. Of the total 620 transactions representing 40 million acres worth $41.6 billion, 369 are in the South with 20.5 million acres worth $24.2 billion (Harris et al. 2012). The peak transaction levels in 2005–2007 are primarily due to Boise's divestiture to

DOI: 10.4324/9781003366737-10

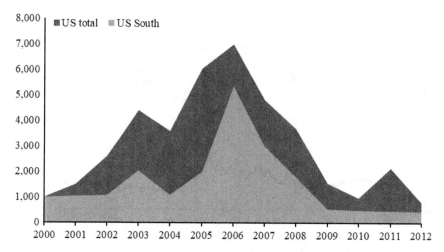

FIGURE 10.1   Total acres (in thousonds) of timberland transactions (large sales of above 1,000 acres) 2000–2012

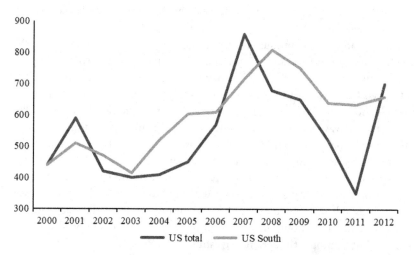

FIGURE 10.2   Average timberland transaction prices in 1982 constant US dollars per acre for 2000–2012

Forest Capital Partners (2.2 million acres), International Paper's massive divestiture (6 million acres) to multiple parties, and Temple-Inland's divestiture to The Campbell Group (1.8 million acres). With an unprecedented increasing influx of capital into the timberland market, timberland price has soared to a historically high level in recent years (Figure 10.2), although timber prices have been flat (pulpwood) or declining (chip-n-saw and sawtimber) over the same time period

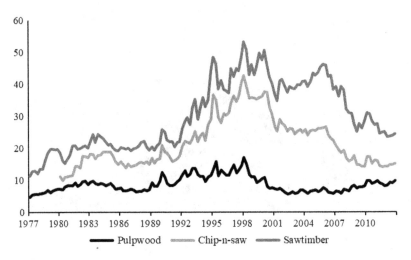

FIGURE 10.3   Nominal stumpage prices in US dollars per ton in Georgia 1977Q1–2012Q4

(Figure 10.3). A big concern of this ownership shift is whether timberland assets have been overpriced.

Static NPV analysis recommends taking any project with a positive NPV. Nonetheless, it ignores managerial options and assumes any investment opportunity is a now-or-never decision. This may result in undervaluation of the timberland assets. Contrasting to the static NPV analysis, the real options approach requires less stringent assumptions and considers managerial flexibility. The option to invest always has a positive value as long as timber price is greater than zero, and this option value should be counted as an opportunity cost when making an irreversible investment decision. In that sense, an investment decision is analogous to a call option—the investor has the right but not the obligation to invest in a project whose value is uncertain within a certain period of time. Once a tree farm is established, the manager has the option to mothball, reactivate, or permanently abandon it should market conditions vary. All these options should also be priced in valuing a timberland investment.

Past research

A number of studies apply real options approach in determining the optimal rotation age. Clarke and Reed (1989) and Reed and Clarke (1990) apply various types of stochastic processes for timber prices and wood volume in establishing the barrier rule of optimal harvesting. Morck et al. (1989) use a contingent claims approach within the context of intertemporal capital asset pricing model to value a hypothetical leased white pine forest, where both prices and inventories follow a standard Ito process. Thomson (1992) models timber prices as a lognormal diffusion process, and, by computing the option values numerically with the binomial procedure, he finds a generally longer rotation length, a higher stand value, and a nonlinear pattern in net present value (NPV) gain as timber price volatility increases. Plantinga (1998) argues that the reservation price strategy per se is equivalent to considering the option value in determining the optimal rotation age. Insley (2002) probes the general numerical solution technique in solving the optimal harvesting problem for an even aged stand of trees within a single rotation. Significantly different stand values and cutting times are found under different timber price assumptions. Insley and Rollins (2005) improve the numerical solution technique by extending it to the multi-rotation case.

Several studies investigate forest real options from other perspectives. Conroy and Miles (1989) find a higher return and a lower variance by setting a benchmark timber price that is 5% above the rolling 12-month trend line. Zinkhan (1991) values timberland conversion options, and posits that neglecting land-use conversion options can lead to underestimation of the intrinsic value of timberland. Reed (1993), Conrad (1997), Forsyth (2000), and Saphores et al. (2002) assume stochastic amenity value or timber prices, and they derive the minimum amenity value required for conserving an old-growth forest. Yin and Newman (1999) address a timber producer's entry, exit, mothballing, and reactivation decisions given random timber prices. Hughes (2000) prices a sale of a New Zealand forestry corporation as a call option, and he argues his approach has advantages in that only volatility of future timber prices needs to be estimated. Yin et al. (2000) use the example of linerboard production to evaluate option values of timberland ownership on operating decisions. Yin (2001) points out the limitations of stand-level analysis in assessing forestry investments, and demonstrates a new framework by combining forest-level analysis with the options valuation approach. Assuming mean-reverting timber prices, Gjolberg and Guttormsen (2002) explain that low discount rates in forestry may indicate rational pricing of comparatively low-risk, long-term investments with real option values included. Schatzki (2003) considers return uncertainty and sunk costs in a real option model, and examines land conversion from agriculture to forest. Yap (2004) models the Philippine forest plantation lease as an option, and asserts that timber price uncertainty could explain why leaseholders have insufficient incentives for immediate planting.

Our analysis differs from previous studies in that we explicitly consider various options associated with a forest investment, and we examine how these option values and timber market combined can be used in evaluating timberland investment and management opportunities.

Real options approach

The basic model

As described in McDonald and Siegel (1986), consider a firm's investment decision as the choice of the optimal time to install an investment with a lump-sum cost I in return for a project with an uncertain value V, given that the capacity installation is irreversible. In timberland investments, I denotes site preparation costs, planting costs, etc., and V denotes future timber sales. From this perspective, a landowner's investment opportunity is just like a call option on the forest with an excise price I. Denoting the value of the timber investment opportunity by F, the optimal rule can be expressed as

$$F = \max_{T} E[(V_T - I)e^{-\rho T}] \tag{10.1}$$

where E represents the expectation, T is the time to invest, ρ is the cost of capital (Dixit and Pindyck 1994). Since V and F are contingent or derivative assets, whose values rely on that of the more basic asset (timber) price P, they are usually expressed as functions of P, i.e., $V(P)$ and $F(P)$. In empirical studies, the geometric Brownian motion is generally assumed for P.

A geometric Brownian motion can be described as

$$dP = \alpha P dt + \sigma P dz \tag{10.2}$$

where α is the drift (growth rate) parameter, σ is the volatility (proportional variance) parameter, dz is the increment of the standard Wiener process defined as $dz = \varepsilon_t \sqrt{dt}$, ε_t being a standard normal random variable. Tsay (2005) demonstrates the way to estimate α and σ by letting $r_t = d\ln(P) = \ln(P) - \ln(P)$ be the continuously compounded return in the tth time interval. Namely, $\hat{\alpha} = \bar{r} / \Delta + s^2 / 2\Delta$ and

$\hat{\sigma} = s / \sqrt{\Delta}$, where $\bar{r}$ and s are the sample mean and standard deviation of the series r_t, and Δ is the equally spaced time interval measured in years.

Solution by contingent claims approach

The contingent claims (option pricing) approach assumes an overall equilibrium in capital markets. It starts by constructing the following dynamic risk-free portfolio: Long one unit of the option to invest $F(P)$, short $F'(P)$ units of the basic assets P. The value of this portfolio is $F - F'(P)P$. The total return on this portfolio over a short time interval dt is $dF - F'(P)dP - \delta PF'(P)dt$, where $\delta = \mu - \alpha$, and μ is the risk-adjusted expected return based on the capital asset pricing model (CAPM). Using Ito's Lemma, the return on the portfolio becomes $[0.5\sigma^2 P^2 F'(P) - \delta PF'(P)]dt$. To avoid arbitrage opportunities, the following equation must hold

$$[0.5\sigma^2 P^2 F'(P) - \delta PF'(P)]dt = r[F - F'(P)P]dt \tag{10.3}$$

Rearranging terms leads to the following differential equation

$$0.5\sigma^2 P^2 F'(P) + (r - \delta)PF'(P) - rF = 0 \qquad (10.4)$$

Entry and exit options

Suppose the payoffs of a forest plantation rely on timber price P, then the value of the forest plantation can be specified as a function of P. Using the contingent claims approach, $V(P)$ can be derived. Since a landowner makes decisions between being idle and being active, the landowner has a call option on the other in either state. Denoting $V_0(P)$ as the value of an idle farm (option value to invest), $V_1(P)$ as the value of active farm (profit from operation plus the option to abandon if the price falls too far), Dixit and Pindyck (1994) show that

$$V_0(P) = A_1 P^{\beta_1}, P \in [0, P_H] \qquad (10.5)$$

$$V_1(P) = B_2 P^{\beta_2} + P / \delta + C / r \qquad (10.6)$$

Where A_1 and B_2 are parameters to be determined, C is the variable cost of operation. Note the term in equation 6.6 represents the option value of abandonment, while the last two terms represent the value of operating profits (losses). Applying the value matching and smooth pasting conditions, the following system of four equations with the four unknowns, A_1, B_2, P_H and P_L, can be established

$$-A_1 P_H^{\beta_1} + B_2 P_H^{\beta_2} + P_H / \delta - C / r = I$$

$$-\beta_1 A_1 P_H^{\beta_1 - 1} + \beta_2 B_2 P_H^{\beta_2 - 1} + 1 / \delta = 0$$

$$-A_1 P_L^{\beta_1} + B_2 P_L^{\beta_2} + P_L / \delta - C / r = -E \qquad (10.7)$$

$$-\beta_1 A_1 P_L^{\beta_1 - 1} + \beta_2 B_2 P_L^{\beta_2 - 1} + 1 / \delta = 0$$

where P_H and P_L are price thresholds for entry (starting a new investment) and exit (abandoning an existent investment), and E is the lump-sum abandoning cost. Given the nonlinear nature, the system of equations should be solved numerically. If mothballing (temporarily suspending production) and reactivation (resuming active production) options are considered, a system of eight equations similar to Equations 10.7 can be established and solved. Accordingly, threshold prices for mothballing and reactivation are denoted as P_M and P_R. Some further discussion on the mothballing option in timberland management are presented in Box 10.1.

BOX 10.1 MOTHBALLING OPTION IN TIMBERLAND MANAGEMENT

In timberland management, the mothballing option implies delaying harvests and storing trees on the stump during unfavorable market conditions. For example, many landowners in the South stopped or reduced harvesting pine sawtimber following the financial crisis of 2007–2009 given the lackluster prices. Historically, pine sawtimber price had been as high as over $50/ton, while after the housing bubble it has been around $25/ton (TMS 2022). Most investors believed that pine sawtimber price should rise in a few years after the crisis, however, it did not happen as promptly as expected. Pine sawtimber price remained flat over the period 2009–2020 and did not show any uptick until recent years.

At the aggregate level, landowners' delay in harvesting resulted in a timber supply overhang. Therefore, even with an increased demand from a recovering housing market, the new equilibrium price of pine sawtimber depends on the relative movement of the supply and demand curves. In our case, the upward pressure on price from an increased demand seems to be offset by the downward pressure from the timber supply overhang so that the market clearing price changed little.

In theory, as long as the output price is volatile, the option to temporarily suspend active production when the price is declining and later reactivate production when the price reverts has some value to an investor. In practice, nevertheless, price movement is out of participants' control in a competitive market and the mothballing option can be costly to exercise. In addition to price volatility, the value of the mothballing option depends on the cost of capital and the expected net gain from waiting.

A numerical example

For illustration, a 25-acre fully regulated loblolly pine (*Pinus taeda* L.) forest as described in Conroy and Miles (1989) is used as an example. That is, at the beginning of each year timber ranges in age from zero to 24 on each acre of the land, while at the end of each year timber ranges in age from one to 25. The 25-year-old acre is harvested and replanted each year so that the landowner will have the same timber yield and age class distribution in any particular time of a year. Although the fully regulated forest is a rather simple and naive assumption, it is consistent with the forest-level analysis in Yin (2001) and Yin and Newman (1999).

Various options related to this fully regulated forest are defined as follows. Investment: An investor buys the 25-acre forest (land plus timber) and plants the one-acre bare land. Mothballing: An existing investor retains the forest but stops harvesting tress and only pays the property tax. Reactivation: An existing investor takes land from a mothballed condition and resumes active management, harvest, and sales of timber. Abandonment: An existing investor sells the forest and pays off all kinds of fees. After an investor has purchased the forest, she will maintain the same management and harvest until the price falls to the mothballing level. When mothballed, the reactivation threshold price could increase or decrease depending on how the forest changes after the mothballing.

Table 10.1 shows timber yield in green tons in three products (pulpwood, chip-n-saw, and sawtimber) for the hypothetical loblolly pine plantation at the end of each year. The volume is simulated by SiMS 2009, a growth-and-yield simulator (ForesTech International 2009). Key parameters used include: 500 trees planted per acre, site index 65 feet (base age 25 years), chemical site preparation, and no thinning. Each year the age 25 stand is harvested producing 203.6 tons of timber (67.1 tons of pulpwood, 118.0 tons of chip-n-saw, and 18.5 tons of sawtimber), whereas the age 1–24 stands are left on the ground and treated as inventory

TABLE 10.1 Timber yield (tons/acre) for the hypothetical loblolly pine plantation

Age	Pulpwood	Chip-n-saw	Sawtimber
1	0.0	0.0	0.0
2	0.0	0.0	0.0
3	0.0	0.0	0.0
4	0.0	0.0	0.0
5	10.6	0.0	0.0
6	22.2	0.1	0.0
7	33.2	1.2	0.0
8	42.3	4.0	0.0
9	49.4	8.4	0.0
10	54.8	14.1	0.0
11	58.9	20.6	0.0
12	62.2	27.5	0.0
13	64.7	34.5	0.2
14	66.6	41.7	0.4
15	67.9	48.8	0.6
16	69.1	55.8	1.0
17	70.2	64.2	1.6
18	69.9	75.4	3.1
19	69.6	84.7	4.8
20	69.2	92.5	6.8
21	68.8	99.1	8.8
22	68.5	104.7	11.2
23	68.1	109.7	13.5
24	67.6	114.1	16.0
25	67.1	118.0	18.5

(1,153.8 tons of pulpwood, 1,001.1 tons of chip-n-saw, and 68.0 tons of sawtimber). Prices for the three timber products are obtained from Timber Mart-South. Average prices, in 1982 constant US dollars, of the last five years are $3.85/ton for pulpwood, $6.97/ton for chip-n-saw, and $12.32/ton for sawtimber. The volumes of each product at age 25 are used as weights to derive the blended price.

Based on previous studies, the following cost parameters are assumed (all values have been deflated by consumer price index (CPI) and stated in constant US dollars as of 1982): site preparation $55/ac; planting and seedling $35/ac; miscellaneous management practices (e.g., fire and insect control) $2/ac; property taxes $2.5/ac; prescribed burning for five times in a rotation $25/ac; bare land value $555/ac; real risk-free rate 4%; and real risk-adjusted rate of return for a southern pine plantation 5%. The annual operating cost is $55 + 35 + (2 + 2.5) \times 25 + 25 = \$227.5$, which includes site preparation and replanting costs for one acre, management cost and taxes for 25 acres, and prescribed burning cost. The annual land rent is $555 \times 25 \times 0.04 = \$555$, and the annual opportunity cost in standing timber is $(1,153.8 \times 3.85 + 1,001.1 \times 6.97 + 68.0 \times 12.32) \times 0.04 = \$490.30$. Therefore, the annual per unit variable cost C is $(227.5 + 555 + 490.30) / 203.6 = \$6.25/ton$. The lump-sum investment cost is $555 \times 25 + 12,257.02 + 55 + 35 = \$26,222.02$, which includes bare land value of 25 acres, current inventory value, and site preparation and planting costs of one acre. On a per unit basis, investment cost I is $26,222.02 / 203.6 = \$128.79/ton$. The abandonment cost $(-\$42.93/ton)$ is assumed to be roughly 1/3 of the investment cost, and the negative sign reflects the salvage value of timber and land sales.[1] Because timber production can be easily suspended and reactivated without incurring heavy expenses, and only property taxes are paid for a mothballed plantation, the mothballing cost (E_M) is assumed to be zero, the reactivation cost (R) is assumed to be $1/ton, and the maintenance cost (M) is calculated as $2.5 \times 25 / 203.6 = \$0.31/ton$. Finally, timber price growth rate α and volatility σ are estimated to be 0.03 and 0.15, respectively. Table 10.2 summarizes key parameter values and the numerical solution to the system of equations given these parameters.

Taking consideration of timber price uncertainty, the entry threshold timber price is higher than the Marshallian long-run average cost $C + rI$, and the exit threshold timber price is lower than the Marshallian threshold $C - rE$. When entry and exit options are considered only, the entry threshold timber price is $3.27 higher and the exit threshold timber price is $3.91 lower than those Marshallian's (Table 10.2). With mothballing and reactivation options considered in addition, both the entry and the exit threshold timber prices are marginally lower than without these options.

Table 10.3 shows the values of the hypothetical loblolly pine plantation at each threshold price. In each state, the option value increases with timber price. At the Marshallian's break-even entry price $11.40/ton, the investment opportunity (V_0) is worth $311.59/ton. This is far larger than zero because of the time premium associated with this "call" option. At the same price, the value of an active forest

TABLE 10.2 Parameter values and numerical solutions to the system of equations

Production parameter	Value	Market parameter	Value
Rotation	25 year	Real risk-free rate r	0.04
Investment cost I	$128.79/ton	Real discount rate μ	0.05
Variable cost C	$6.25/ton	Timber price growth rate α	0.03
Abandonment cost E	−$42.93/ton	Timber price volatility σ	0.15
Mothballing cost E_M	$0/ton	Convenience yield $\delta = \mu - \alpha$	0.02
Maintenance cost M	$0.31/ton	β_1	1.54
Reactivation cost R	$1/ton	β_2	−2.31
Marshallian entry threshold $C + rI$	$11.40/ton		
Marshallian exit threshold $C - rE$	$7.97/ton		
Entry and exit		Entry, lay-up, reactivation, and exit	
A_1	7.31	A_1	7.31
B_2	1,556.45	B_2	1,596.22
P_H	$15.96/ton	D_1	10.66
P_L	$4.49/ton	D_2	560.43
		P_H	$15.95/ton
		P_R	$6.82/ton
		P_M	$5.13/ton
		P_L	$4.20/ton

TABLE 10.3 Values of the hypothetical loblolly pine plantation at each threshold price

Threshold price		Idle V_0	Mothballed V_M	Active V_1	Description
Exit	$P_L = 4.20$	67.51	110.45	—	$V_M = V_0 - E$
Mothball	$P_M = 5.13$	86.66	132.22	132.22	$V_1 = V_M (E_M = 0)$
Reactivate	$P_R = 6.82$	137.43	199.45	200.44	$V_M = V_1 - R$
Entry	$P_H = 15.95$	517.53	—	646.32	$V_0 = V_1 - I$

plantation (V_1) is far larger than $128.75/ton $(P - C)/r$ because of the managerial flexibility in mothballing, reactivating, and abandoning the forest plantation. At each threshold price, the value-matching rule applies to prevent any arbitrage opportunities. For example, when $P_H = $15.95/ton, the value of an active forest plantation (V_1) exceeds that of the investment opportunity (V_0) by the investment cost (I). That is, when timber price is as high as $15.95/ton, an investor can forgo the waiting opportunity by exercising her "call" option with a strike price $128.79/ton and lock in the value of an active forest plantation.

Robustness and sensitivity analysis

The sensitivity analysis is conducted in Table 10.4. Row 1 corresponds to the base case with parameter values specified in Table 10.2. Rows 2–11 correspond to some alternative cases, each row representing a case in which only one parameter changes values while the others remain constant. When the real risk-free rate (r) drops to 3%, it implies that the present value of the exercise cost is higher. Therefore, investors are more likely to exercise their options resulting in lower threshold prices, and these option values approach their intrinsic values more. When the real risk-adjusted rate of return (μ) increases, it implies the convenience yield increases.[2] From the contingent claims perspective, the portfolio holder has to pay more dividends on the short positions. This essentially increases the cost of holding the portfolio, thus increasing all threshold prices, decreasing the option values of investment and reactivation, and increasing the option values of mothballing and reactivation. A decline in the price growth rate (α) is equivalent to a rise in the real risk-adjusted rate of return in that both lead to an increase in the convenience yield. Hence, similar effects are observed in rows 3 and 4.

When price volatility increases (σ), more uncertainty is involved. Investors will be more reluctant to invest but less likely to abandon an existing project. Thus, threshold prices for investment and reactivation increase and those for mothballing and abandonment decrease. All else being equal, higher price volatility results in higher option values. If lump-sum investment cost (I) decreases, an investment becomes cheaper, so the threshold price for investment decreases and the option to invest becomes more valuable. In the meantime, a lower investment cost implies a relatively higher salvage value, so investors are more willing to abandon a project. That is, investors may choose to exit at a higher abandonment threshold price.

TABLE 10.4 Sensitivity analysis of the real options analysis

No.	Case	Variable	Base	New	P_H	P_R	P_M	P_L
1	Base				15.95	6.82	5.13	4.20
2	Δr	Real risk-free rate	0.04	0.03	13.60	5.44	3.99	3.46
3	$\Delta\mu$	Real discount rate	0.05	0.06	16.86	6.86	5.16	4.78
4	$\Delta\alpha$	Price growth rate	0.03	0.02	16.86	6.86	5.16	4.78
5	$\Delta\sigma$	Price volatility	0.15	0.20	18.27	7.05	4.99	3.81
6	ΔI	Investment cost	128.79	85	13.14	6.82	5.13	4.93
7	ΔC	Variable cost	6.25	8	18.25	8.73	6.72	5.06
8	ΔE	Abandonment cost	−42.93	−60	15.80	6.82	5.13	5.09
9	ΔE_M	Mothballing cost	0	1	15.97	7.03	4.89	4.23
10	ΔM	Maintenance cost	0.31	1	15.96	6.06	4.50	4.48
11	ΔR	Reactivation cost	1	2	15.96	7.08	4.92	4.26

Since investment cost is sunk, it has little impact on the mothballing and reactivation decisions. Using the same rationale, similar effects are observed for a decrease in the exit cost (*E*, rows 6 and 8). However, even if the investment cost is reduced by 34% from $128.79/ton to $85/ton, the average timber price level in Georgia in the last five years is still below the entry threshold price but above the abandonment threshold price.

When variable cost (*C*) rises, production becomes more expensive, so all threshold prices go up. Investment and reactivation options become less attractive, while mothballing and abandonment options become more feasible. When mothballing cost increases (E_M), mothballing becomes a less valuable option. In the extreme case, if mothballing cost exceeds abandonment cost, there will be no mothballing option at all. Higher mothballing cost indicates less managerial flexibility thus less option value, which, in turn, results in a higher entry threshold price to adjust for the risk, a higher reactivation threshold price to offset the mothballing cost, a lower mothballing threshold price to delay temporarily lay-up, and a lower exit threshold price to expand the life of an active project in hope that sunk costs can be recovered when more favorable information arrives.

When maintenance cost increases (*M*), the mothballed state of a project becomes less preferable. Accordingly, investors will respond by delaying entry (a higher entry threshold price), advancing reactivation for a mothballed project (a lower reactivation threshold price), postponing suspension (a lower mothballing threshold price), and considering earlier termination (a higher exit threshold price). In other words, option values of investment and mothballing will decrease, and those of reactivation and abandonment will increase. An increase in the reactivation cost (*R*) has effects similar to an increase the mothballing cost (rows 9 and 11). Again, in the extreme case, if the reactivation cost exceeds the initial investment cost, there will be no reactivation option at all since an investor can simply choose to start from scratch.

Finally, an alternative geometric Ornstein-Uhlenbeck process has been attempted to fit the timber price series. However, the value of the mean-reverting speed parameter is very small, and the value of the volatility parameter is similar to that from geometric Brownian motion. Therefore, our results are generally robust to different price assumptions. This is consistent with the findings in Metcalf and Hassett (1995).

Discussion and conclusions

Results from the numerical example of a hypothetical loblolly pine plantation in Georgia show that it is not optimal to make new investments on relatively young stands with current timberland and stumpage prices. In other words, the low stumpage prices cannot justify the high timberland price and timberland assets tend to be overpriced. For existing timberland investors, however, timber prices fall close to the mothballing threshold.[3] Therefore, some timberland investors may have temperately suspended timber production, which implies less harvesting activities. Actually, this has been evidenced by lower levels of timber production in recent years, especially for larger-size timber (Schiller et al. 2009; TMS 2022).

Results from the static NPV analysis are in stark contrast to those from the real options analysis. With the NPV analysis, the entry price is lower than that from the real options analysis albeit above the current timber price level, and the exit price is higher than the current timber price level. The differences can be owed to market uncertainty and managerial flexibility. Facing volatile prices, investors are less willing to get in, and existing landowners are less willing to walk away. This is especially true given the considerably large initial lump-sum costs and the long-term management regime in timberland investments. That is, the options to wait for more information, to temporarily shut down, to resume production, and to abandon a tree farm to prevent further losses, all have values. Results from the real options analysis can help investors make better capital budgeting decisions in the timberland industry.

It should be noted that our analysis is based on pure timber production. It may be true that certain timberland properties may have higher-and-better uses, such as residential or commercial development opportunities, or they may be embedded with mineral, oil, or gas leasing opportunities. All these have values and affect an investor's decision. In addition, the hypothetical loblolly pine plantation is a rather simplified example for illustration purpose only. In practice, investors must factor into their analyses age class distribution, product mix, site quality, and accuracy of the inventory estimate, to name a few. Various aspects can be improved in future studies. For instance, commercial thinnings can be added in the forest management efforts; biological growth and/or real risk-free rate can be assumed to be stochastic rather than deterministic; and a timberland portfolio that has different species and is geographically diversified can be examined likewise. Finally, the 25-year harvest strategy can be interrupted when the mothballing option is exercised. However, on a forest-level basis, this has minor effects in valuating timberland investments.

Questions

1. How is an investment decision like a financial call option?
2. How would various managerial options affect the exit decision of timberland investors?
3. Why should uncertainty be considered in decision making?

Notes

1 We assume a 100% equity investment. By abandoning, a timberland investor will sell off her properties (probably below their fair market values) regardless of market conditions. In addition to the bankruptcy cost, there may be extra costs to settle the

potential adverse impact on the environment. We assume that the value exceeds the total cost by 1/3, and the abandonment decision results in a cash inflow (negative cost). Sensitivity analysis on the abandonment cost is conducted later.

2 Convenience yield is the benefit or premium associated with holding an underlying product or physical good, rather than the contract or derivative product. Users of a consumption asset may obtain a benefit from physically holding the asset (as inventory) prior to maturity, which is not obtained from holding the futures contract. Here, convenience yield (δ) equals the risk-adjusted return (μ) minus the growth rate (α).

3 As suggested by the sensitivity analysis, price thresholds depend on each individual investor's situation (realized values of production parameters and market parameters).

Bibliography

Clarke, H.R., and W.J. Reed. 1989. The tree-cutting problem in a stochastic environment: The case of age-dependent growth. *J. Econ. Dyn. Control* 13(4):569–595.

Conrad, J.M. 1997. On the option value of old-growth forest. *Ecol. Econ.* 22(2):97–102.

Conroy, R., and M. Miles. 1989. Commercial forestland in the pension portfolio: The biological beta. *Financ. Anal. J.* 45(5):46–54.

Dixit, A.K., and R.S. Pindyck. 1994. *Investment under uncertainty.* Princeton University Press, Princeton, NJ, 468p.

ForesTech International. 2009. *SiMS 2009: Growth and yield simulator for southern pine.* ForesTech International, Watkinsville, GA.

Forsyth, M. 2000. On estimating the option value of preserving a wilderness area. *Can. J. Econ.* 33(2):413–434.

Gjolberg, O., and A.G. Guttormsen. 2002. Real options in the forest: What if prices are mean-reverting? *For. Policy Econ.* 4(1):13–20.

Harris, T., S. Baldwin, and J. Siry. 2012. *United States Timberland markets 2000 to mid-2012: Transactions, values & market research.* Timber Mart-South, Athens, GA, 320p.

Hughes, R. 2000. Valuing a forest as a call option: The sale of forestry corporation of New Zealand. *For. Sci.* 46(1):32–39.

Insley, M. 2002. A real options approach to the valuation of a forestry investment. *J. Environ. Econ. Manag.* 44(3):471–492.

Insley, M., and K. Rollins. 2005. On solving the multirotational timber harvesting problem with stochastic prices: A linear complementarity formulation. *Am. J. Agri. Econ.* 87(3):735–755.

McDonald, R., and D. Siegel. 1986. The value of waiting to invest. *Q. J. Econ.* 101(4):707–728.

Metcalf, G.E., and K.A. Hassett. 1995. Investment under alternative return assumptions - comparing random-walks and mean reversion. *J. Econ. Dyn. Control* 19(8):1471–1488.

Morck, R., E. Schwartz, and D. Stangeland. 1989. The valuation of forestry resources under stochastic prices and inventories. *J. Financial Quant. Anal.* 24(4):473–487.

Plantinga, A.J. 1998. The optimal timber rotation: An option value approach. *For. Sci.* 44(2):192–202.

Reed, W.J. 1993. The decision to conserve or harvest old-growth forest. *Ecol. Econ.* 8(1):45–69.

Reed, W.J., and H.R. Clarke. 1990. Harvest decisions and asset valuation for biological resources exhibiting size-dependent stochastic growth. *Int. Econ. Rev.* 31(1):147–169.

Saphores, J.-D., L. Khalaf, and D. Pelletier. 2002. On jumps and ARCH effects in natural resource prices: An application to Pacific Northwest stumpage prices. *Am. J. Agri. Econ.* 84(2):387–400.

Schatzki, T. 2003. Options, uncertainty and sunk costs: An empirical analysis of land use change. *J. Environ. Econ. Manag.* 46(1):86–105.

Schiller, J.R., N. McClure, and R.A. Willard. 2009. *Georgia's timber industry—An assessment of timber product output and use, 2007.* USDA Foreign Service, Asheville, NC, 35.

Thomson, T.A. 1992. Optimal forest rotation when stumpage prices follow a diffusion process. *Land Econ.* 68(3):329–342.

TMS. 2022. *TimberMart-South.* Norris Foundation, Athens, GA.

Tsay, R.S. 2005. *Analysis of financial time series.* John Wiley & Sons, Hoboken, NJ, 640p.

Yap, R.C. 2004. Option valuation of Philippine forest plantation leases. *Environ. Dev. Econ.* 9(3):315–333.

Yin, R. 2001. Combining forest-level analysis with options valuation approach—A new framework for assessing forestry investment. *For. Sci.* 47(4):475–483.

Yin, R., T.G. Harris, and B. Izlar. 2000. Why forest products companies may need to hold timberland. *For. Prod. J.* 50(9):39–44.

Yin, R., and D.H. Newman. 1999. A timber producer's entry, exit, mothballing, and reactivation decision under market risk. *J. For. Econ.* 5(2):305–320.

Zinkhan, F.C. 1991. Option pricing and timberland's land-use conversion option. *Land Econ.* 67(3):317–325.

11

VALUING TIMBER HARVEST CONTRACTS

Highlights

- Timber harvest contract is like an American call option, in which the wood user (option-holder or buyer) has the right but not obligation to harvest the landowner's (option writer or seller) timber within a given period of time.
- The underlying asset is timber, and the exercise price is periodically decided based on certain widely used market index.
- The option is multidimensional in that there are three timber products produced simultaneously from a southern pine plantation.
- Timber harvest contracts are often off the balance sheets but do have values.

With the shift of timberland ownership, forest products companies rely more on the open market for timber. To mitigate market risks, many wood users have timber harvest contracts with forest landowners. In this chapter, we are going to investigate the pricing of certain short-term timber harvest contract as a high-dimensional American call option via least-squares Monte Carlo simulation.

Background

Using the Black-Scholes model, a group of researchers have examined a variety of contractual and real options in the forest industry. Shaffer (1984) evaluated two actual long-term timber cutting contracts used by forest industry companies. Restrepo et al. (2020) updated the pricing framework of Shaffer (1984) by using some more advanced financial modeling techniques. Zinkhan (1991) investigated timberland conversion options in a timberland bid. Hughes (2000) priced the sale of Forestry Corporation of New Zealand as a call option. Petrasek and

DOI: 10.4324/9781003366737-11

Perez–Garcia (2010) used modified least-squares Monte Carlo simulation (LSM) to evaluate timber harvest contracts offered by the Department of Natural Resources in the state of Washington.

A summary of the past research reveals three limitations in the field of valuing contractual options in the forest industry. First, timber harvest contracts were often treated as European call options rather than American call options (e.g., Burnes et al. 1999; Shaffer 1984). American options differ from European options in that the former can be exercised any time up to the expiration date whereas the latter can be exercised only on the expiration date. In timber harvest contracts, contract holders usually have the managerial flexibility to cut trees any time prior to the expiry date and, hence, such contracts should be treated as American options. Second, the values of timber harvest contracts were derived based on certain price indices rather than actual timber prices (e.g., Morck et al. 1989; Petrasek and Perez–Garcia 2010). Although this assumption simplified the option pricing algorithm, it ignored the fact that multiple timber products are produced simultaneously. Take a southern pine plantation as an example. Three products—pulpwood, chip-n-saw, and sawtimber—can be produced in the final harvest. Although stumpage prices for the three products evolve through time with some similar patterns, they are not perfectly correlated. Third, with a few exceptions, e.g., Binkley et al. (2001), Insley (2002), and Insley and Rollins (2005), most previous studies assumed timber price to follow either a random walk or a mean-reverting process but did not compare the results under different price assumptions.

We contribute to the existing literature in the field of valuing timber harvest contracts in two ways. First, we considered multiple timber products simultaneously in the LSM method. This is equivalent to pricing high-dimensional American options, as described in Broadie and Glasserman (1997). Second, we compared two alternative stochastic processes for timber prices: random walk vs. mean-reverting and examined their impact on the contract values.

Timber harvest contract as American call option

To optimize their revenues from auctioning off the timber cut rights, government agencies have designed timber harvest contracts for a variety of timber sales, such as lump-sum sales, scale sales, and individual sales (Petrasek and Perez–Garcia 2010). Within a time period defined in the contract, the winner in a public auction has to harvest the trees offered for sale by the government agency, or otherwise face a penalty fee. These contracts share some similarities with those used by forest products companies or timber brokers. In this study, we proposed a privately negotiated timber harvest contract between a forest products company and a landowner of a southern pine plantation, in which the company is obligated to cut the landowner's trees any time before the predetermined date at a fixed price, or it has to compensate the forest landowner by paying a liquidation damage fee based on the strike price in the contract. All the contractual commitments are fulfilled upon the removal of the timber. This type of contract can be viewed as a high-dimensional American call option on the three timber products. Besides the liquidation damage fee, another major difference between timber harvest contracts and financial options is that cutting trees off incurs sales and administration costs. Our goal is to properly determine the value of such a contract.

The terms of the timber harvest contract are given as follows. First, the contract is based on a scale sale, in which all timber is sold by weight in tons. Second, the length of the contract is set to be three years. When the contract is written, both parties have assessed and therefore known the standing timber volume. Third, given the ongoing debate on the stochastic properties of timber prices (e.g., Binkley et al. 2001; Prestemon 2003; Washburn and Binkley 1990), two alternative models are used: a geometric Brownian motion (random walk model) vs. a modified Ornstein-Uhlenbeck process (mean-reverting model). Last, price correlations among the three timber products are built into the models, and the strike price of the contract is the average stand value calculated using the estimated long-run equilibrium timber prices and the average timber volumes over the three-year window. Box 11.1 shows the applications of certain fiber supply contracts by one of the world's largest and most experienced forest products companies, International Paper.

BOX 11.1 SOME REAL-WORLD APPLICATIONS OF FIBER SUPPLY CONTRACTS

In 2006, International Paper sold 4.2 million acres of timberland for about $5 billion to two TIMOs, Resource Management Service and Forest Investment Associates. Coming together with the sales were a 20-year fiber supply agreement for International Paper's pulp and paper mills in the South, a, ten-year fiber supply agreement for its coated paper facilities in Michigan, and a ten-year fiber supply agreement for its wood products facilities, all at market prices.

In the meantime, International Paper sold 900,000 acres for about $1.1 billion to TimberStar, a joint venture owned by commercial real estate financial firm iStar Financial and a group of equity investors. This sale included a 50-year fiber supply agreement for International Paper's pulp and paper mills and a 30-year fiber supply agreement for its wood products facilities, both at market prices. These combined transactions represent the largest private forestland sale in US history.

Despite the change of land ownership, the forestlands would continue to be managed and third-party certified under the requirements of the Sustainable Forestry Initiative. David Liebetreu, vice president of forest resources for International Paper at that time, said, "We are very pleased with the terms of both agreements, which allow us to capture about 20% of our annual soft-wood fiber requirements from these lands for our pulp and paper facilities, which is only slightly lower than our historic levels. In addition, the agreements we have negotiated ensure the lands will be sustainably managed and we will have no interruptions in this important segment of our supply chain."

"We are excited about the relationship with International Paper," said Jerry Barag, managing director of TimberStar. "Its excellent stewardship of these lands over the last half century made this an especially compelling opportunity for our company. This transaction, with its combination of prime forest-lands and significant, long-term supply agreements, diversifies and extends the TimberStar franchise into the epicenter of one of the most sought-after regions of the US forest products industry. We are confident that this will be a strong and mutually beneficial relationship between International Paper and TimberStar."

Deemed as a win-win situation at the initiation time, the fiber supply agreements may turn out to be more in favor of a particular party. For example, TimberStar properties were later sold in a whole to Manulife Investment Management (former Hancock Timber Resource Group) for $1.7 billion in 2008, and then partially (about 295,000 acres) sold to Forest Investment Associates and Molpus Woodlands Group in 2016, both with the fiber supply agreements inherited. From our conversations with those market players, there were diverging opinions on the perceived gains and losses for the fiber supply agreements.

Shaffer (1984) and Restrepo et al. (2020) proposed a framework in pricing certain long-term cutting contracts and identified timber price volatility to be a crucial factor. Overall, timber prices have been less volatile in the recent decade, resulting in lower values of the fiber supply agreements for the wood user's (International Paper) perspective.

Data sources: International Paper's 10 K reports.

Methodology

Valuation framework

The general framework of derivative pricing can be found in Black and Scholes (1973) and Merton (1973). The following description is based on the notations as in Longstaff and Schwartz (2001). First, a complete probability space (Ω, Λ, P) and a finite time horizon $[0,T]$ are defined, where Ω is the set of all potential realizations of the evolving economy (ω's) over time $[0,T]$, Λ is the space of distinguishable events, and P is the probability associated with each event in Λ. Then, the problem is to determine the value of an American option with stochastic cash flows $C(\omega, s; t, T)$ conditional on the option being alive at or before time t and on the option-holder following the optimal stopping rule for all $s \in (t, T]$.

Theoretically, an American option can be exercised any time before the expiration date. To be more intuitive, however, we consider its approximation where the American option can be executed only at the K discrete times $0 < t_1 < t_2 < \cdots < t_K = T$. This simplification mimics the continuously exercisable American option well when K is adequately large. At the expiration date $t_K = T$, the option-holder either exercises the option if it is in-the-money or lets it expire otherwise. Before that, at time t_k, $k = 1, 2, \cdots, K-1$, the option-holder will decide whether to exercise the option right away or hold on to make the decision one time period later at t_{k+1}. The option value is maximized unconditionally if it is exercised whenever the immediate exercise value exceeds the continuation value (Duffie 2001).

In terms of a timber harvest contract, Ω denotes the realizations of future stumpage prices and the contract holder will decide the optimal time to exercise the option so as to maximize his/her profit

$$\pi_t = \max\left\{P_t'Q_t - C; E\left[m_t \pi_{t+1}\right]\right\} \tag{11.1}$$

where π denotes the profit, P is the vector of stumpage prices, Q is the vector of timber volumes, C is the total cost of sales, m is the discount factor, $E[\cdot]$ is the expectation operator, and subscript t indicates time. On the expiration date T, an American option is the same as a European option and the cash flow equals either zero if the option is out-of-the-money or the intrinsic value if it is in-the-money. Besides the harvest cost, there is an extra liquidation damage cost F, and the optimal strategy becomes

$$\pi_T = \max\left\{P_T'Q_T - C - F; 0\right\}. \tag{11.2}$$

Least-squares Monte Carlo simulation

The LSM approach has been widely used in pricing American options. As the expiration date arrives, the optimal strategy for an American option-holder is to exercise the option if it is in-the-money. Before that, the optimal strategy is to weigh the immediate exercise value against the anticipated cash flows from continuing and then exercise if the former is greater than the latter. As such, a central part of the LSM algorithm is to approximate the continuation values by the conditional expected values at $t_{K-1}, t_{K-2}, \cdots, t_1$ prior to the expiration date. The algorithm works backwards recursively to get the path of cash flows $C(\omega, s; t, T)$ generated by the option. Therefore, $C(\omega, s; t_k, T)$ can be different from $C(\omega, s; t_{k+1}, T)$ as it may be better to exercise at time t_{k+1}, changing all succeeding cash flows on a realized path ω. After all the cash flows associated with the option are identified, the value of the option can be calculated as the present value of each cash flow averaged over all paths.

Typically, the conditional expectation function $F(\omega; t)$ can be specified as a linear combination of a set of measurable basis functions $L_i(X)$,

$$F(\omega; t) = \sum_{i=0}^{\infty} a_i L_i(X). \tag{11.3}$$

One candidate set for the basis functions that is widely used is the Laguerre polynomials: $L_n(X) = e^{-X/2} \dfrac{e^X}{n!} \dfrac{d^n}{dX^n}\left(X^n e^{-X}\right)$, where X is the value of the asset underlying the option (Longstaff and Schwartz 2001). Regarding the timber harvest contract, X's are stumpage values in three timber products. An intuitive numerical example using the LSM method can be found in the Appendix.

Models for timber prices

In an efficient market, competition creates an equilibrium in which it is extremely difficult to achieve excess returns over the market on a risk-adjusted basis. In other words, asset prices impound all relevant information and respond only to news releases (Fama 1970). Since the proposition of the efficient market hypothesis, a large number of empirical studies have been conducted to test it but have resulted in conflicting findings (Fama 1991). However, most agree that capital markets are efficient in the weak or semi-strong but not in the strong form (Copeland et al. 2005). One implication of market efficiency is that asset prices evolve almost randomly over time. With respect to the US timber market, mixed evidence of market efficiency has also been found (Prestemon 2003). Part of the reason is that although forces such as population-driven shifts in demand or supplies from old-growth forests can be anticipated (Hardie et al. 1984), substantial short-run fluctuations in demand remain unpredictable (Brazee and Mendelsohn 1988). Hence, we considered two alternative timber price assumptions, a random walk model vs. a mean-reverting process.

A random walk is a mathematical formulization of a path made by taking successive random steps. The geometric Brownian motion model is one of the most widely used stochastic processes in modeling security or commodity prices in finance theory and practice for its desirable properties including (Hull 2009): (1) Expected returns from a geometric Brownian motion do not rely on prices, which is consistent with the efficient market hypothesis; (2) A geometric Brownian motion takes positive values only, which is appropriate for prices; (3) A geometric Brownian motion can mimic well the tracks of asset prices; and

(4) Analytical solutions with a geometric Brownian motion are relatively easy. Nonetheless, a geometric Brownian motion has some constraints as well. First, a geometric Brownian motion assumes constant volatility of assets. Second, a geometric Brownian motion assumes returns to be normally distributed. Both of these assumptions tend to be violated in the real world (Wilmott 2006). Like the geometric Brownian motion, the modified Ornstein-Uhlenbeck process has the same constraints in terms of return volatility and normality.

Random timber prices in this study were modeled by a geometric Brownian motion

$$dP_t = \alpha P_t dt + \sigma P_t dw_t \qquad (11.4)$$

where P_t is pine stumpage price, α and σ are the drift and volatility parameters, and dw_t is the increment of a Wiener process defined as $dw_t = \varepsilon_t \sqrt{dt}$, with ε_t being standard normal. Expressing $r_t = d\ln(P_t) = \ln(P_t) - \ln(P_{t-1})$ as the continuously compounded return in the tth time interval, it was shown that $\hat{a} = \bar{r}/\Delta + s^2/2\Delta$ and $\hat{\sigma} = s/\sqrt{\Delta}$, where $\bar{r}$ and s are the sample mean and standard deviation of the series r_t and Δ is the equally spaced time interval measured in years (Tsay 2005).

Mean-reverting timber prices were modeled by a modified Ornstein-Uhlenbeck process

$$dP_t = \eta(\bar{P} - P_t)dt + \delta P dw_t \qquad (11.5)$$

where $\bar{P}$ is the long-run equilibrium level of pine stumpage prices, η is the reversion speed parameter, and δ and dw_t are likewise defined as in a geometric Brownian Motion. A mean-reverting process differs from a geometric Brownian motion in the drift parameter—it is positive when current price is below $\bar{P}$ and negative vice versa. That is, the long run, equilibrium level draws prices in its direction despite short-run vacillations. Some researchers asserted that a mean-reverting process ought to be a better option because commodity prices should mirror their marginal costs of production, e.g., Schwartz (1997) and Mei et al. (2011). A discrete time approximation of the modified Ornstein-Uhlenbeck process is $P_t - P_{t-1} = \eta \bar{P} \Delta t - \eta \Delta t P_{t-1} + \delta P_{t-1} \sqrt{\Delta t} \varepsilon_t$. Rearranging the terms results in

$$(P_t - P_{t-1})/P_{t-1} = c(1) + c(2)/P_{t-1} + e_t \qquad (11.6)$$

where $c(1) \equiv -\eta \Delta t$, $c(2) \equiv \eta \bar{P} \Delta t$, and $e_t \equiv \delta \sqrt{\Delta t} \varepsilon_t$ (Insley and Rollins 2005). The relevant parameters can be calculated by running a regression on Equation 10.6.

Simulated future prices for the three timber products were assumed to have the same correlations as the historical data. For both stochastic processes, the correlations were incorporated into the models by the Cholesky decomposition method described as follows (Greene 2017). The problem is to generate $X = (X_1, X_2, \ldots, X_n)$ so that $X \quad MN(0, \pounds)$. In this study $n = 3$ since there are three timber products. The variance-covariance matrix being symmetric positive-definite, it can be written as

$$\pounds = U'DU = \left(U'\sqrt{D}\right)\left(\sqrt{D}U\right) = \left(\sqrt{D}U\right)'\left(\sqrt{D}U\right) \tag{11.7}$$

where U is an upper triangular matrix and $\mathbf{D}$ is a diagonal matrix with positive diagonal elements. Denoting matrix $\mathbf{C} = \sqrt{D}U$, $\mathbf{X}$ can be generated as $\mathbf{X} = \mathbf{C}'z$, where $z \sim MN(0, 1)$.

An example and discussion

Suppose a three-year timber harvest contract is written on a 30-year-old loblolly pine (*Pinus taeda*) plantation with a known standing volume. The growth and yield data for the next three years (Table 11.1) were simulated by SiMS (ForesTech International 2009) and agreed upon by both parties. Estimates of the key parameters for timber prices are the same as in Chapter 4, which were based on southern Georgia (GA2) pine stumpage prices over 1977Q1–2010Q4 as reported by TimberMart-South (TMS 2022). The starting values of timber prices in the simulation were set at the average levels in the past five years. Using the average timber volume over the next three years and the estimated long-run equilibrium timber prices, the strike price was set at $4,355/ac. Further, it was assumed that the risk-free rate is 6% and the option could be exercised four times per year ($K = 4$), that is, once per quarter. Accordingly, the growth and yield data were linearly

TABLE 11.1 Growth and yield (tons/acre) for the southern pine plantation over age 30–32 years

Age	pulpwood	chip-n-saw	sawtimber
30Q1	84.1	126.0	12.4
30Q2	83.6	127.2	13.1
30Q3	83.2	128.4	13.8
30Q4	82.2	130.7	15.1
31Q1	81.7	131.8	15.9
31Q2	81.3	132.8	16.6
31Q3	80.8	133.9	17.4
31Q4	80.3	134.9	18.1
32Q1	79.9	135.8	19.0
32Q2	79.4	136.7	19.8
32Q3	79.0	137.6	20.7
32Q4	78.5	138.5	21.5

interpolated between years. The total cost of sales C included a sale fee of $225/ac and an administration fee of $12/ac (Petrasek and Perez-Garcia 2010), and this cost was assumed to increase with an expected inflation of 2% per year (Federal Reserve Bank of Cleveland 2011). The liquidation damage fee was assumed to be 10% of the strike price. The conditional expectation function was specified using the second order Laguerre polynomials. In total, 100 simulations were run with 1,000 iterations (price paths) in each simulation.

The simulated values of the timber harvest contract are shown in Figure 11.1. The simulated contract values were $1,829 – $1,984/ac with an average of $1,901/ac for random walk timber prices and $1,693 – $1,846/ac with an average of $1,785/ac for mean-reverting timber prices. The average contract value was higher in the former case because with the random walk assumptions timber prices tend to be more volatile. The wider the spread of stumpage values, the higher contract values can reach in good times because the lower values can be truncated and ignored. The 95% confidence intervals around the median (the shaded area) of the contract values under both price assumptions are shown in Figure 11.2. Overall, the value of such a timber harvest contract should be somewhere between $1,693/ac and $1,984/ac. This estimate will become more precise with larger numbers of total simulations and iterations, which is commonly known as the trade-off between the accuracy and the computational cost in a Monte Carlo simulation. Lastly, ignoring the possibility of early exercises and using simulated cash flows

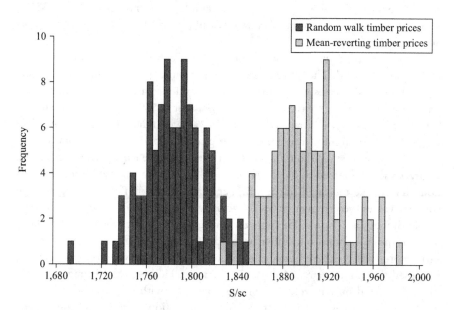

FIGURE 11.1   Distributions of simulated contract values with two alternative timber price assumptions

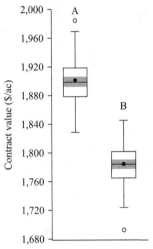

A: Random walk timber prices
B: Mean-reverting timber prices

FIGURE 11.2 Box plots of the simulated contract values with two alternative timber price assumptions

at the expiration date only, we calculated the value of the timber harvest contract as a European option. For this numerical example, an average premium of $320/ac was found when the contract is viewed as an American rather than a European option.

To examine the impact of key parameters on the contract value, sensitivity analyses were conducted. The results were all within our expectation in that the value of a call option decreases with transaction costs and increases with the value of the underlying asset. First, we increased the harvest cost to $500/ac. All else equal, this led to a lower average contract value of $1,694/ac with random walk timber prices and $1,580/ac with mean-reverting timber prices. Second, we eliminated the liquidation damage fee. Without this threat of exercise at the expiry date, the average contract value increased to $1,954/ac and $1,829/ac under the two price assumptions. Third, we increased starting timber prices by 20%. The resulting average contract values were higher at $3,178/ac and $2,974/ac, respectively. Intuitively, higher timber prices resulted in higher stumpage values, which increased the likelihood of the call option on timber to be in-the-money. Higher timber prices, in turn, more likely triggered early exercise of the timber harvest contract. Fourth, we raised the interest rate to 10%, a 67% increase. However, the average contract values increased only marginally. This is consistent with the "rho" effect in the Black-Scholes model in that the response of the option value to a change of the interest rate is usually trivial.

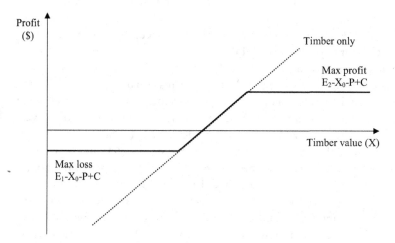

FIGURE 11.3   Payoffs from the collar strategy used by a forest landowner

In a similar way, private forest landowners can negotiate various timber sales contracts with forest products companies (or timber brokers), in which landowners have the right but not the obligation to sell their timber to forest products companies within a specified time period at a predetermined price. This type of contract is just like an American put option on the timber assets and can be used by forest land-owners to protect themselves against a loss from market downturns. Properly combined, these various contracts can be used to design more sophisticated supply chain instruments for those with advanced financial knowledge. For instance, if a forest landowner writes a timber harvest contract (a short position in a call) and at the same time holds a timber sales contract (a long position in a put), he/she is actually using a collar strategy. As such, upfront cash flows will be limited or even zero (zero-cost collar), whereas the potential loss and gain will be truncated (Figure 11.3).

Summary and conclusions

Securing the raw material supply is a crucial issue for forest products companies. With the shifting landscape of timberland ownership in the United States, forest products companies relied more heavily on the open market for timber. Among various timber procurement vehicles, timber cut contracts have been the most commonly used within the forest industry. Because most of such contracts are not reported on the corporate balance sheet, it is necessary and important for the stakeholders of forest products companies to understand the economic values of these "off-balance-sheet" assets. In this study, we treated a three-year timber harvest contract on a 30-year-old loblolly pine plantation as a high-dimensional American call option and calculated its value by the LSM approach. This method can be easily adapted to evaluate other privately negotiated timber cut contracts with different contract terms.

One of the key assumptions in valuing a timber cut contract is about the stochastic behavior of timber prices. Like many other commodity prices, timber prices are determined by the market supply and demand. In the long run, timber prices should be mean-reverting, reflecting the marginal costs of production in equilibrium, whereas the short run, large movement in timber prices is not uncommon. The results in this study showed that the value of the three-year timber harvest contract was higher with random walk timber prices. This is because random walk timber prices have a wider spread of values and higher contract values in good times can be realized by simply exercising the options. Therefore, timber price assumptions should be carefully considered in determining the value of a timber harvest contract. For a short-term contract, the random walk assumption may be a better choice. Next, a timber cut contract differs from a financial call option in that the former involves considerable transaction costs. To enhance the gain from holding such contracts, forest products companies can try to minimize the sales and administration costs. Moreover, private forest landowners should realize that the liquidation damage fee acts as a two bladed sword. On the one hand, it increases the possibility that the timber cut contract will be exercised and therefore alleviates their downside risk. On the other hand, however, it reduces the upfront profits from writing such contracts. Hence, landowners have to weigh one effect against another before making their decisions. Finally, moderate changes in the interest rate have minor effects on the contract values.

Overall, the valuation approach presented in this study provides an alternative way to the Black-Scholes model to price timber cut contracts. The simulation process can help participants in the forest industry better understand and thus appropriately use various types of timber harvest contracts to manage their business risks. This method can also be used to value long-term wood supply agreements by breaking them down into a series of short-term timber harvest contracts. Furthermore, different contracts can be combined to construct more complex strategies. Properly applied, both upside and downside risks can be controlled and a win-win solution may be reached between forest products companies and private forest landowners.

Appendix

Consider an American call option on a share of stock without dividend. Current price for the stock is 1.80. The option can be exercised at times 1 and 2 with a strike price of 2.00, and time 2 is the expiration date. The risk-free rate is 6%. For illustration purpose, we use ten sample paths for the stock price shown in the following matrix.

Price paths		
Path	Time 1	Time 2
1	2.20	2.16
2	2.32	2.50
3	2.44	2.15
4	1.80	1.95
5	2.22	3.10
6	1.54	1.60
7	1.85	1.68
8	1.76	2.40
9	1.98	2.05
10	2.19	1.99

The goal is to find the stopping rule that maximizes the option value at each point along each price path. Conditional on not exercising the option before time 2, the cash flows at time 2 following the optimal strategy are given below.

Cash flows at time 2		
Path	Time 1	Time 2
1	–	0.16
2	–	0.50
3	–	0.15
4	–	0
5	–	1.10
6	–	0
7	–	0
8	–	0.40
9	–	0.05
10	–	0

If the option is in-the-money at time 1, the option-holder has to choose whether to exercise or continue holding the option until expiration. Let X be the stock prices at time 1 when the option is in-the-money and Y be the corresponding discounted cash flows realized at time 2 if the option is alive at time 1. The vectors X and Y are given below.

Regression at time 1

Path	Y	X
1	$0.16 \times e^{-0.06}$	2.20
2	$0.50 \times e^{-0.06}$	2.32
3	$0.15 \times e^{-0.06}$	2.44
4	–	–
5	$1.11 \times e^{-0.06}$	2.22
6	–	–
7	–	–
8	–	–
9	–	–
10	$0 \times e^{-0.06}$	2.19

Only in-the-money paths are used so as to improve the efficiency of the LSM algorithm (Longstaff and Schwartz 2001). The conditional expectation function is based on a regression of Y on a constant, X and X^2, i.e., $E[Y \mid X] = -179.24 + 156.08X - 33.84X^2$. We then compare the immediate exercise values (intrinsic values) with those conditional expectations (fitted values using the above equation) for the in-the-money paths. If the former is larger, it's optimal to exercise; otherwise, it's optimal to delay. Once exercised, all subsequent cash flows along that price path are set to zero since an option can be exercised only once.

Optimal decision at time 1

Path	Exercise	Hold
1	0.2	0.32
2	0.32	0.69
3	0.44	0.09
4	–	–
5	0.22	0.45
6	–	–
7	–	–
8	–	–
9	–	–
10	0.19	0.25

With the comparison, it is optimal to exercise at time 1 only for the third path. Therefore, the stopping rule and the option cash flow matrices are given as follows. Note that the cash flow at time 2 for path 3 has been set to zero.

Stopping rule

Path	Time 1	Time 2
1	0	1
2	0	1
3	1	0
4	0	0
5	0	1
6	0	0
7	0	0
8	0	1
9	0	1
10	0	0

Option cash flows

Path	Time 1	Time 2
1	0	0.16
2	0	0.50
3	0.44	0
4	0	0
5	0	1.10
6	0	0
7	0	0
8	0	0.40
9	0	0.05
10	0	0

The value of an American option can be calculated by discounting each cash flow in the option cash flow matrix back to time 0 and averaging across all paths. For this specific example, the value of such an American call option is calculated at 0.24. If, instead, the option can be exercised only at time 2, then, the optimal rule reduces to exercising the option at expiration if it is in-the-money. Hence, the cash flows at time 2 will be either the option's intrinsic value or zero. The value of such a European option can be calculated by discounting time 2 cash flows and averaging across all paths. With the above price path matrix, the European call option is valued at 0.21, which is very close to that reported by the Black–Scholes model. For larger numbers of total paths and time periods, this LSM algorithm can be realized via computer programming.

Questions

1. Explain how a timber harvest contract is like a call option.
2. Who is the owner (buyer) and who is the writer (seller) in a timber harvest contract?
3. When should an American option be exercised prior to the expiry date?

Bibliography

Binkley, C.S., C.I. Washburn, and M.E. Aronow. 2001. *Stochastic simulation in timberland investment. Research Note R-01-2.* Hancock Timber Resource Group, Boston, MA. 6.

Black, F., and M. Scholes. 1973. The pricing of options and corporate liabilities. *J. Polit. Econ.* 81(3):637–654.

Brazee, R.J., and R. Mendelsohn. 1988. Timber harvesting with fluctuating prices. *For. Sci.* 34(2):359–372.

Broadie, M., and P. Glasserman. 1997. Pricing American-style securities using simulation. *J. Econ. Dyn. Control* 21(8–9):1323–1352.

Burnes, E., E. Thomann, and E.C. Waymire. 1999. Arbitrage-free valuation of a federal timber lease. *For. Sci.* 45(4):473–483.

Copeland, T.E., J.F. Weston, and K. Shastri. 2005. *Financial theory and corporate policy.* Pearson Addison Wesley, Boston, MA, 1000p.

Duffie, D. 2001. *Dynamic asset pricing theory.* Princeton University Press, Princeton, NJ.

Fama, E.F. 1970. Efficient capital markets: A review of theory and empirical work. *J. Financ.* 25(2):383–417.

Fama, E.F. 1991. Efficient capital markets: II. *J. Financ.* 46(5):1575–1617.

Federal Reserve Bank of Cleveland. 2011. *Cleveland fed estimates of inflation expectations.* https://www.clevelandfed.org/. Last accessed August 20, 2022.

ForesTech International. 2009. *SiMS 2009: Growth and yield simulator for Southern pine.* ForesTech International, Watkinsville, GA.

Greene, W.H. 2017. *Econometric analysis,* 8th ed. Pearson, New York.

Hardie, I.W., J.N. Daberkow, and K.E. Mcconnell. 1984. A timber harvesting model with variable rotation lengths. *For. Sci.* 30(2):511–523.

Hughes, R. 2000. Valuing a forest as a call option: The sale of forestry corporation of New Zealand. *For. Sci.* 46(1):32–39.

Hull, J.C. 2009. *Options, futures, and other derivatives.* Pearson Prentice Hall, Upper Saddle River, NJ, 822p.

Insley, M. 2002. A real options approach to the valuation of a forestry investment. *J. Environ. Econ. Manag.* 44(3):471–492.

Insley, M., and K. Rollins. 2005. On solving the multirotational timber harvesting problem with stochastic prices: A linear complementarity formulation. *Am. J. Agri. Econ.* 87(3):735–755.

Longstaff, F.A., and E.S. Schwartz. 2001. Valuing American options by simulation: A simple least-squares approach. *Rev. Financ. Stud.* 14(1):113–147.

Mei, B., D. Swinarski, M.L. Clutter, and T.G. Harris. 2011. Investment decisions of a new linerboard mill under market uncertainty. *J. For. Prod. Bus. Res.* 8:1–7.

Merton, R.C. 1973. Theory of rational option pricing. *Bell J. Econ. Manag. Sci.* 4(1):141–183.

Morck, R., E. Schwartz, and D. Stangeland. 1989. The valuation of forestry resources under stochastic prices and inventories. *J. Financ. Quant. Anal.* 24(4):473–487.

Petrasek, S., and J.M. Perez-Garcia. 2010. Valuation of timber harvest contracts as American call options with modified least-squares Monte Carlo algorithm. *For. Sci.* 56(5):494–504.

Prestemon, J.P. 2003. Evaluation of U.S. southern pine stumpage market informational efficiency. *Can. J. For. Res.* 33(4):561–572.

Restrepo, H.I., B. Mei, and B.P. Bullock. 2020. Long-term timber contracts in the southeastern United States: Updating the primer valuation framework. *For. Sci.* 66(6):653–665.

Schwartz, E.S. 1997. The stochastic behavior of commodity prices: Implications for valuation and hedging. *J. Financ.* 52(3):923–973.

Shaffer, R.M. 1984. Valuation of certain long-term timber cutting contracts. *For. Sci.* 30(3):774–787.

TMS. 2022. *TimberMart-South.* Norris Foundation, Athens, GA.

Tsay, R.S. 2005. *Analysis of financial time series.* John Wiley & Sons, Hoboken, NJ, 640p.

Washburn, C.L., and C.S. Binkley. 1990. Informational efficiency of markets for stumpage. *Am. J. Agri. Econ.* 72(2):394–405.

Wilmott, P. 2006. *Paul Wilmott on quantitative finance.* John Wiley & Sons Ltd, West Sussex, 363p.

Zinkhan, F.C. 1991. Option pricing and timberland's land-use conversion option. *Land Econ.* 67(3):317–325.

12

BENEFIT AND COST ANALYSIS OF FOREST CARBON

Highlights

- Benefit and cost of forest carbon storage from a landowner's standpoint is illustrated by a hypothetical southern pine plantation.
- The inclusion of carbon into the total profit function usually leads to a longer rotation.
- A landowners' decision on forest carbon is most sensitive to the discount rate, and relative timber and carbon prices.
- When the economic uncertainty is incorporated into the decision making, the landowners' decisions on forest carbon tend to be sustained albeit the carbon additionality is slightly reduced.

Although the United States has an active and competitive timber market, it has only a nascent carbon market, which dampens the effective functioning of forest carbon sinks as a climate mitigation tool. In this chapter, we are going to examine the benefit and cost of forest carbon sequestration from a landowner's standpoint based on a southern pine plantation.

Background

Forests not only provide fiber and fuel for humans, but also fix the majority of the total terrestrial carbon. In fact, covering 65% of the total land surface, forests contain 90% of the total vegetation carbon, hold 80% of the total soil carbon, and account for 67% of the total CO_2 assimilated from the atmosphere by all terrestrial ecosystems (Hou et al. 2020; Landsberg and Gower 1997). Since the preindustrial era, nevertheless, the concentration of CO_2 in the atmosphere has increased by

DOI: 10.4324/9781003366737-12

more than 30% (Pan et al. 2011; Wenzel et al. 2016). The increased concentrations of CO_2 and other greenhouse gases have been widely recognized as the major cause of global warming. As a result, a considerable public attention has been paid to forests as a carbon sink, and more discussion has been initiated on how to use forest carbon effectively to combat climate change in recent years (van der Gaast et al. 2018). It has been expected that planting trees to remove atmospheric CO_2 would be more cost efficient than developing and implementing technologies or carbon taxes to reduce the emissions of existing industries (Dang Phan et al. 2014; Gren and Aklilu 2016; Li et al. 2022; Lin and Ge 2019). Unfortunately, there is a lack of research on these topics, although it is the biome that global models associate with the largest potentials of carbon removal (Fuss et al. 2018).

The United States has abundant forest resources, with forestland occupying about 766 million acres or 34% of the total land area in the country. Out of the total forestland, about 58% is privately owned and this proportion is even higher at about 90% in the US South (Oswalt et al. 2019). The southern United States supplies a significant portion of wood products to the country as well as provides a wide variety of ecosystem services, such as water quality and quantity, soil stabilization, wildlife habitat protection, and biodiversity, to name a few. For example, in Georgia the total economic impact of the forest industry in 2018 was estimated to be $36.3 billion (Enterprise Innovation Institute 2018), while the non-timber and non-recreation ecosystem service value of forestland was estimated to be $37.6 billion (Moore et al. 2011). Despite an active and competitive timber market in the southern United States, there is only a nascent carbon market, which impedes the effective provision of forest carbon from vast private landowners as a climate mitigation tool. The goal of this study is to examine the benefit and cost of forest carbon for landowners in the voluntary carbon market. The analysis is based on a southern pine plantation for two reasons. First, southern pine is a major species in the US South (Oswalt et al. 2019). Second, pine forests are often intensively managed as plantations, which not only produce traditional industrial wood products, but also contain a significant portion of forest carbon in the United States (Johnsen et al. 2001).

Past research

The forest carbon literature has been rapidly snowballing in the last three decades. Gower (2003) reviewed the key components of the forest carbon cycle and inspected how global changes might influence the carbon dynamics between forests and the atmosphere. Helin et al. (2013) concluded that biomass carbon stored in the products and the timing of sinks and emissions should be taken into consideration in the life-cycle analysis in order to accurately measure greenhouse gas emissions and the related climate impacts. They also recommended the use of dynamic forest models rather than carbon stock values taken from the literature. Forest modeling having gone beyond the domain of scientific discovery into the policy arena, Prisley and

Mortimer (2004) synthesized the literature on the application of models for forest carbon accounting, discussed validation, verification and evaluation as applied to modeling, and concluded that forest carbon models should abide by scientifically relevant and judicially proven guidelines. Gren and Aklilu (2016) reviewed the economics literature on efficient policy design for forest carbon and associated the difficulties in policy design with site-specific sequestration conditions, uncertainty in sequestration, additionality, and permanence. While an exclusive synthetization of the forest carbon literature is not the emphasis here, these review papers provide us a solid background to endeavors in forest carbon analyses.

Regarding the economics of forest carbon, many studies have found that forest carbon could reduce net emission with a relatively low cost (Cho et al. 2018; Vass and Elofsson 2016). Newell and Stavins (2000) examined the sensitivity of carbon sequestration costs to the nature of management and deforestation regimes, silvicultural species, relative prices, and discount rates. They found higher costs of carbon sequestration for (1) periodically harvested rather than permanently established forests, (2) higher discount rates, (3) higher agricultural prices, and (4) increased forestation instead of retarded deforestation. Richards and Stokes (2004) pointed out that carbon sequestration cost studies were not directly comparable because of the inconsistent use of terms, geographic scope, assumptions, program definitions, and methods. They further claimed that market interactions need more attention when analyzing carbon sequestration programs. Using meta-analysis, van Kooten and Sohngen (2007) found a wide range of cost from \$2 to \$80 per ton of CO_2 equivalent for creating carbon offsets using forestry in North America. Given the great uncertainty in model scenarios and the difficulty of contracting, van Kooten and Johnston (2016) claimed that caution would be needed to identify carbon offsets from forestry activities should they be traded in the emission markets.

A summarization of the forest carbon literature reveals two primary features. One is that most analyses were conducted on forest carbon markets outside the United States. The other is that stand-level analyses centered around the optimal forest rotation. Thus, our study intends to examine the economic feasibility of forest carbon supply by landowners at the stand level in the US South, given its rapid developing carbon market and its primary private timberland ownership. Because an intensively managed forest is a more effective approach in mitigating climate change (van Kooten and Johnston 2016; van Kooten and Sohngen 2007), and more of the assimilated carbon is allocated to aboveground pools in managed than in unmanaged forests (Noormets et al. 2015), our study focuses on benefit and cost of forest carbon for landowners using a carbon accounting model based on a hypothetical southern pine plantation. Following the recommendations of Prisley and Mortimer (2004), our model aims to be clearly defined, clearly documented, sensitized on key parameters, available for testing or evaluation, and updatable with new knowledge and data.

In this chapter, we evaluate the potential supply of forest carbon from private landowners at the stand level in the voluntary carbon market. Such information can shed light on the aggregate supply of both timber and carbon at the regional or higher level. Our analysis explicitly examines incremental cash flows from forest carbon and contrasts those with the timber production only scenario to identify changes in the optimal forest management and the resulting additional carbon storage. As the timber and carbon markets are both volatile, incorporating price volatility into the analysis under the Monte Carlo simulation or the real options framework can help us better understand landowners' decision making in an uncertain environment. Box 12.1 has some basic information on the trading mechanism of forest carbon on the Natural Capital Exchange (NCX).

BOX 12.1 FOREST CARBON TRADED ON THE NATURAL CAPITAL EXCHANGE (NCX)

NCX strives to address the climate challenge by delivering large-scale, near-term impact through its carbon program. Its goal is to enable widespread, equitable landowner participation and bring carbon credits to market. These credits provide direct benefit to landowners, and they give carbon buyers confidence that they are creating a real climate impact.

The NCX program pays landowners with mature forests to defer harvests for one year. Thus, carbon is held longer on the ground, not being released into the atmosphere. Note that only forests that realistically would likely be harvested are eligible to participate, because such a deferred harvest represents a departure from business as usual or generate "additionality" for that property. The impact is enlarged when many such one-year delays are packaged together into one carbon program. NCX has no minimum (or maximum) acreage requirement, and it does not require a management plan for eligibility.

At the end of the year, the landowner can seek another assessment and bid to reenroll with NCX or move forward with the timber harvest. Regarding the carbon measurement, NCX combines remote-sensing technology with available boots-on-the-ground inventories and machine learning. As such, NCX is able to estimate forest composition, carbon, and timber value on an acre-by-acre basis. This comes free to the landowner.

From the landowner's point of view, there is a cost associated with a harvest delayed by one year. The marginal cost equals the timber rent (interest on the proceeds from the immediate harvest) and the land rent (interest on future rotations), whereas the marginal benefit equals the payment for carbon and the expected change in timber value, which is often negative because it might be beyond the optimal rotation. A landowner needs to compare the marginal cost with the marginal benefit to make the optimal decision on enrollment in the NCX's forest carbon program.

Data sources: NCX's website.

Data and methods

An aboveground forest carbon regime is illustrated based on a hypothetical southern pine plantation in the state of Georgia. Timber yield data are generated from the current version of the Plantation Management Research Cooperative forest growth and yield simulator with a site index of 65 (base age 25) and an initial planting density of 680 trees per acre (1 acre = 0.4047 hectares) (PMRC 2022). Forest carbon storage at the stand level is positively related to the site quality, all else equal (Gonzalez-Benecke et al. 2015; Sampo et al. 2014; West et al. 2019). As the average site index of timberland in the US South is around 60–80 (Gopalakrishnan et al. 2019; PMRC 2022; Zhao et al. 2016a), the hypothetical southern pine plantation is representative of the region. Yield is categorized into three product classes, by the diameter at breast height, as pulpwood 6 inches (1 inch = 2.54 cm) and up, chip-n-saw 8 to 11 inches, and sawtimber 12 inches and up (TMS 2022).[1] Total yield is the sum of yield by product and marginal yield is the annual change in total yield.

Equation 12.1 is used to convert timber yield in green tons to total carbon stored in the aboveground biomass in metric tons,

$$AC = TY \times BEF \times (1 - MC) \times CT \tag{12.1}$$

where AC is aboveground carbon in metric tons, TY is total yield of merchantable timber in green tons, BEF is biomass expansion factor (the ratio of the total aboveground tree biomass to the biomass of merchantable timber), MC is moisture content, and CT is carbon content in dry wood. Based on the literature (PMRC 2022; Smith et al. 2006; Zhao et al. 2016b), the followings parameter values are used: $BEF = 1.20$, $MC = 0.54$, and $CT = 0.47$.

Annual carbon value is marginal carbon stored multiplied by carbon price. A carbon price of \$20 per metric ton, or \$5.45 per ton of CO_2 equivalent is used based on the average transacted price in the voluntary carbon market (Donofrio et al. 2021). Perpetual carbon value is the present value of carbon credits for a given rotation with a carbon release factor ($\delta(T) = 0.70205 - 0.001266T + 0.0000168T^2$) at harvest time T (Creedy and Wurzbacher 2001). Based on the past research (e.g., Baral et al. 2020; Cascio and Clutter 2008) and TimberMart-South data (TMS 2022), our baseline land expectation value (LEV) for timber production only is calculated with a regeneration cost of \$200 per acre, a pulpwood price of \$10 per green ton, a chip-n-saw price of \$18 per green ton, a sawtimber price of \$26 per green ton, and a discount rate of 4% as in Equation 12.2,

$$LEV(T) = \frac{P_T Y_T - E(1+r)^T}{(1+r)^T - 1} \tag{12.2}$$

where rotation length T is the decision variable, P_T and Y_T are the respective price and yield vectors of the three timber products, E is the regeneration cost, and r is the discount rate. Equation 12.2 is also known as the Faustmann model (Faustmann 1995). The profit function $\pi(T)$ for both timber and carbon provision is the net present value of all future cash flows associated with timber production and carbon sequestration. The calculation is shown in Equation 12.3,

$$\pi(T) = LEV(T) + \frac{\sum_{t=1}^{T}(P_c \cdot \Delta W_t)(1+r)^{(T-t)} - P_c \cdot \delta(T) \cdot \Delta W_T}{(1+r)^T - 1} \tag{12.3}$$

where P_c is carbon price in dollars per metric ton, ΔW_t is the marginal weight of carbon captured in metric tons, and $\delta(T)$ is the carbon release factor at harvest. A brief summarization of all parameters and variables is presented in Table 12.1. Note that all costs, prices, and the discount rate are in real terms as of year 2022.

Based on the LEV framework, two scenarios of forest carbon are analyzed. In the first scenario, a landowner contemplates whether to offer forest carbon credits starting from an afforestation. In the second scenario, a landowner has some mature trees standing on the land and decides whether to delay timber harvest for carbon credits. In the first scenario, sensitivity analysis is conducted on the key parameters, and a Monte Carlo simulation is used for the risk assessment. A Monte Carlo simulation is a computational algorithm that uses repeated random

TABLE 12.1 A brief summarization of all parameters and variables for forest carbon analysis

Parameter or variable	Definition	Value
Variable		
P_t	Timber prices	$10/green ton, pulpwood
		$18/green ton, chip-n-saw
		$26/green ton, sawtimber
P_c	Carbon price	$20/metric ton
E	Regeneration cost	$200/acre
Discount rates		
r	Discount rate	0.04
Parameter		
BEF	Biomass expansion factor	1.20
MC	Moisture content of loblolly pine	0.54
CT	Carbon content in dry wood	0.47
$\delta(T)$	Carbon release at harvest	$\delta(T) = 0.70205 - 0.001266T + 0.0000168T^2$

sampling to obtain numerical results. The idea is to use randomness to solve problems that might be deterministic in principle. That is, financial uncertainty is taken into account in the simulation. For timber and carbon prices, a lognormal distribution is used to guarantee that prices are positive. For the discount rate, a triangular distribution is used, which is a continuous probability distribution with a lower limit, an upper limit, and a mode. This setting enables us to examine the impact of most likely discount rates on the valuation.

In addition, the option to wait for a year to make the decision about the enrollment of a 30-year carbon contract is evaluated under the real options framework. In general, an investment decision in an uncertain world is similar to a financial call option in that it incurs the initial investment cost to exercise the option, and, in return, the investor holds a risky asset whose value is stochastic over time. In our case, the cost for entering into a carbon contract arises from the deviation from the optimal rotation; and the underlying asset value is the net present value of cash flows associated with carbon sequestration during the contract period. Other key inputs for the option pricing are the time to maturity, the volatility of the underlying asset, and the risk-free rate. Then, the call option price C can be determined by the Black-Scholes model expressed in Equation 12.4 (Black and Scholes 1973),

$$C = N(d_1)S_t - N(d_2)Ke^{-rt} \tag{12.4}$$

where $N(\cdot)$ is the cumulative distribution function of the standard normal distribution, $d_1 = \dfrac{\ln(S_t / K) + (r + .5\sigma^2)t}{\sigma\sqrt{t}}$, S_t is the spot price of an asset, K is the strike price, r is the risk-free rate, t is time to maturity, σ is the volatility of the asset, and $d_2 = d_1 - \sigma\sqrt{t}$. Observing the uncertainty of forest carbon, risk averse landowners will value the option to wait to make the enrollment decision. The investment timing option itself can be valued as a financial call option.

In the second scenario, incremental cash flows are analyzed to help the landowner with a mature stand decide whether to enter into a short-term carbon contract. The cost arises from a reduced LEV due to a delayed harvest, whereas the benefit comes from payments for carbon credits. Whenever the net present value of the incremental cash flows is positive, the carbon contract will add value to the landowner.

Results

The growth and yield data for the hypothetical southern pine plantation together with the valuation results are reported in Table 12.2. Columns 2–4 are timber yield in green ton in three products (i.e., pulpwood, chip-and-saw, and sawtimber) based on the PMRC model. Column 5 is the total timber yield, i.e., the

TABLE 12.2 Growth and yield of a southern pine plantation and valuation of forest carbon

(1) Age	(2) Pulpwood yield	(3) Chip-n-saw yield	(4) Sawtimber yield	(5) Total yield	(6) Marginal yield	(7) Annual carbon value	(8) Perpetual carbon value	(9) LEV	(10) Profit with carbon
1	0.00	0.00	0.00	0.00	0.00	0.00			
2	0.00	0.00	0.00	0.00	0.00	0.00			
3	0.00	0.00	0.00	0.00	0.00	0.00			
4	0.00	0.00	0.00	0.00	0.00	0.00			
5	0.10	0.00	0.00	0.10	0.10	0.52			
6	2.30	0.00	0.00	2.30	2.20	11.42			
7	8.50	0.00	0.00	8.50	6.20	32.17			
8	17.70	0.00	0.00	17.70	9.20	47.74			
9	28.00	0.30	0.00	28.30	10.60	55.00			
10	38.10	1.20	0.00	39.30	11.00	57.08	156.51	221.87	378.37
11	47.10	2.80	0.00	49.90	10.60	55.00	187.29	395.79	583.07
12	54.70	5.40	0.00	60.10	10.20	52.93	214.45	539.06	753.52
13	60.90	8.90	0.00	69.80	9.70	50.33	238.46	655.85	894.31
14	65.70	13.30	0.00	79.00	9.20	47.74	259.84	751.79	1011.62
15	69.30	18.50	0.00	87.80	8.80	45.66	279.19	831.28	1110.47
16	71.90	24.20	0.00	96.10	8.30	43.07	296.61	893.49	1190.10
17	73.50	30.10	0.40	104.00	7.90	40.99	312.51	946.96	1259.47
18	74.40	36.40	0.70	111.50	7.50	38.92	327.06	986.76	1313.83
19	74.60	42.80	1.30	118.70	7.20	37.36	340.56	1019.86	1360.42
20	74.40	49.10	2.00	125.50	6.80	35.28	352.97	1042.36	1395.32
21	73.70	55.30	3.10	132.10	6.60	34.25	364.63	1061.37	1426.00
22	72.80	61.20	4.50	138.50	6.40	33.21	375.63	1074.97	1450.59
23	71.50	66.70	6.20	144.40	5.90	30.61	385.66	1081.34	1467.00
24	70.10	71.70	8.40	150.20	5.80	30.10	395.23	1085.74	1480.96
25	68.50	76.10	11.00	155.60	5.40	28.02	404.06	1085.12	1489.18

(Continued)

TABLE 12.2 Continued

(1) Age	(2) Pulpwood yield	(3) Chip-n-saw yield	(4) Sawtimber yield	(5) Total yield	(6) Marginal yield	(7) Annual carbon value	(8) Perpetual carbon value	(9) LEV	(10) Profit with carbon
26	66.80	79.90	14.10	160.80	5.20	26.98	412.40	1082.28	1494.68
27	65.00	83.10	17.70	165.80	5.00	25.94	420.27	1077.50	1497.77
28	63.20	85.60	21.80	170.60	4.80	24.91	427.71	1070.62	1498.33
29	61.40	87.50	26.30	175.20	4.60	23.87	434.73	1061.56	1496.29
30	59.60	88.70	31.30	179.60	4.40	22.83	441.37	1050.96	1492.33
31	57.90	89.20	36.70	183.80	4.20	21.79	447.64	1038.36	1486.01
32	56.10	89.20	42.50	187.80	4.00	20.76	453.57	1024.69	1478.26
33	54.50	88.60	48.70	191.80	4.00	20.76	459.29	1010.55	1469.84
34	52.90	87.50	55.20	195.60	3.80	19.72	464.70	995.00	1459.70
35	51.30	86.00	61.90	199.20	3.60	18.68	469.82	977.97	1447.79
36	49.80	84.10	68.80	202.70	3.50	18.16	474.71	960.01	1434.72
37	48.40	81.80	75.90	206.10	3.40	17.64	479.38	941.28	1420.65
38	47.10	79.30	83.10	209.50	3.40	17.64	483.89	922.19	1406.08
39	45.90	76.60	90.30	212.80	3.30	17.12	488.21	902.10	1390.31
40	44.80	73.70	97.70	216.20	3.40	17.64	492.43	882.55	1374.98
41	43.70	70.60	104.90	219.20	3.00	15.57	496.34	860.64	1356.98
42	42.70	67.50	112.20	222.40	3.20	16.60	500.21	839.69	1339.90
43	41.80	64.40	119.30	225.50	3.10	16.09	503.91	817.84	1321.75
44	40.90	61.20	126.30	228.40	2.90	15.05	507.42	795.21	1302.63
45	40.20	58.10	133.20	231.50	3.10	16.09	510.89	773.11	1284.00
46	39.50	55.00	139.90	234.40	2.90	15.05	514.18	750.26	1264.44
47	38.80	52.00	146.50	237.30	2.90	15.05	517.36	727.64	1245.00
48	38.30	49.00	153.10	240.40	3.10	16.09	520.51	705.77	1226.28
49	37.70	46.20	159.30	243.20	2.80	14.53	523.47	682.92	1206.40
50	37.30	43.50	165.40	246.20	3.00	15.57	526.40	660.76	1187.16

Note: Yield for the three timber products is in green tons per acre. Total yield is the sum of yield of the three timber products. Marginal yield is the annual change in total yield. Annual carbon value is based on marginal yield and a carbon price of $20 per metric ton. Perpetual carbon value is the present value of carbon for a given rotation. LEV is land expectation value owed to timber production with a regeneration cost of $200 per acre, a pulpwood price of $10 per green ton, a chip-n-saw price of $18 per green ton, and a sawtimber price of $26 per green ton. The discount rate is 4%. Profit with carbon is LEV plus perpetual carbon value.

summation of the previous three columns. Column 6 is the marginal timber yield, i.e., the annual incremental gain in the total timber yield. Column 7 is the dollar value of annual carbon sequestered, calculated as the weight of marginal carbon sequestered in metric ton times carbon price in dollar per metric ton. Column 8 is the dollar value of carbon sequestered on a perpetual basis for a given rotation. According to Column 9, the optimal rotation for timber production only is 24 years, resulting in a maximum LEV of $1,085.74 per acre.[2] When carbon is also considered, the optimal rotation is four years longer, resulting in a maximum profit of $1,498.33 per acre at age 28. The result is consistent with previous research in that the inclusion of carbon only makes the rotation a bit longer than the Faustmann rotation (e.g., Dong et al. 2020; Hoel et al. 2014; Ning and Sun 2019; van Kooten and Binkley 1995). As such, it could be a win-win situation in that the landowner realizes a higher profit from the timberland by lengthening the rotation by four years, and the society has four-year additional carbon fixed in the trees.

Next, the results are sensitized on the key parameters or variables (Table 12.3). First, all three timber prices are increased by 20%, corresponding to the price levels prior to the 2008 financial crisis. With higher timber prices, LEV increases to $1,368.47 per acre at age 24, and the maximum total profit of $1,774.51 per acre occurs at age 27. Thus, one less year of carbon is sequestered compared with the base case. Second, carbon price is increased to $30 per metric ton. Then, the total profit increases to $1,713.66 per acre at age 28. Therefore, one additional year of carbon sequestration can be achieved with a higher carbon price.

Third, when the regeneration cost is increased to $300 per acre, LEV is reduced to $925.86 per acre with a 26-year rotation. The total profit is maximized at $1,349.09 with a 29-year rotation. The net result is one-year carbon additionality. Fourth, a carbon administration cost of $1 per year is considered in the model. This has a similar impact on the total profit as a decrease in carbon price. The total profit falls to $1,473.33 per acre at age 28. Thus, carbon additionality remains the same as the base case. Lastly, when the discount rate is increased to 5%, the maximized LEV is $707.20 per acre at age 22 and the maximum total profit is $1,037.29 per acre at age 25. Thus, a higher discount rate reduces the rotation length and the profit compared with the base case.

Third, the regeneration cost is increased to $300 per acre. Accordingly, LEV is reduced to $925.86 per acre with a 26-year rotation. The total profit is maximized at $1,015.65 with a 27-year rotation. The net result is still a one-year carbon additionality. Fourth, carbon administration cost is reduced to zero. This has a similar impact on the total profit as an increase in carbon price. The total profit rises to $1,184.66 per acre but the rotation length remains at age 25. Thus, carbon additionality remains the same as the base case. Fifth, the carbon release factor at harvest is lowered to 0.5. While LEV is unchanged, the total profit increases to $1,180.98 per acre with a 25-year rotation. Lastly, the discount rate is set to be equal at 0.04 for both timber and carbon. With a lower opportunity cost, carbon is

TABLE 12.3 Sensitivity analysis of key variables on forest carbon analysis

	Assumptions						Results			
	P_t		P_c	E	E_c	r	Timber rotation	LEV	Carbon rotation	Total profit
Base	18	26	20	200	0	0.04	24	1085.74	28	1498.33
1	21.6	31.2					24	1368.47	27	1774.51
2			30				24	1085.74	29	1713.66
3				300			26	925.86	28	1398.48
4					1		24	1085.74	28	1473.33
5						0.05	22	707.20	25	1037.29

Note: P_t for timber prices (pulpwood, chip-n-saw and sawtimber) in dollars per green ton; P_c for carbon price in dollars per metric ton; E for regeneration cost in dollars per acre; E_c for annual carbon administration cost in dollars per acre; and r for discount rate. Rotation is in years, and land expectation value (LEV) and total profit are in dollars per acre.

more valuable compared to the base case. The maximum total profit of $1,238.87 per acre occurs at age 26, resulting in a one more year of carbon fixed compared with the base case.

Given that the decision on forest carbon is most sensitive to prices and the discount rate, a Monte Carlo simulation is conducted on the base case analysis. Prices are specified to be lognormal with mean values the same as those used in the static analysis. Regarding the standard deviation, $2, $3, and $6 per green ton are used for pulpwood, chip-n-saw, and sawtimber prices (TMS 2022), and $6 per metric ton is used for the carbon price (Donofrio et al. 2021). In addition, the discount rate is assumed to follow a triangular distribution with a mean 4%, a minimum of 3% and a maximum of 5%.

The simulated total profit for timber and carbon with a 28-year rotation is presented in Figure 12.1. With 0,000 iterations, the respective mean and standard deviation are $1,524.88 and $323.63 per acre. Compared with the base case, there is a 48.2% chance that the total profit exceeds that from the static analysis on the upside; and there is a 6.7% chance that the total profit falls below the maximized LEV from the static analysis on the downside. As shown in the tornado chart (Figure 12.2), discount rate is the most sensitive factor on total profit, followed by chip-n-saw and carbon prices. The sensitivity of chip-n-saw price can be explained by the fact that, with a 28-year rotation, chip-n-saw is the major timber product that accounts for a significant portion of the total output.

Other useful information from the simulation is the impact of the economic uncertainty on the optimal rotation age. The mean rotation age for timber production only is 25.64 with a standard deviation of 4.59; that for both timber production and carbon sequestration is higher at 28.47 with a standard deviation of 4.76 (Figure 12.3). Compared with the static analysis, about one less year of carbon additionality can be achieved from the voluntary carbon trading when the economic uncertainty is considered. Figure 12.4 shows the sensitivity of the

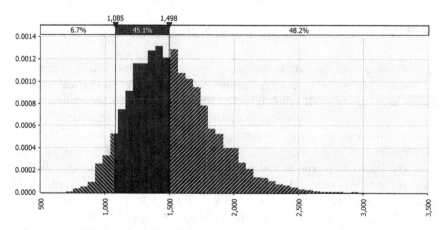

FIGURE 12.1   Simulated total profit for timber and carbon with a 28-year rotation

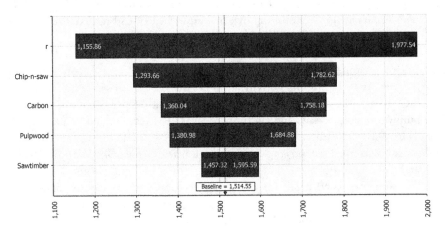

FIGURE 12.2   Sensitivity of simulated total profit on different factors

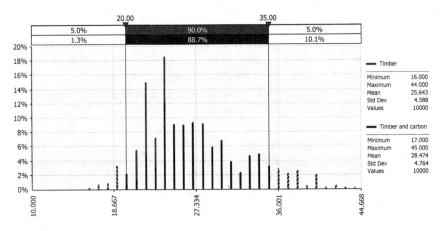

FIGURE 12.3   Impact of economic uncertainty on the optimal rotation

optimal rotation on different factors under the economic uncertainty. Compared with timber prices, carbon price has a much lower impact on the optimal rotation due to its relatively small value. In short, landowners tend to be risk averse and behave more conservatively on forest carbon when facing financial risks.

If the additionality is the ultimate goal, a 30-year carbon contract from an afforestation may still be appealing to a landowner. Without the carbon contract, the landowner expects the maximum LEV of $1,085.47 per acre with a 24-year rotation (Column 9 of Table 12.2); with the carbon contract, the landowner expects a total profit of $1,492.33 per acre with a 30-year rotation (Column 10 of Table 12.2). Thus, the net gain is $1,492.33 – $1,085.47 = $406.59 per acre. Alternatively, if the cash flows of timber are separated from carbon, the cost of the

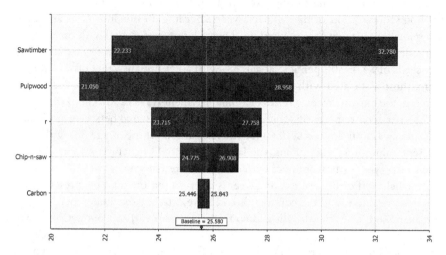

FIGURE 12.4   Sensitivity of the optimal rotation for both timber production and carbon sequestration on different factors under economic uncertainty

30-year carbon contract results from the change in LEV due to a delayed harvest ($1,085.47 − $1,050.96 = $34.78), the gain comes from carbon credit ($441.37), and the net present value is $406.59. The longer the term of the contract, the larger the cost of a delayed harvest and the smaller the gain from carbon credit due to the law of diminishing marginal returns of forest growth and yield.[3]

From the option pricing perspective, the 30-year carbon contract is like a financial call option. The strike price is the change in LEV due to a delayed harvest that is converted to a cost every 30 years (K = $24.06).[4] The underlying asset price (S_t = $305.29) is the net present value of carbon-related cash flows over 30 years (Column 8 of Table 12.2, with carbon release at harvest incorporated). Time to maturity is the period that landowners can afford to wait and is assumed to be one year (t = 1) when there is no merchantable timber on the ground. The risk-free rate is set to 2% (r = 2%), and the volatility is assumed to be 15% (σ = 15%). With these inputs, the value of the investment timing option is calculated to be $281.71 per acre by the Black-Scholes model. As discussed before, for a longer-term carbon contract, both the strike price and the asset price increase, with the former rising at a more rapid rate. Thus, the option value will decrease. However, this option value can offset some of the negative impact of the longer duration of a carbon contract on its static net present value. Therefore, landowners should still keep a reasonably longer-term carbon contract in mind when doing an afforestation.

Next, decision making is examined for a landowner who has a mature forest and has not been paid yet for any forest carbon.[5] The landowner has the option to enroll in a carbon contract in which he/she has to postpone harvest for five years, will be paid for existing carbon fixed in the forest, and will be paid for marginal carbon sequestration in the next five years. Because all previous costs are sunk, incremental cash flows are focused on. The cash flows associated with timber are a forgone harvest proceeds of $3,406.00 per acre at age 33 and an expected harvest proceeds of $4,059.00 per acre at age 38, with a net present value of -$69.80 per acre; those associated with carbon are a payment of $995.21 per acre for carbon fixed in the existing trees, a series of annual payments ($19.72, $18.68, $18.16, and $17.64 per acre, respectively) for marginal carbon sequestered between age 34 and 37, and a cash outflow of $719.60 for the net carbon release at age 38, with a net present value of $471.21. Thus, the landowner should benefit from enrolling in such a five-year carbon contract with a total net present value of $401.41 per acre. Nevertheless, if carbon on existing trees is not paid for, the total net present value becomes negative, and the contract should be rejected by the landowner.

Examined last is the benefit and cost of a one-year carbon contract similar to what is being offered by Natural Capital Exchange (NCX 2022). Under the contract, the landowner agrees to delay harvest for a year in exchange for a payment for carbon. On an incremental basis, the cash flows associated with timber are forgone harvest proceeds of $3,406.00 per acre at age 33 and an expected harvest proceeds of $3,539.20 per acre at age 34, with a net present value of -$2.92 per acre. Thus, a payment larger than $2.92 per acre for a year would trigger a landowner's enrollment in this carbon program.

Discussion and conclusions

Given the importance of southern pine to the forestry industry in the US South, the benefit and cost of forest carbon to landowners in the voluntary carbon market are examined based on a hypothetical southern pine plantation. Carbon value being defined according to marginal growth of trees, its inclusion into the objective function usually leads to longer rotations and higher total profits. In our baseline analysis, the rotation age increases by four years when both timber and carbon are considered. Therefore, landowners benefit from extra cash flows from carbon credits and additional carbon is fixed in the forests for four years.

Landowners' decision on forest carbon is most sensitive to the discount rate and timber and carbon prices. When the discount rate is higher, future cash flows become less valuable and the optimal rotation shortens. When timber prices exceed carbon price by a large margin, as is the current market condition, timber value dominates carbon value, and the optimal rotation age does not deviate much from that defined by the Faustmann model. Therefore, with a higher discount rate and higher timber prices, voluntary carbon trading results in little additionality. When the economic uncertainty is incorporated into the decision making, results tend to be sustained albeit carbon additionality is slightly reduced.

The analysis of a 30-year carbon contract starting from the afforestation shows that landowners can benefit from such a long-term contract. If a landowner can wait for a year prior to making the enrollment decision, the benefit is even larger given the uncertainty of carbon price. That is, landowners should keep forest carbon in mind when making the afforestation decision. However, as the contractual period lengthens (e.g., to 100 years), the incremental gain from carbon is not enough to offset the cost from delayed harvest because of the law of diminishing marginal returns of forest yield. Therefore, subsidies are needed to incentivize landowners' enrollment in longer-term carbon contracts.

For landowners who have mature forests but have not been paid yet for forest carbon, a five-year carbon contract that pays for carbon already sequestered in the existing trees as well as marginal carbon sequestration over the next five years will benefit the landowners. However, if the five-year carbon contract only pays for marginal carbon during the contractual period, such a contract provides additional carbon but at the cost of the landowners. In this case, government interventions are needed again to guide and regulate the provision of forest carbon. Given that delaying harvest has a lower opportunity cost on a less productive site, both the cost of conserving such a stand and the amount of carbon stored are lower. Therefore, when facing a flat payment for forest carbon (e.g., a fixed payment per acre of enrollment), landowners with lower site qualities are more willing to participate in the voluntary carbon market.

In closing, forest carbon being a crucial nature-based solution to climate change, additionality does not always autonomously occur from voluntary carbon trading. Hence, government interventions are often needed in sustaining forest carbon. Results from this study can help landowners better understand the economics, the contractual design, and the trading mechanism of the voluntary forest carbon market. Future research can integrate silvicultural management into the forest carbon analysis, extend the current analysis to a landscape level by considering multiple tree species and geographic locations, or consider possible land use changes.

Questions

1. Why does forest carbon sequestration often lead to a longer rotation?
2. What is the opportunity cost of a landowner for a delayed harvest for carbon storage?
3. What incentive payment programs are more cost effective in inducing forest carbon sequestration, those that are site quality based or those based on a flat rate in dollars per acre?

Notes

1 Smaller-size timber is used to produce pulp and paper products, while larger-size timber is used to produce lumber and veneer products.
2 Annual property tax is ignored in the analysis, or it will reduce the LEV.

3 Forests have a sigmoid growth curve. The law of diminishing marginal returns of forest growth and yield means that the marginal growth (current annual increment) declines when a forest passes the inflection point and approaches maturity.
4 K is solved by setting $34.78 = K / (1 - (1 + r)^{-30})$, assuming K occurs at the beginning of a year every 30 years.
5 At age 33, the net present value of the single rotation is maximized. At this age, a landowner considers whether or not to enter into a carbon contract. Similar analysis can be conducted for ages around 33.

Bibliography

Baral, S., Y. Li, and B. Mei. 2020. Financial effects of the 2017 Tax Cuts and Jobs Act on nonindustrial private forest landowners: A comparative study for 10 southern States of the United States. *J. For.* 118(6):584–597.

Black, F., and M. Scholes. 1973. The pricing of options and corporate liabilities. *J. Polit. Econ.* 81(3):637–654.

Bluffstone, R., J. Coulston, R.G. Haight, J.D. Kline, S. Polasky, D.N. Wear, and K. Zook. 2017. Chapter 3: Estimated values of carbon sequestration resulting from forest management scenarios. The Council on Food, Agricultural and Resource Economics (C-FARE), Washington, DC, 25.

Cascio, A.J., and M.L. Clutter. 2008. Risk and required return assessments of equity timberland investments in the United States. *For. Prod. J.* 58(10):61–70.

Cho, S.-H., J. Lee, R. Roberts, E.T. Yu, and P.R. Armsworth. 2018. Impact of market conditions on the effectiveness of payments for forest-based carbon sequestration. *For. Policy Econ.* 92:33–42.

Creedy, J., and A.D. Wurzbacher. 2001. The economic value of a forested catchment with timber, water and carbon sequestration benefits. Ecol. Econ. 38(1):71-83.

Dang Phan, T.-H., R. Brouwer, and M. Davidson. 2014. The economic costs of avoided deforestation in the developing world: A meta-analysis. *J. For. Econ.* 20(1):1–16.

Dong, L., W. Lu, and Z. Liu. 2020. Determining the optimal rotations of larch plantations when multiple carbon pools and wood products are valued. *For. Ecol. Manag.* 474:118356.

Donofrio, S., P. Maguire, K. Myers, C. Daley, and K. Lin. 2021. State of the Voluntary Carbon Markets 2021. Forest Trends Association, Washington, DC. 40.

Enterprise Innovation Institute. 2018. *Economic benefits of the forest industry in Georgia.* Georgia Institute of Technology, Atlanta, GA, 2.

Faustmann, M. 1995. Calculation of the value of which forest land and immature stands possess for forestry (Orriginally published in German Journal of Forest Research in 1849). *J. For. Econ.* 1(1):7–44.

Fuss, S., W.F. Lamb, M.W. Callaghan, J. Hilaire, F. Creutzig, T. Amann, T. Beringer, W. de Oliveira Garcia, J. Hartmann, T. Khanna, G. Luderer, G.F. Nemet, J. Rogelj, P. Smith, J.L.V. Vicente, J. Wilcox, M. del Mar Zamora Dominguez, and J.C. Minx. 2018. Negative emissions—Part 2: Costs, potentials and side effects. *Environ. Res. Lett* 13(6):063002.

Gonzalez-Benecke, C.A., L.J. Samuelson, T.A. Martin, W.P. Cropper, K.H. Johnsen, T.A. Stokes, J.R. Butnor, and P.H. Anderson. 2015. Modeling the effects of forest management on in situ and ex situ longleaf pine forest carbon stocks. *For. Ecol. Manag.* 355:24–36.

Gopalakrishnan, R., J.S. Kauffman, M.E. Fagan, J.W. Coulston, V.A. Thomas, R.H. Wynne, T.R. Fox, and V.F. Quirino. 2019. Creating landscape-scale site index maps for the southeastern US is possible with airborne LiDAR and landsat imagery. *Forests* 10(3):234.

Gower, S.T. 2003. Patterns and mechanisms of the forest carbon cycle. *Ann. Rev. Environ. Resour.* 28(1):169–204.

Gren, I.-M., and A.Z. Aklilu. 2016. Policy design for forest carbon sequestration: A review of the literature. *For. Policy Econ.* 70:128–136.

Helin, T., L. Sokka, S. Soimakallio, K. Pingoud, and T. Pajula. 2013. Approaches for inclusion of forest carbon cycle in life cycle assessment – A review. *GCB Bioenergy* 5(5):475–486.

Hoel, M., B. Holtsmark, and K. Holtsmark. 2014. Faustmann and the climate. *J. For. Econ.* 20(2):192–210.

Hou, G., C.O. Delang, X. Lu, and R. Olschewski. 2020. Optimizing rotation periods of forest plantations: The effects of carbon accounting regimes. *For. Policy Econ.* 118:102263.

Johnsen, K.H., D. Wear, R. Oren, R.O. Teskey, F. Sanchez, R. Will, J. Butnor, D. Markewitz, D. Richter, T. Rials, H.L. Allen, J. Seiler, D. Ellsworth, C. Maier, G. Katul, and P.M. Dougherty. 2001. Meeting global policy commitments: carbon sequestration and southern pine forests. J. For. 99(4):14-21.

Landsberg, J.J., and S.T. Gower. 1997. *Applications of physiological ecology to forest management.* Academic Press, San Diégo, CA, 354p.

Li, R., B. Sohngen, and X. Tian. 2022. Efficiency of forest carbon policies at intensive and extensive margins. *Am. J. Agri. Econ.* 104(4):1243-1267.

Lin, B., and J. Ge. 2019. Valued forest carbon sinks: How much emissions abatement costs could be reduced in China. *J. Clean. Prod.* 224:455–464.

Moore, R., T. Williams, E. Rodriguez, and J. Hepinstall-Cymmerman. 2011. *Quantifying the value of non-timber ecosystem services from Georgia's private forests.* Georgia Forestry Foundation, Forsyth, GA, 51.

NCX. 2022. Natural Capital Exchange. https://www.ncx.com. Last accessed July 19, 2022.

Newell, R.G., and R.N. Stavins. 2000. Climate change and forest sinks: Factors affecting the costs of carbon sequestration. *J. Environ. Econ. Manag.* 40(3):211–235.

Ning, Z., and C. Sun. 2019. Carbon sequestration and biofuel production on forestland under three stochastic prices. *For. Policy Econ.* 109:102018.

Noormets, A., D. Epron, J.C. Domec, S.G. McNulty, T. Fox, G. Sun, and J.S. King. 2015. Effects of forest management on productivity and carbon sequestration: A review and hypothesis. *For. Ecol. Manag.* 355:124–140.

Oswalt, S.N., W.B. Smith, P.D. Miles, and S.A. Pugh. 2019. *Forest resources of the United States, 2017: A technical document supporting the Forest Service 2020 update of the RPA assessment.* U.S. Forest Service, Washington, DC, 223.

Pan, Y., R.A. Birdsey, J. Fang, R. Houghton, P.E. Kauppi, W.A. Kurz, O.L. Phillips, A. Shvidenko, S.L. Lewis, J.G. Canadell, P. Ciais, R.B. Jackson, S.W. Pacala, A.D. McGuire, S. Piao, A. Rautiainen, S. Sitch, and D. Hayes. 2011. A large and persistent carbon sink in the world's forests. *Science* 333(6045):988–993.

PMRC. 2022. *Plantation management research cooperative.* Warnell School of Forestry and Natural Resources, University of Georgia, Athens, GA.

Prisley, S.P., and M.J. Mortimer. 2004. A synthesis of literature on evaluation of models for policy applications, with implications for forest carbon accounting. *For. Ecol. Manag.* 198(1):89–103.

Richards, K.R., and C. Stokes. 2004. A review of forest carbon sequestration cost studies: A dozen years of research. *Clim. Change* 63(1):1–48.

Sampo, P., T. Olli, and N. Sami. 2014. The economics of timber and bioenergy production and carbon storage in scots pine stands. *Can. J. For. Res.* 44(9):1091–1102.

Smith, J.E., L.S. Heath, K.E. Skog, and R.A. Birdsey. 2006. Methods for calculating forest ecosystem and harvested carbon with standard estimates for forest types of the United States. *USDA Forest Service. GTR NE-343*:222.

Sun, C., B. Mei, and Y. Li. 2022. Optimal contract arrangements for conservation on working forests. *Nat. Res. Model.* 35(4):e12351 .

TMS. 2022. *TimberMart-South.* Norris Foundation, Athens, GA.

van der Gaast, W., R. Sikkema, and M. Vohrer. 2018. The contribution of forest carbon credit projects to addressing the climate change challenge. *Clim. Policy* 18(1):42–48.

van Kooten, G.C., and C.S. Binkley. 1995. Effect of carbon taxes and subsidies on optimal forest rotation age and supply of carbon services. *Am. J. Agri. Econ.* 77(2):365.

van Kooten, G.C., and C.M.T. Johnston. 2016. The economics of forest carbon offsets. *Annual Rev. Resour. Econ.* 8(1):227–246.

van Kooten, G.C., and B. Sohngen. 2007. Economics of forest ecosystem carbon sinks: A review. *Int. Rev. Environ. Resour. Econ.* 1(3):237–269.

Vass, M.M., and K. Elofsson. 2016. Is forest carbon sequestration at the expense of bioenergy and forest products cost-efficient in EU climate policy to 2050? *J. For. Econ.* 24:82–105.

Wenzel, S., P.M. Cox, V. Eyring, and P. Friedlingstein. 2016. Projected land photosynthesis constrained by changes in the seasonal cycle of atmospheric CO2. *Nature* 538(7626):499–501.

West, T.A.P., C. Wilson, M. Vrachioli, and K.A. Grogan. 2019. Carbon payments for extended rotations in forest plantations: Conflicting insights from a theoretical model. *Ecol. Econ.* 163:70–76.

Zhao, D., M. Kane, R. Teskey, T.R. Fox, T.J. Albaugh, H.L. Allen, and R. Rubilar. 2016. Maximum response of loblolly pine plantations to silvicultural management in the southern United States. *For. Ecol. Manag.* 375:105–111.

13

EMERGING WOODY BIOMASS MARKET

Highlights

- Replacing fossil fuel with wood pellets in generating electricity can reduce net CO_2 emission.
- The European Union and the United Kingdom have government mandates in cofiring wood pellets with coal.
- Without a government intervention, it is not economically feasible to cofire wood pellets with coal for electricity for most time periods of 2009–2015 in the United States.
- A subsidy of $1.40/mmbtu to the 10% wood pellets cofiring or a coal tax of $1.50/mmbtu would trigger the conversions of coal-only power plants to cofiring ones.

Unlike the European Union, US power plants are not cofiring wood pellets with coal. Applying a regime switching model under the theoretical framework of real options, we inspect the optimal timing boundaries for coal and coal mixed with wood pellets as two alternative fuels in this chapter.

Background

Historically, coal is the major fuel type for power plants. Electricity generated from coal-fired power plants accounts for more than 40% and 39% globally and within the United States, respectively (EIA 2016). On a per-unit energy basis, coal is one of the largest emitters of carbon dioxide among all fossil fuels, and coal-fired power plants represent a major source of man-made carbon dioxide emissions. To reduce greenhouse gas (GHG) emissions, most countries have set

DOI: 10.4324/9781003366737-13

reduction targets. The world-leader in this effort is the European Union (EU) and the United Kingdom (UK). In recent years, the EU in general and the UK in particular have burned an increasing amount of biomass for electricity generation. In 2015, the United States launched the Clean Power Plan aimed to lower carbon dioxide emitted by electrical power generation by 32% within 25 years relative to the 2005 level. The plan is focused on reducing emissions from coal-burning power plants, as well as increasing the use of renewable energy, and energy conservation.[1] Given the fact that electricity produced from renewable resources is less than 7% in the United States (EIA 2016), there remains a great expansion potential in the bioenergy market.

BOX 13.1 THE AFFORDABLE CLEAN ENERGY RULE REPLACING THE CLEAR POWER PLAN

On June 19, 2019, the US Environmental Protection Agency issued the final Affordable Clean Energy rule, which replaced the prior administration's overreaching Clean Power Plan with a rule that restores rule of law, empowers states, and supports energy diversity. The Affordable Clean Energy rule establishes emission guidelines for states to use when developing plans to limit CO_2 at their coal-fired electric generating units. In this notice, the Environmental Protection Agency also repealed the Clean Power Plan and issued new implementing regulations for affordable clean energy and future rules under section 111(d).

On January 19, 2021, the D.C. Circuit vacated the Affordable Clean Energy rule and remanded to the Environmental Protection Agency for further proceedings consistent with its opinion. On February 12, 2021, the Environmental Protection Agency did not expect states to take any further action to develop and submit plans under Clean Air Act section 111(d) with respect to greenhouse gas emissions from power plants at this time.

We acknowledge the political debates on clean energy and, in particular, on burning woody biomass for electricity. However, the focus of this chapter is on the economic feasibility of cofiring wood pellets for a traditional coal-fired power plant. The model is updatable with new data and policies.

A typical coal-fired power plant bears a huge capital investment with a design life of 20–50 years. Therefore, it is usually not economical to totally abandon a coal-fired power plant and replace it with cleaner technology prior to the end of its useful life. Nonetheless, it is feasible to substitute some portion of the coal by biomass (cofire coal with biomass) so as to reduce carbon emissions. In particular, wood pellets[2] are easily adaptable to automated combustion systems and the cost to convert existing coal boilers to mixed fuel burning is less prohibitive than plant retirement (Zhang et al. 2010). The saving of GHG emissions from wood pellets ranges from 72.6% to 82.4% for each kWh of electricity (Dwivedi et al. 2011). Within the EU and specifically in the UK, many power plants are cofiring wood pellets with coal as a transition option toward a carbon-free power sector. This has created a rapidly growing international market for wood pellets. Given the high productivity of the forest sector in the US Southeast, much of this market is supplied by southeastern wood pellet mills (Spelter and Toth 2009). Forisk Consulting (2015) projects that US wood pellet production could grow from about five million tons in 2009 to near 18 million tons by 2018, of which, 97% would be intended for export markets.

Corresponding to the expanded supply, real wood pellet prices have been generally declining from 2009 to 2012 and have since stabilized (Figure 13.1). In the same period, coal prices have steadily declined, primarily because of the competition from declining natural gas prices, resulting from the advent of commercially viable hydraulic fracturing technologies and horizontal drilling methods. In terms of price volatility, both wood pellet and natural gas exhibit higher variations than coal. Therefore, an intriguing question for coal power-plant managers is how to make the optimal decision on fuel selection. In the energy economics literature, a few studies have examined this issue. Specifically, applying real options analysis, Pederson and Zou (2009) evaluate ethanol plant investments; Lee and Shih (2010), Lima et al. (2013), and Monjas–Barroso and Balibrea-Iniesta (2013) study solar- and wind-energy projects; Song et al. (2011), and Gazheli and Corato (2013) examine the conversion option of traditional farmland for energy crops; Bednyagin and Gnansounou (2011), Detert and Kotani (2013), and Zambujal-Oliveira (2013)

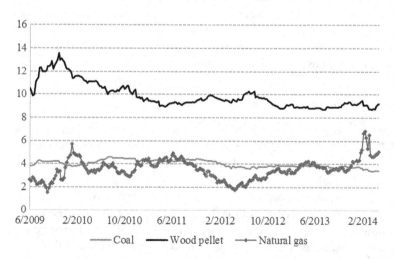

FIGURE 13.1 Weekly real energy prices ($/mmbtu) for 06/05/2009–04/25/2014 (base time period January 2013)

investigate the investment decisions among combined-cycle, coal-fired, wind, solar, and nuclear power plants; Cheng et al. (2011) assess the clean-energy mix policy; and Siddiqui and Fleten (2010) analyze the staged commercialization and deployment of alternative energy technologies.

Past research on wood pellets mainly focuses on decentralized household heating systems (e.g., Claudy et al. 2011; Hyysalo et al. 2013; Michelsen and Madlener 2012). Studies on wood pellets for electricity generation, however, have been limited. Steininger and Voraberger (2003) employ a computable general equilibrium model of the Austrian economy and demonstrate that fostering the use of cofiring could lead to a decline in both gross domestic product (GDP) and employment. Ehrig and Behrendt (2013) assert that cofiring wood pellets with coal represents one of the most cost-attractive ways to reach the EU 2020 carbon targets. Dwivedi et al. (2014) reveal that the use of wood pellets for electricity generation could reduce the UK's GHG emissions by 50–68% relative to fossil fuels. Xian et al. (2015) account for uncertain energy markets and examine the economic feasibility of cofiring wood pellets with coal for electricity generation.

In this study, we apply a regime switching model under the framework of real options analysis to investigate the economic boundary conditions between coal and coal mixed with wood pellets as the fuel for power plants. We intend to contribute to the current literature by considering reciprocal switch options between coal-only and cofiring for a power plant, and incorporating the switch cost explicitly as a function of the energy prices. Considering the shifting energy patterns in the US market (Figure 13.1), we conduct analyses on two distinct periods in addition to the whole sample period. One is the infancy period (2009–2011), which is the early stage when coal prices are relatively high and wood pellet prices are declining because of initial rapid supply expansion. The other is the substitution period, when cheap natural gas undermines coal's dominance as the fuel for US power plants. The null hypothesis is both coal-only and cofiring are economically viable options for US power plants, which solely depends on contemporary market situations but not government involvement.[3]

Regime switch framework

Based upon the classic real options approach proposed by Dixit and Pindyck (1994), Adkins and Paxson (2011) examine the reciprocal energy-switching options and provide a quasi-analytical solution for the case of two competing energy inputs. Extending their analysis, we adopt a general regime switching model, which incorporates price uncertainty of two alternative fuels to investigate a power plant's optimal choice of the fuel type. Consider an active, perpetual operating power plant that turns the chemical energy in coal into electricity and has an option to exchange the incumbent fuel (coal) with a substitute fuel (coal mixed with wood pellets). The switch is reciprocal and incurs a known sunk cost

K_{ij}, $i,j \in \{c,m\}$ and $i \neq j$.[4] Gains from a switch include the net cost saving from using cheaper fuel and the option value of switching back.

Price for fuel, X_i, $i \in \{c,m\}$, is assumed to follow a geometric Brownian motion,

$$dX_i = \alpha_i X_i dt + \sigma_i X_i dz_i \qquad (13.1)$$

where α is the drift rate, σ is the volatility rate and dz is the increment of a standard Wiener process. Correlation between the two price variables is described by ρ ($|\rho| \leq 1$), so that $\mathrm{cov}(dX_c, dX_m) = \rho\sigma_c\sigma_m dt$. To state the valuation relationship in terms of one unit of output, price for each fuel can be adjusted by a conversion factor.[5]

The function $F_i(X_c, X_m)$, $i \in \{c,m\}$, denotes the plant value from using fuel i and the embedded switch option, which depends on prices of both the incumbent and the substitute fuels. Using the dynamic programming approach, the following partial differential equation can be obtained:

$$\frac{1}{2}\sigma_c^2 X_c^2 \frac{\partial^2 F_i}{\partial X_c^2} + \frac{1}{2}\sigma_m^2 X_m^2 \frac{\partial^2 F_i}{\partial X_m^2} + \rho\sigma_c\sigma_m X_c X_m \frac{\partial^2 F_i}{\partial X_c X_m}$$

$$+ \alpha_c X_c \frac{\partial F_i}{\partial X_c} + \alpha_m X_m \frac{\partial F_i}{\partial X_m} - \mu F_i + Y - X_i = 0 \qquad (13.2)$$

where μ is the discount rate, Y is the output (electricity) price net of operating costs. The generic valuation function F_i takes the form

$$F_i(X_c, X_m) = A_i X_c^{\beta_i} X_m^{\eta_i} + \frac{Y}{\mu} - \frac{X_i}{\mu - \alpha_i} \qquad (13.3)$$

where A ($A \geq 0$), β and η are unknown parameters of the product power function. The first term in (3) represents the option value of switching fuel inputs, and the last two terms represent the value of operation without any switch option. By applying the limiting boundary conditions, it can be shown that

$$F_c = A_{c4} X_c^{\beta_{c4}} X_m^{\eta_{c4}} + \frac{Y}{\mu} - \frac{X_c}{\mu - \alpha_c} \qquad (13.4)$$

$$F_m = A_{m2} X_c^{\beta_{m2}} X_m^{\eta_{m2}} + \frac{Y}{\mu} - \frac{X_m}{\mu - \alpha_m} \qquad (13.5)$$

where $\beta_{c4} > 0$, $\eta_{c4} \leq 0$, $\beta_{m2} \leq 0$, and $\eta_{m2} > 0$. Using the value-matching conditions, smooth-pasting conditions, and the two characteristic root equations, a system of eight equations can be established and the switch timing boundaries can be determined numerically. The price ratios along the two discriminatory boundaries are given by

$$W_{cm} = \frac{X_c}{X_m} > 1 \text{ and } W_{mc} = \frac{X_m}{X_c} > 1 \qquad (13.6)$$

where W_{ij} designates the price ratio when fuel i currently in use should be replaced by fuel j. Imposing the property of homogeneity of degree one on the value functions (i.e., $\beta_{c4} + \eta_{c4} = 1$ and $\beta_{m2} + \eta_{m2} = 1$) and the conversion cost function, the value-matching and the smooth-pasting conditions are

$$A_{c4}W_{cm}^{\beta_{c4}} - \frac{W_{cm}}{\mu - \alpha_c} = A_{m2}W_{cm}^{\beta_{m2}} - \frac{1}{\mu - \alpha_m} - k_c W_{cm}^{\phi_c}$$

$$A_{m2}W_{mc}^{1-\beta_{m2}} - \frac{W_{mc}}{\mu - \alpha_m} = A_{c4}W_{mc}^{1-\beta_{c4}} - \frac{1}{\mu - \alpha_c} - k_m W_{mc}^{\phi_m}$$

$$\beta_{c4}A_{c4}W_{cm}^{\beta_{c4}-1} - \frac{1}{\mu - \alpha_c} = \beta_{m2}A_{m2}W_{cm}^{\beta_{m2}-1} - \phi_c k_c W_{cm}^{\phi_c-1} \qquad (13.7)$$

$$(1 - \beta_{m2})A_{m2}W_{mc}^{-\beta_{m2}} - \frac{1}{\mu - \alpha_m} = (1 - \beta_{c4})A_{c4}W_{mc}^{-\beta_{c4}} - \phi_m k_m W_{mc}^{\phi_m-1}$$

where k_i and ϕ_i are parameters in the conversion cost function $K_{ij} = k_i X_i^{\phi_i} X_j^{1-\phi_i}$, and the implied characteristic root equation has closed-form solutions for β_{c4} and β_{m2}

$$\beta_{c4} = \frac{1}{2} - \frac{\alpha_c - \alpha_m}{\sigma_H^2} + \sqrt{\left(\frac{1}{2} - \frac{\alpha_c - \alpha_m}{\sigma_H^2}\right)^2 + \frac{2(\mu - \alpha_m)}{\sigma_H^2}} > 0, \qquad (13.8)$$

$$\beta_{m2} = \frac{1}{2} - \frac{\alpha_c - \alpha_m}{\sigma_H^2} - \sqrt{\left(\frac{1}{2} - \frac{\alpha_c - \alpha_m}{\sigma_H^2}\right)^2 + \frac{2(\mu - \alpha_m)}{\sigma_H^2}} < 0, \qquad (13.9)$$

where $\sigma_H^2 = \sigma_c^2 - 2\rho\sigma_c\sigma_m + \sigma_m^2$. Equations 13.7 can be solved numerically.

The conversion cost is an increasing function of ϕ_i, which indicates the relative importance of the two price levels in determining the converting cost ϕ_i. When ϕ_i approaches one, the conversion cost almost only depends on the price of the incumbent but not the substitute fuel. That is, when $\phi_i = 1$ the conversion cost is proportional to the price of the incumbent, prevailing fuel but not the potential

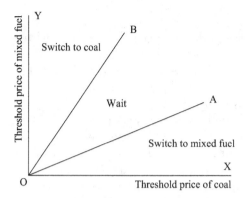

FIGURE 13.2 Switching boundaries between two fuel types for a power plant

substitute because of the lack of production using the latter during the transition period.

The optimal switch decisions can be illustrated in Figure 13.2. The locus OA denotes the optimal switching boundary from coal as the current fuel to mixed fuel as the substitute, whereas the locus OB denotes that from mixed fuel as the current fuel to coal as the substitute. If a price pair falls into the region OAX and the incumbent fuel is coal, it is optimal to switch to mixed fuel. Instead, if a price pair falls into the region OBY and the incumbent fuel is mixed fuel, it is optimal to switch to coal. Therefore, the continuance region is OAY if the incumbent is coal and OBX if the incumbent is mixed fuel.

Data and variable description

All energy prices, expressed as of $/mmbtu, are of weekly frequency and range from June 5, 2009, to April 25, 2014. Coal prices of US Central Appalachian are used because more than 33% of total coal burned by power plants in the Southeast is supplied by this region. Natural gas prices of the Henry Hub are used because of its importance to the North American natural gas market. Both coal and natural gas prices are obtained from the US Energy Information Administration (EIA 2016). Wood pellet prices (energy density 17 GJ/ton and free on board US Southeast) are from Argus Media (2015). All prices are deflated by the Producer Price Index (PPI) for crude material and stated in January 2013 dollars. A transportation cost of $1.15/mmbtu, which is the average railway cost from Central Appalachian to Atlanta, Georgia, in 2013 (EIA 2016), is added to the real price of coal to make it comparable to wood pellet price.

Mixed fuels are defined as 10%, 15%, and 25% of wood pellets cofiring with coal. Their price series (X_{mi}) are weighted averages of wood pellet (X_w) and coal (X_c) prices, and adjusted for fuel efficiency

$$X_{mi} = \lambda_i \left[w_{wi} X_w + (1 - w_{wi}) X_c \right] \tag{13.10}$$

where w_{wi} is the share of wood pellets in the cofiring and λ_i is the efficiency multiple defined as the ratio of coal-to-electricity efficiency over mixed-fuel-to-electricity efficiency. The net efficiency of coal-to-electricity is 32.67% based on the average heat rate of 10,444 btu/kWh of a coal power plant (EIA 2016). The efficiency loss for low-level cofiring is about 0.5% per each 10% of wood pellet input (Robinson et al. 2003). Therefore, the efficiency multiples for 10%, 15%, and 25% wood pellet cofiring are 1.016, 1.024, and 1.040, respectively.

Summary statistics of energy prices are reported in Table 13.1. Over the whole sample period, wood pellet has the highest average price and volatility, and natural gas has the lowest average price but a relatively moderate volatility. Blending more wood pellets with coal increases the mixed fuel cost and volatility. Note that the impact on volatility is less than proportional, given wood pellet prices are not perfectly correlated with coal prices. Considering the overall evolvement of the energy market, two sub-sample periods are investigated. In the infancy period, 2009–2011, US wood pellet production was primarily consumed domestically for home heating (EIA 2016). In contrast, during the substitution period, 2012–2014, wood pellet exports from the United States to the EU increased dramatically and relatively cheap natural gas began to substitute coal in US power plants. Energy prices in the substitution period are lower than those in the infancy period resulting from a more intense competition of alternative fuels in the energy market. In addition, the volatility of mixed fuel in the two sub-samples are comparable or even lower than that of coal due to the low correlations between these two-price series.

Parameters in Equation 13.1 are estimated and calibrated as follows.[6] Let $r_t = d \ln(X_t) = \ln(X_t) - \ln(X_{t-1})$ be the continuously compounded return in the tth time interval, then $\hat{\alpha} = \bar{r} / \Delta + s^2 / 2\Delta$ and $\hat{\sigma}_1 = s / \sqrt{\Delta}$, where $\bar{r}$ and S are the sample mean and standard deviation of the series r_t and Δ is the equally spaced time interval measured in years (i.e., $\Delta = 1/52$ year for weekly data). As indicated by the magnitudes of the drift parameters (Table 13.2), all energy price series show a declining trend during the whole sample and the substitution periods. In contrast, for the infancy period, all energy price series except for wood pellets exhibit a rising trend.

Regarding the variation, coal prices have a fairly constant volatility, whereas wood pellet prices stabilize over time and become less volatile than coal prices during the substitution period. The correlation coefficient estimates remain low at 0.327–0.348 and therefore volatilities of mixed fuel prices are generally lower than those of wood pellets and coal. Because of the portfolio effect, the correlation coefficient decreases as the percentage of wood pellets in the mixed fuels increases. Finally, the values of parameters k's and ϕ's in the conversion cost function are based on Adkins and Paxson (2011), where $k_c = k_m = 0.5$ means

TABLE 13.1 Summary statistics of real energy prices in $/mmbtu

Fuel type	Whole period 2009–2014		Infancy period 2009–2011		Substitution period 2012–2014	
	Mean	SD	Mean	SD	Mean	SD
Coal	4.01	0.29	4.22	0.21	3.77	0.15
Natural gas	3.54	0.88	3.61	0.76	3.45	0.99
Wood pellet	9.89	1.09	10.47	1.18	9.23	0.40
WP10	4.67	0.31	4.92	0.17	4.38	0.14
WP15	5.01	0.34	5.28	0.19	4.70	0.15
WP25	5.70	0.41	6.01	0.28	5.34	0.16

TABLE 13.2 Parameter estimates of the geometric Brownian motion for real energy prices in $/mmbtu

Fuel type	Whole period 2009–2014			Infancy period 2009–2011			Substitution period 2012–2014		
	α	σ	ρ	α	σ	ρ	α	σ	ρ
Coal	−0.009	0.103	1.000	0.050	0.100	1.000	−0.075	0.105	1.000
Wood pellet	−0.011	0.123	0.327	−0.001	0.149	0.348	−0.019	0.085	0.329
WP10	−0.013	0.093	0.959	0.035	0.095	0.942	−0.065	0.090	0.981
WP15	−0.014	0.091	0.915	0.029	0.096	0.886	−0.061	0.085	0.957
WP25	−0.015	0.092	0.808	0.021	0.102	0.765	−0.053	0.079	0.886

TABLE 13.3 Description of the variables used in the regime switch analysis

Symbol	Definition	Value
μ	Discount rate for US power plants	0.08
k_c	Parameter of the conversion cost function from coal to mixed fuel	0.5
k_m	Parameter of the conversion cost function from mixed fuel to coal	0.5
ϕ_c	Parameter of the conversion cost function from coal to mixed fuel	1
ϕ_m	Parameter of the conversion cost function from mixed fuel to coal	1
Y	Electricity price net of operating costs	0.050
X_c	Coal price	0.014
X_m	Mixed fuel price (10% wood pellets)	0.016
	Mixed fuel price (15% wood pellets)	0.017
	Mixed fuel price (25% wood pellets)	0.019

switch options are equally reciprocal and $\phi_c = \phi_m = 1$ means the conversion cost merely depends on the price of the incumbent fuel. Other key variables and their adopted values are presented in Table 13.3, including a discount rate of 8% for US power plants, an average retail electricity price of $0.050/kWh net of operating costs, an average coal price of $0.014/kWh, and average mixed fuel prices of $0.016/kWh, $0.017/kWh, and $0.019/kWh with 10%, 15%, and 25% wood pellets, respectively.

Results and discussion

Base case results

Numerical solutions for Equations 13.7 are presented in Table 13.4. Parameters β's and A's are of expected signs and all price ratios are greater than one. The total value per kWh of a coal power plant and a mixed fuel power plant can be calculated according to Equations 13.4 and 13.5 for a given coal and mixed fuel price pairs. For example, the total value of a coal (mixed fuel with 10% wood pellets) power plant using the whole sample parameter values and average energy prices is $0.7837/kWh ($0.8052/kWh) and the option value to switch to mixed fuel with 10% wood pellets (coal) is $0.0014/kWh ($0.0081/kWh).

The threshold price ratios W_{cm} and W_{mc} define the optimal switching boundaries between coal and mixed fuel as fuel options for a power plant for nine different scenarios. The boundaries together with historical mixed fuel and coal price ratios are plotted in Figure 13.3. In most cases, the price pairs fall into the switch-to-coal region, meaning that it is not economical to cofire wood pellets with coal

TABLE 13.4 Results of the regime switching model

Symbol	WP10			WP15			WP25		
	Whole period 2009–2014	Infancy period 2009–2011	Substitution period 2012–2014	Whole period 2009–2014	Infancy period 2009-2011	Substitution period 2012–2014	Whole period 2009–2014	Infancy period 2009–2011	Substitution period 2012–2014
β_{c4}	11.022	2.809	46.028	8.293	2.276	32.430	6.097	1.894	22.703
β_{m2}	−19.057	−28.428	−10.787	−13.048	−20.325	−7.448	−8.289	−12.983	−4.564
A_{c4}	0.372	10.684	0.0001	0.550	13.310	0.004	0.804	16.007	0.0013
W_{om}	1.100	1.051	1.178	1.121	1.064	1.211	1.157	1.090	1.268
A_{m2}	0.040	0.002	0.190	0.088	0.005	0.359	0.205	0.018	0.750
W_{mc}	1.138	1.199	1.102	1.164	1.244	1.110	1.201	1.302	1.121

Note: WP10, WP15, and WP25 represent 10%, 15%, and 25% wood pellet cofiring with coal.

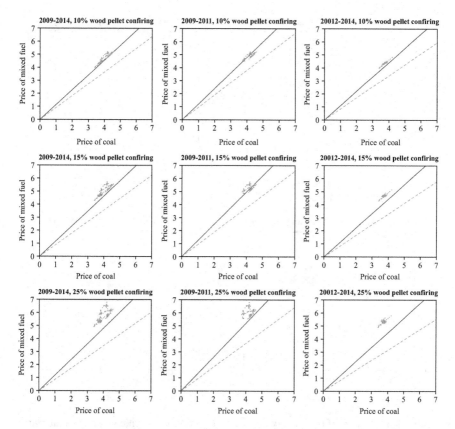

FIGURE 13.3 Optimal switching boundaries for nine different wood pellet and coal cofiring scenarios for electricity generation

because the mixed fuel cost increases with the share of wood pellets. Exceptions are 10% and 15% cofiring during the infancy period, where some portion of the price pairs fall into the continuation region. In these two exceptions, a power plant should continue to use whichever is its incumbent fuel. Consequently, a cofiring power plant could have operated efficiently during that time period. In general, Table 13.4 suggests that cofiring wood pellets with coal is not economically feasible in the United States over the 2009–2014 period with high wood pellet prices.

Next, we consider the impact of potential government interventions on the renewable resource energy market (Figure 13.4). First, we include a direct subsidy of $1.40/mmbtu to the mixed fuel with 10% wood pellets, which essentially cuts the input cost of a cofiring power plant. As such, all the energy price pairs move just under the coal-to-mixed-fuel switch boundary. Second, we impose a tax of $1.50/

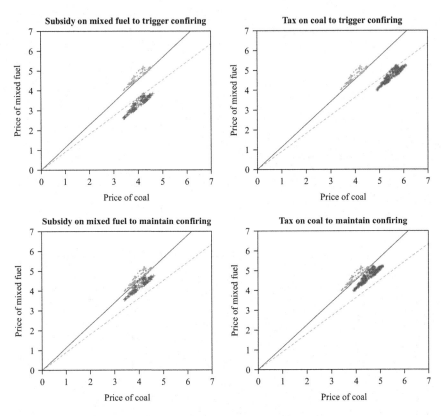

FIGURE 13.4   Impact of the subsidy on mixed fuel and the tax on coal on optimal switch decisions. A subsidy of $1.40/mmbtu to the 10% mixed fuel or a coal tax of $1.50/mmbtu would trigger the conversions of coal-only power plants to cofiring ones, and a subsidy of $0.45/mmbtu to the 10% mixed fuel or a tax of $0.50/mmbtu on coal would maintain existing cofiring power plants in the status quo.

mmbtu on a coal-only power plant, which is equivalent to increasing the cost of coal. Accordingly, all the energy price pairs fall just below the coal-to-mixed-fuel switch boundary. In both scenarios, a coal power plant should convert to wood pellets and coal cofiring. Therefore, a minimum tax of $1.50/mmbtu on coal has a similar effect as a minimum subsidy of $1.40/mmbtu on mixed fuel in triggering the investment in cofiring power plants. Given an average cost of $0.12/kWh ($35/mmbtu) in the United States, the mixed fuel subsidy or coal tax represents about 4% of the electricity rate. Alternatively, a minimum subsidy of $0.45/mmbtu on the mixed fuel or a minimum tax of $0.50/mmbtu on the coal could maintain existing cofiring power plants in the status quo, which represents about 1.3% of the electricity rate.

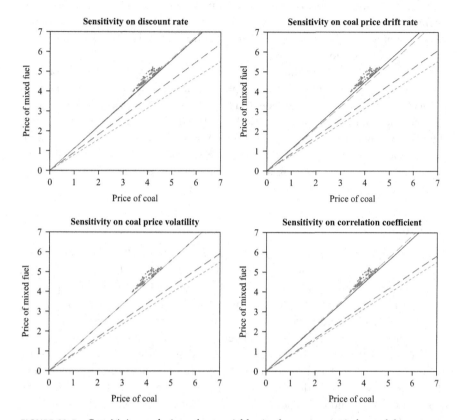

FIGURE 13.5   Sensitivity analysis on key variables in the regime switch model

Sensitivity analysis

Sensitivity analysis is conducted on the discount rate, drift and volatility parameters of coal price, correlation coefficient, and wood pellet price for the whole
sample period and the case of 10% wood pellet cofiring (Figure 13.5). When the
discount rate is reduced from 8% to 6%, the major impact is on the switch boundary from coal to mixed fuels. A lower discount rate yields higher cost mixed fuels
more affordable and thus shifts the switch boundary up. When the drift parameter
of coal price is reduced from −0.009 to −0.020, both coal price and mixed fuel
price tend to fall over time, so that the wait region narrows and both switches are
more likely to occur. When the volatility parameter of coal is lowered from 0.103
to 0.050, the volatility of mixed fuel decreases as well. With less uncertainty in the
mixed fuel cost, a coal power plant is more willing to switch to mixed fuel. When
the correlation coefficient is reduced from 0.959 to 0.800, the portfolio effect
becomes more significant. Hence, the impact is quite similar to that of a reduction
in the volatility of mixed fuel.

In summary, when values of the key variables in the switch regime model change by a significant amount, the optimal decision for a power plant does not change appreciably. Specifically, cofiring wood pellets with coal is not an economically viable option.

At the plant level, heat rates and delivered fuel prices can deviate from the industry averages. A lower heat rate implies higher operation efficiency and thus reduces fuel input cost, all else equal. This means that the price pairs in Figure 13.3 fall more into the "switch to coal" region. Similarly, the same would occur if a plant can negotiate a lower coal delivered price. In other words, plants with lower heat rates or better control of delivered coal prices are less willing to switch to wood pellets cofiring and larger incentives are needed to induce the conversion.

Conclusions

Using the regime switching model under the theoretical framework of real options, we examine the optimal timing boundaries for coal and mixed fuel as two alternative fuels for a US power plant. Results indicate that cofiring wood pellets with coal is not a commercially viable option in most cases. However, lower-level (with wood pellets less than 15%) cofiring could have been feasible during the infancy period when wood pellet price is declining. Sensitivity analysis indicates that our conclusions are robust and the most important factors are relative prices of coal and mixed fuel. Therefore, we reject the null hypothesis that cofiring is economically feasible and suggest using subsidies to stimulate the bioenergy market and meet the GHG emission reduction target.

Specifically, a subsidy of $1.40/mmbtu to the 10% mixed fuel[7] or a coal tax of $1.50/mmbtu would trigger the conversions of coal-only power plants to cofiring ones, and a subsidy of $0.45/mmbtu to the 10% mixed fuel or a tax of $0.50/mmbtu on coal would maintain existing cofiring power plants in the status quo. Given the total electricity of 1,596 billion kWh generated from coal (EIA 2016), the estimated government spending is about $8 billion to prompt the conversion to mixed fuel and $2.7 billion to retain current cofiring power plants. This spending will increase as the share of wood pellets in the mixed fuel enlarges. These numbers are roughly comparable to the subsidy levels of $0.03–0.20/kWh or $8.82–58.82/mmbtu to solar energy (Fthenakis et al. 2009), and the production tax credit of $0.019/kWh or $5.59/mmbtu toward wind energy (Greenblatt et al. 2007). Therefore, we urge that renewable energy policies should give equal priorities to wood pellets cofiring as to solar and wind energy in the United States.

Unlike most countries in Europe, where domestic cost of manufacturing wood pellets is not competitive with the import price, the US Southeast has a productive forest industry and well-established infrastructure. Hence, producing wood pellets from intensively managed timberland in this region is likely to increase local employment as well as GDP. For example, a 500-megawatt coal power plant takes about 2,540 jobs, whereas a same-sized power plant with mixed fuel is estimated to take 3,480 jobs, or a 37% increase in employment (Strauss 2014). In addition, a long-term demand for wood pellets can help preserve existing working forests and attract more investments in commercial forests, which, in turn, increases carbon sequestration. Thus, the government expenditure on boosting wood pellets usage by power plants does not simply represent a cost but has some benefits and can potentially improve the rural economy.

Questions

1. How does fuel cost uncertainty affect fuel adoption decision at the plant level?
2. What instruments can be used to stimulate the woody biomass market?

Notes

1 Specifically, the Environmental Protection Agency requires individual states to implement their plans by focusing on three building blocks: increasing the generation efficiency of existing fossil fuel plants, substituting lower carbon dioxide-emitting natural gas generation for coal-powered generation, and substituting generation from new zero carbon dioxide-emitting renewable sources for fossil fuel-powered generation. This study focuses on the last one.
2 Wood pellets are small nuggets of compressed, sawdust-sized wood fiber that have higher energy density and lower moisture content than their raw input. The sustainability of wood pellets as feedstock for energy is largely a matter of carbon cycle calculations, which depends on the origin and type of trees used for wood pellets. We believe that burning wood pellets locally for energy is more carbon efficient than burning coal, even after accounting for the emissions for collecting and processing biomass.
3 The EU biomass market is driven by government mandates. The same has not been mirrored in the US.
4 Letter c for coal and m for mixed fuel (coal mixed with wood pellets). K_c denotes the conversion cost from coal to mixed fuel and K_m denotes the conversion cost from mixed fuel to coal. For example, for a coal-burning power plant to burn wood and meet emission requirements, some accommodations to facility operation and physical structure are necessary, including ash and air emission control, hard coating cleaning, wood storage, and grinding and blowing systems.
5 1 kwh = 0.0034 mmbtu.
6 For completeness, we conducted unit root tests on the energy price series and find mixed results for or against the null hypothesis of unit roots. An alternative stochastic model for price series is the geometric Ornstein-Uhlenbeck process. We also estimate the parameters for the geometric Ornstein-Uhlenbeck process and find low rates of mean reversion and similar volatility estimates. Therefore, we conclude that the geometric Brownian motion well captures the short-run stochastic nature of the energy price series.
7 On a hypothetical 100% carbon reduction basis, a multiple of 10 should be applied. So, roughly speaking, the corresponding subsidy should be $14/mmbtu to trigger the switch from coal to 100% wood pellets burning.

Bibliography

Adkins, R., and D. Paxson. 2011. Reciprocal energy-switching options. *J. Energy Markets* 4(1):91–120.

Argus Media. 2015. *Argus biomass markets (various issues)*. Argus Media, London, United Kingdom.

Bednyagin, D., and E. Gnansounou. 2011. Real options valuation of fusion energy R&D programme. *Energy Policy* 39(1):116–130.

Cheng, C.T., S.L. Lo, and T.T. Lin. 2011. Applying real options analysis to assess cleaner energy development strategies. *Energy Policy* 39(10):5929–5938.

Claudy, M.C., C. Michelsen, and A. O'Driscoll. 2011. The diffusion of microgeneration technologies – assessing the influence of perceived product characteristics on home owners' willingness to pay. *Energy Policy* 39(3):1459–1469.

Detert, N., and K. Kotani. 2013. Real options approach to renewable energy investments in Mongolia. *Energy Policy* 56:136–150.

Dixit, A.K., and R.S. Pindyck. 1994. *Investment under uncertainty*. Princeton University Press, Princeton, NJ, 468p.

Dwivedi, P., R. Bailis, T. Bush, and M. Marinescu. 2011. Quantifying GWI of wood pellet production in the Southern United States and its subsequent utilization for electricity production in the Netherlands/Florida. *Bioenerg. Res.* 4(3):180–192.

Dwivedi, P., K. Madhu, B. Robert, and G. Adrian. 2014. Potential greenhouse gas benefits of transatlantic wood pellet trade. *Environ. Res. Lett* 9(2):024007.

Ehrig, R., and F. Behrendt. 2013. Co-firing of imported wood pellets – an option to efficiently save CO2 emissions in Europe? *Energy Policy* 59:283–300.

EIA. 2016. *U.S. Energy Information Administration*. Washington, DC.

Forisk Consulting. 2015. Wood bioenergy in the US: Pellet volumes grow; biofuel projects stall. https://forisk.com/blog/2015/02/22/wood-bioenergy-u-s-pellet-volumes-grow-biofuel-projects-stall/. Last assessed August 20, 2022.

Fthenakis, V., J.E. Mason, and K. Zweibel. 2009. The technical, geographical, and economic feasibility for solar energy to supply the energy needs of the US. *Energy Policy* 37(2):387–399.

Gazheli, A., and L.D. Corato. 2013. Land-use change and solar energy production: A real option approach. *Agri. Financ. Rev.* 73(3):507–525.

Greenblatt, J.B., S. Succar, D.C. Denkenberger, R.H. Williams, and R.H. Socolow. 2007. Baseload wind energy: Modeling the competition between gas turbines and compressed air energy storage for supplemental generation. *Energy Policy* 35(3):1474–1492.

Hyysalo, S., J.K. Juntunen, and S. Freeman. 2013. User innovation in sustainable home energy technologies. *Energy Policy* 55:490–500.

Lee, S.C., and L.H. Shih. 2010. Renewable energy policy evaluation using real option model – the case of Taiwan. *Energy Econ.* 32:S67–S78.

Lima, D., G. Colson, B. Karali, B. Guerrero, S. Amosson, and M. Wetzstein. 2013. A new look at the economic evaluation of wind energy as an alternative to electric and natural gas-powered irrigation. *J. Agri. Appl. Econ.* 45(04):739–751.

Michelsen, C.C., and R. Madlener. 2012. Homeowners' preferences for adopting innovative residential heating systems: A discrete choice analysis for Germany. *Energy Econ.* 34(5):1271–1283.

Monjas-Barroso, M., and J. Balibrea-Iniesta. 2013. Valuation of projects for power generation with renewable energy: A comparative study based on real regulatory options. *Energy Policy* 55:335–352.

Pederson, G., and T. Zou. 2009. Using real options to evaluate ethanol plant expansion decisions. *Agri. Financ. Rev.* 69(1):23–35.

Robinson, A.L., J.S. Rhodes, and D.W. Keith. 2003. Assessment of potential carbon dioxide reductions due to biomass-coal cofiring in the United States. *Environ. Sci. Technol.* 37(22):5081–5089.

Siddiqui, A., and S.E. Fleten. 2010. How to proceed with competing alternative energy technologies: A real options analysis. *Energy Econ.* 32(4):817–830.

Song, F., J. Zhao, and S.M. Swinton. 2011. Switching to perennial energy crops under uncertainty and costly reversibility. *Am. J. Agri. Econ.* 93(3):768–783.

Spelter, H., and D. Toth. 2009. *North America's wood pellet sector.* USDA Forest Service, Madison, WI. Research paper FPL-RP-656, 21.

Steininger, K., and H. Voraberger. 2003. Exploiting the medium term biomass energy potentials in Austria: A comparison of costs and macroeconomic impact. *Environ. Resource Econ.* 24(4):359–377.

Strauss, W. 2014. *The many benefits of replacing coal with wood pellet fuel.* https://biomassmagazine.com/articles/10750/the-many-benefits-of-replacing-coal-with-wood-pellet-fuel. Last accessed August 20, 2022.

Xian, H., G. Colson, B. Mei, and M.E. Wetzstein. 2015. Co-firing coal with wood pellets for U.S. electricity generation: A real options analysis. *Energy Policy* 81:106–116.

Zambujal-Oliveira, J. 2013. Investments in combined cycle natural gas-fired systems: A real options analysis. *Int. J. Elec. Power Energy Sys.* 49:1–7.

Zhang, Y., J. McKechnie, D. Cormier, R. Lyng, W. Mabee, A. Ogino, and H.L. MacLean. 2010. Life cycle emissions and cost of producing electricity from coal, natural gas, and wood pellets in Ontario, Canada. *Environ. Sci. Technol.* 44(1):538–544.

14

CASE STUDY: WEYERHAEUSER AND PLUM CREEK MERGER

Highlights

- Consolidations in the form of mergers and acquisitions in the timberland industry have been increasing since 2015.
- Cost saving is one of the major drivers of value creation.
- The valuation of Weyerhaeuser and Plum Creek merger is illustrated by the discount cash flow and the comparable company analyses.

Mergers and acquisitions (M&As) have been common in corporation restructuring. In the forest products industry alone, there have been more than 70 M&As over 1990–2004. For example, Georgia-Pacific acquired Great Northern Nekoosa in 1990 for $3.8 billion; Kimberly-Clark acquired Scott Paper in 1995 for $9.4 billion; International Paper acquired Union Camp in 1998 for $7.9 billion and Champion International in 2000 for $9.6 billion; and Weyerhaeuser acquired Willamette Industries in 2004 for 7.8 billion (Mei and Sun 2008b). In 2016, the world largest two timber REITs—Weyerhaeuser (WY) and Plum Creek (PCL)—merged with a market value of $23 billion. A key question of any M&A is the valuation of the target company. In this chapter, we will investigate this question and use the WY & PCL merger as a case study.

BOX 14.1 FINANCIAL OUTCOME OF MERGERS AND ACQUISITIONS

Using an event study, the financial performance of the acquirer and the target can be assessed (MacKinlay 1997). In terms of M&As, it is the targets, not

---

DOI: 10.4324/9781003366737-14

the acquirers, that usually have short-term abnormal returns. The abnormal performance of the targets is most related to the control premium paid by the acquirer, which is about 20%–40% above the market value depending on the industry (Rosenbaum and Pearl 2020). For the targets of the M&As in the timber REIT segment thus far (i.e., Plum Creek, Pope Resources, Deltic Timber, and CatchMark), all had positive abnormal returns on the merger announcement date.

The performance of the acquirers depends on a number of factors, such as means of payment, market competition, transaction size, and geographic scope. A major consideration is whether the projected synergies from cost savings, and the economies of scale and scope can be realized. It turns out that acquirers may secure some gains in the short run but have no abnormal returns on average in the long run after M&As (Alexandridis et al. 2010).

Review of valuation methods

In general, there are three valuation methods: The comparable company analysis (including precedent transaction analysis), the DCF approach, and the leveraged buyout (LBO) analysis. The comparable company analysis is simple in its logic in that two otherwise similar companies should be worth the same price. Values of companies are typically expressed as multiples of a metric of the cash flow (e.g., EBITDA, EBIT, FCF, or sales).[1] Once a close comparable company, or a group of close comparable companies are identified, the (average) multiple of the comparable company (companies) can be applied to the target based on the selected metric of cash flow. For example, if the target company has an EBITDA of $100 million, the close comparable company has an EV/EBITDA[2] ratio of 8.0, then the target should have an EV of 100 × 8.0 = $800 million.

Despite the quickness and convenience of the comparable company analysis on intuition, there may be lack of relevant comparable companies. Also, the multiples depend on business cycles and are sometimes subjective. Finally, there might be disconnection between the EV and the cash flow, which measures the profitability of a company. The DCF approach, in contrast, discount all future cash flows back to present at the weighted average cost of capital (WACC) and, thus, gives the intrinsic value of a company. In practice, FCF is projected for the next five to ten years and all future values are captured in the terminal value. The discount rate WACC is determined at the optimal capital structure as determined by comparable companies. The detailed procedure will be described in the WY and PCL case study.

The third valuation method, LBO analysis, is a return driven process. To enhance return, the transaction is typically financed with a significant portion of debt (over 2.0 Debt/Equity ratio). The purchase price is determined in such a way that a target IRR can be obtained within the next five years or so. Similar to the DCF approach, five years of FCF and a terminal value need to be estimated. One important constraint is that the new entity, after the LBO, ought to have the ability to cover all debt obligations, including interest expenses and principal repayments. Since the DCF approach is a fundamental method, we will discuss it in length in the next section.

DCF approach

The conceptual framework of the DCF approach is illustrated in Figure 14.1. Enterprise value (EV) equals sum of present values of free cash flows of the next five years and a terminal value.

$$EV = \frac{FCF_1}{1+WACC} + \frac{FCF_2}{\left(1+WACC\right)^2} + \frac{FCF_3}{\left(1+WACC\right)^3} + \frac{FCF_4}{\left(1+WACC\right)^4} + \frac{FCF_5+TV}{\left(1+WACC\right)^5}$$

FCF is calculated as net operating profit after tax (NOPAT) minus change in total net operating capital (ΔCAPITAL), i.e., FCF = NOPAT – ΔCAPITAL.[3] NOPAT is usually directly available from the income statement or can be derived from EBIT. ΔCAPITAL consists of two components: Net operating working capital (NOWC) and net operating long-term assets (i.e., fixed assets or property, plant and equipment). NOWC equals operating current assets (OCA) minus operating current liabilities (OCL). OCA includes cash, inventory, and receivables but excludes short-term investments because they are not related to the core business.[4] OCL includes accounts payable and accruals but excludes notes payable because that is a financial decision.

Calculation of ΔCAPITAL needs two years of balance sheet information in a roll. For example, given the balance sheet information of GoGreen Inc. of 2016 and 2017 in Table 14.1, change in total net operating capital can be calculated step by step as follows. $NOWC_{2016} = (15 + 315 + 415) - (30 + 130) = \$585$ million, $CAPITAL_{2016} = 585 + 870 = \$1,455$ million, $NOWC_{2017} = (10 + 375 + 615) - (60 + 140) = \$800$ million, $CAPITAL_{2017} = 800 + 1,000 = \$1,800$ million. Thus, $\Delta CAPITAL = CAPITAL_{2017} - CAPITAL_{2016} = 1,800 - 1,455 = \$345$ million.

	FCF_1	FCF_2	FCF_3	FCF_4	FCF_5
					Terminal value (TV)
Year	1	2	3	4	5 (Terminal year)

FIGURE 14.1 Conceptual framework of the DCF approach

TABLE 14.1 Financial data of GoGreen Inc.

Balance sheet ($ million)

Assets	2017	2016	Liabilities and equity	2017	2016
Cash	$10	$15	Accounts payable	$60	$30
Short-term investment	0	65	Notes payable	110	60
Accounts receivable	375	315	Accruals	140	130
Inventories	615	415	Total current liabilities	310	220
Total current assets	1,000	810	Long-term bonds	754	580
Net plant & equipment	1,000	870	Total liabilities	1,064	800
			Preferred stock	40	40
			Common stock	130	130
			Retained earnings	766	710
			Total common equity	896	840
Total assets	2,000	1,680		2,000	1,680

Income statement ($ million)

	2017	2016
Net sales	$3,000	$2,850
Operating costs excluding depreciation and amortization	2,617	2,500
EBITDA	383	350
Depreciation and amortization	100	90
EBIT	283	260
Less interest	88	60
Earnings before taxes (EBT)	195	200
Taxes (40%)	78	80
Net income before preferred dividends	117	120
Preferred dividends	4	4
Net income	113	116
Additional information		
Common dividends	57	53
Addition to retained earnings	56	63

Provided an $EBIT_{2017}$ of $283 million, a tax rate of 40%, $FCF_{2017} = 283 \times (1 - 0.4)$ − 345 = −$175.2 million.

TV can be calculated in two ways. One way is to use an exit multiple on FCF of the last year (year five in this case), which is similarly defined as in the comparable company analysis. It is worth noting that the exit multiple must be normalized to a steady state, reflecting a long-term trend. The other way is to assume a perpetual growth rate (g) of last year's FCF, then $TV = \dfrac{FCF_5(1+g)}{WACC - g}$.

Lastly, WACC is calculated as $WACC = w_d R_d (1-T) + (1-w_d)R_e$, where w_d is the optimal weight on debt as revealed by comparable companies, R_d is the required rate of return on debt, $1 - w_d$ is the optimal weight on equity, and R_e is the required rate of return on equity. Cost of debt is reduced by a factor of $1 - T$ because interest expenses are tax deductible. Cost of equity is generally determined by the CAPM, $E[R_e] = R_f + \beta_{L,t}[R_m - R_f]$, where $\beta_{L,t}$ is leveraged beta of the target company at the optimal capital structure.[5] To derive $\beta_{L,t}$, betas of comparable companies need to be unleveraged, $\beta_{U,i} = \dfrac{\beta_{L,i}}{\left(1+\left(D/E\right)\left(1-T\right)\right)}$.

Then, average is taken on these unleveraged betas, denoted as β_U. Finally, leveraged beta of the target company is releveraged at the optimal capital structure as $\beta_{L,t} = \beta_U\left(1+\left(D/E\right)\left(1-T\right)\right)$. Once again, for the WACC calculation, capital structure should be at their optimal level regardless of the target company's status quo.

Valuation of Weyerhaeuser and Plum Creek merger

Weyerhaeuser was incorporated in the state of Washington in 1900. Starting from 2010, WY elected to be taxed as a REIT. In 2014, WY owned 7 million acres of timberlands primarily in the South and Pacific Northwest of the United States, and it managed another 14 million acres of timberlands under long-term licenses in Canada. With $13.5 billion of total assets, WY generated a total revenue of $7,403 million and a net income of $1,782 million.

Plum Creek (PCL) was founded as a small business in the state of Minnesota in the 1930s. In 1999, PCL became the first timber REIT in the United States. In 2014, PCL had 6.6 million acres of timberlands in 19 states located in the North, South, and West Coast of the United States. With $5.1 billion of total assets, PCL had a total revenue of $1,476 million and a net income of $214 million.

On November 9, 2015, WY and PCL announced that they had entered into a definitive agreement to create a new WY with an equity value of $23 billion and over 13 million acres of timberland in the United States. The deal was described as an all-stock transaction, with PCL's shareholders receiving 1.6 shares of WY's common stock for each share of PCL.[6] The closing price of WY on the announcement day was $30 per share. Regarding the benefits of the merger, executives counted on new WY's ability to capitalize on the housing recovery, best-in-class management team, and $100 million synergies (cost savings). In this section, we are going to use the comparable company analysis and the DCF approach to price the target company PCL.

With respect to data, there are a number of sources for publicly traded companies like WY and PCL. Financial database Wharton Research Data Services (WRDS) is widely used in academic research (WRDS 2020). Specifically, database CRSP has all information about common stocks (e.g., price, return, total shares outstanding, dividends, etc.), and database Compustat has all information about the financial statements. Despite the reliability and efficiency of WRDS, access to the data is available to authorized users only.[7] Alternatively, one can use data from public sources like SEC/EDGAR, Zacks.com, Yahoo Finance, and

Google Finance. One drawback of using public sources is that financial statements are not standardized even within the same industry. Many subjective decisions need to be made before conducting any financial analysis.

Comparable company analysis on Plum Creek

In the timber REIT industry, there are two other major players, Rayonier (RYN) and Potlach (PCH). RYN was incorporated in the state of Washington in 1926. Since 2004, RYN has been operating as a REIT. In 2014, RYN owned 2.7 million acres of timberlands in nine states (Washington, New York, Florida, Georgia, Alabama, Arkansas, Louisiana, Oklahoma, and Texas). With $2.5 billion of total assets, RYN made a total revenue of $604 million and a net income of $99 million. PCH was incorporated in the state of Delaware and started its business in 1903. Since 2006, PCH has been operating as a REIT. In 2014, PCH owned 1.6 million acres of timberlands in Arkansas, Idaho, and Minnesota. With $1 billion of total assets, PCH created a total revenue of $607 million and a net income of $90 million. Key financial terms of RYN and PCH are listed in Table 14.2. Trading multiples are calculated in Table 14.3.

Given PCL's data in the past three years (with more emphasis on 2013 and 2014), PCL's value can be calculated in Table 14.4. We focus more on EBIT and EBITDA multiples as they are better cash flow measures than sales and net income. Therefore, per share value of PCL is narrowed down to $38–$45.

DCF analysis on Plum Creek

DCF approach begins with projecting the growth rate of sales, usually based on historical sales data and analysts' outlook. Second, a set of assumptions on operating and financial efficiency needs to be made so that income statement and balance sheet items can be projected one by one for the projection window (typically five years). Finally, FCF is calculated and discounted to year 0. For illustration purpose, we omitted the details of the second step and made a rough assumption that FCF grows at the same rate as sales in the next five years and show how the DCF approach works.

In the past four years, PCL realized an average growth of 5.5% on sales. With a rational expectation on the gradual recovery of US housing starts, which is the key determining factor of lumber demand, we suspect that PCL's sales should grow with some momentum in the near term. Thus, a 6% growth rate is assumed for sales and FCF in the next five years. After that, we assume sales still grow on average but at a much more steady rate of 2%, comparable to the consensus forecast of GDP growth. Provided a FCF of $570 on the base year (2014),[8] future FCF can be derived.

Next, we work on the WACC, which utilizes information from comparable companies, as shown in Table 14.5. Over 2012–2014, RYN's and PCH's D/E ratios averaged 0.209 and 0.256, respectively.[9] Given RYN's and PCH's leveraged betas

TABLE 14.2 Key financial terms of RYN and PCH as PCL's comparable companies

Year	LT Debt	D&A	Sales	NI	EBIT	EBITDA	Inte-rest	Market Cap	EV
Comparable companies									
RYN									
2012	1120.05	148.72	1571.00	278.69	397.80	546.52	45.00	6392.30	7512.35
2013	1461.72	191.27	1707.82	371.90	396.67	587.94	44.00	5315.38	6777.10
2014	621.85	119.98	603.52	99.34	71.78	191.76	44.00	3540.72	4162.57
PCH									
2012	349.16	24.30	525.13	42.59	85.05	109.35	26.00	1581.19	1930.36
2013	320.09	25.50	570.29	70.58	111.12	136.62	23.00	1692.01	2012.11
2014	606.47	25.40	606.95	89.91	132.51	157.91	23.00	1700.13	2306.60
Target company									
PCL									
2012	3197.00	115.00	1340.00	214.00	306.00	421.00	140.00	8232.27	11429.27
2013	2759.00	136.00	1476.00	214.00	307.00	443.00	141.00	7526.76	10285.76
2014	2759.00	133.00	1445.00	197.00	266.00	399.00	166.00	8312.82	11071.82

TABLE 14.3 Trading multiples of RYN and PCH 2012–2014

		EV/Sales	EV/NI	EV/EBIT	EV/EBITDA
RYN	2012	4.78	26.96	18.88	13.75
	2013	3.97	18.22	17.09	11.53
	2014	6.90	41.90	57.99	21.71
PCH	2012	3.68	45.32	22.70	17.65
	2013	3.53	28.51	18.11	14.73
	2014	3.80	25.65	17.41	14.61
	High	4.80	38.00	30.00	17.00
	Mean	4.44	31.09	25.36	15.66
	Low	4.00	28.00	20.00	14.00

Note: High and low values are based on subjective judgment.

TABLE 14.4 Value of PCL based on comparable company analysis

Metric		Sales	NI	EBIT	EBITDA
Market Cap	high	6758.40	8132.00	9195.00	7344.00
	mean	6254.28	6654.16	7773.57	6765.73
	low	5632.00	5992.00	6130.00	6048.00
EV	high	9736.40	11110.00	12173.00	10322.00
	mean	9232.28	9632.16	10751.57	9743.73
	low	8610.00	8970.00	9108.00	9026.00
Per share	high	38.82	46.71	52.82	42.18
	mean	35.92	38.22	44.65	38.86
	low	32.35	34.42	35.21	34.74

Note: PCL has 174,096,000 shares outstanding. Market Cap and EV are in $ million, and per share value is in $.

TABLE 14.5 Capital structure of RYN and PCH, and beta deleveraging and releveraging

		D/E	$\beta_{L,i}$	$\beta_{U,i}$
RYN	2012	0.175		
	2013	0.275		
	2014	0.176		
	Avg	0.209	0.41	0.34
PCH	2012	0.221		
	2013	0.189		
	2014	0.357		
	Avg	0.256	1.41	1.12
	Avg	0.232		0.73

0.41 and 1.12, their unleveraged betas are 0.34 and 1.12, with an average of 0.73 (equity beta). Next, we need to re-leverage this equity beta at the optimal capital structure. The optimal D/E ratio is averaged across comparable companies (i.e., RYN and PCH) and is found to be 0.232. Thus, the releveraged beta is calculated to be 0.90. With a risk-free rate of 2% and an average market premium of 10%, the required rate of return on equity, according to the CAPM, is $0.02 + 0.90 \times 0.10 = 11.01\%$.

The other component of WACC is cost of debt. It is common to use total interest expense over total long-term debt as a proxy. During 2012–2014, the cost of debt of RYN, PCH, WY, and PCL averaged about 6%, and we decided to use the same rate in our analysis. The tax rate is assumed to be zero given the REIT structure, and an optimal D/E ratio of 0.232 implies an optimal weight on debt of 0.188. Hence, WACC is calculated as $0.6 \times 0.188 + 0.1101 \times 0.812 = 10\%$. Finally, TV is calculated to be \$10,107 million using the perpetual growth method (Figure 14.2). The present value of the cash flows (EV), as shown in Figure 14.2, is \$8,829.38 million. Taking out long-term debt, market capitalization is \$6,853 million, or \$39 per share. We further conducted sensitivity analysis on WACC (9.5%–10.5%), sales growth rate (5.5%–6.5%), and perpetual growth rate (1.5%–2.5%), resulting a range of \$36–\$43 per share of PCL.

Finalizing the valuation

Given WY's stock price of \$30 and a fixed exchange ratio of 1.6:1, the implied per share value of PCL is \$48. This is higher than the upper bound value estimated by both methods. However, synergies are not considered yet. When the \$100 million cost savings are added to the cash flows in both methods, \$48 per share falls into the upper range of values of our estimation.

In the investor meeting on September 19, 2017, WY confirmed that they achieved \$125 million cost synergies, or \$25 million more than the projected \$100 million. This means WY was able to operate more efficiently after the transaction. WY also showed that it had even more superior adjusted EBITDA per acre compared with Rayonier, Deltic Timber, and the NCREIF Timberland Index following the merger. Compared with the dividend of \$0.15 per share in 2011Q1,

	FCF_1	FCF_2	FCF_3	FCF_4	FCF_5
	570×1.06	570×1.06^2	570×1.06^3	570×1.06^4	570×1.06^5
	$=604.20$	$=640.45$	$=678.88$	$=719.61$	$=762.79$
					$TV=(762.79\times1.02)/(0.10-0.02)$
					$=10,107$
Year	1	2	3	4	5
	2016	2017	2018	2019	2020

FIGURE 14.2   Timeline and projected cash flows of PCL

the dividend of $0.31 per share in 2017Q3 was more than doubled. In addition, WY completed 80% of its proposed 2.5 billion share repurchase in 2017Q3. A share repurchase plan is often viewed as a value-enhancing strategy when the management believe its stocks are undervalued. It also reduces the share dilution. All in all, it can be concluded that the merger has added value to the new WY.

There might be some other advantages not disclosed publicly. For instance, it is demonstrated that the US forest products industry was less competitive after the recent waves of M&As (Mei and Sun 2008a). Given its absolutely dominant size in the timber REIT sector after the acquisition of PCL, WY is likely to process some oligopoly and oligopsony power after the merger. The market power might enable WY to make some super profits in certain timber regions or certain wood product markets.

Discussion and conclusions

Restructuring activities within the forest products industry have been unprec-edented in the past few decades. How to attach a dollar value to the target com-pany is an important yet challenging question. Using the WY & PCL merger, we demonstrate how to value a target using the comparable company analysis and DCF approach. A sound understanding of the valuation methods requires in-depth familiarity of the financial statements, the target industry, and quanti-tative software like MS Excel. Nonetheless, keep in mind that, for any forecast, assumptions are needed. The quality of the results from any model, no matter how sophisticated it is, is only as good as the quality of the assumptions themselves.

Questions

1. Describe the three methods in valuing a company?
2. What is the optimal capital structure and how is that related to determining WACC?

Notes

1 EBITDA for earnings before interest, taxes, depreciation, and amortization. FCF for free cash flow.
2 EV for enterprise value. EV = Equity + Debt + Preferred Stock + Noncontrolling Interest − Cash. Equity value is measured by market capitalization as year-end closing price times total shares outstanding. Debt is measured by the book value of long-term debt.
3 NOPAT = EBIT × (1 − T), where T is corporate tax rate.
4 In terms of M&As, no cash of the target company will be left on the table as cash is used to pay off existing debt or pay a special dividend.
5 For small-size companies, a size premium is often added to the CAPM.
6 This is known as fixed exchange ratio. Another way of stock exchange is via floating exchange ratio, where the number of shares needed to finance the transaction by the acquiring firm depends on both parties' share price at the time of closing.

7 At the University of Georgia, it is Terry College of Business that is in charge of managing the users.

8 We downloaded PCL's financial statements from SEC/EDGAR and calculated FCF accordingly. Some subjective judgements were used in this process.

9 D/E ratio is calculated as long-term debt over market capitalization.

Bibliography

Alexandridis, G., D. Petmezas, and N.G. Travlos. 2010. Gains from mergers and acquisitions around the world: New evidence. *Financ. Manag.* 39(4):1671–1695.

MacKinlay, A.C. 1997. Event studies in economics and finance. *J. Econ. Lit.* 35(1):13–39.

Mei, B., and C. Sun. 2008a. Assessing time-varying oligopoly and oligopsony power in the U.S. paper industry. *J. Agri. Appl. Econ.* 40(3):927–939.

Mei, B., and C. Sun. 2008b. Event analysis of the impact of mergers and acquisitions on the financial performance of the U.S. forest products industry. *For. Policy Econ.* 10(5):286–294.

Rosenbaum, J., and J. Pearl. 2020. *Investment banking: Valuation, LBOs, M&A, and IPOs,* 3rd ed. Wiley, Hoboken, NJ.

WRDS. 2020. *Wharton research data services.* The Wharton School at the University of Pennsylvania. Philadelphia, PA.

15

CONCLUDING REMARKS

Timberland investments in the United States have been unprecedentedly active since the 1980s, when timberland ownership started shifting from industrial firms to institutional investors (via TIMOs) and REITs. Not echoing this trend, the top 100 forest products companies in the world have increased timberland holdings between 2007 and 2012 in order to reduce risks associated with the flow of raw materials (Korhonen et al. 2016). An example is IKEA's recent acquisition of US timberlands as part of a broad strategy to invest in the sustainable production of resources that IKEA consumes. The increased vertical integration in the global forest products industry presents both opportunities and challenges for timberland investors in the United States. Forest products companies usually have different valuation models than TIMOs or REITs in that the inclusion of the insurance value of internal wood supply often adds a premium to timberland's intrinsic value. Therefore, this provides existing landowners an incentive to exit and secure a portion of the premium. For new investors, nonetheless, this trend of vertical integration implies a higher demand for timberland and eventually a higher acquisition cost, which dampens the expected future returns.

In addition to vertical integration, there has been a trend toward timberland investments for climate change mitigation purposes (e.g., carbon offsets) at the global level. In theory, this has similar implications to timberland investors as those from vertical integration; however, in practice, the impact differs substantially by region. In the United States, attitudes toward climate change mitigation are significantly influenced by the emergence of climate change legislation at the federal level (Thompson and Hansen 2012). In other words, most organizations are taking a passive approach toward climate change mitigation projects in the United States, and the development of this market will be an iterative process

DOI: 10.4324/9781003366737-15

that requires global collaborations given the integrated nature of climate change mitigation (Thompson and Hansen 2012). For timber production itself, returns and costs for major timber plantation species as well as other institutional, forestry, and policy factors that affect investments for a set of countries are compared and reported in Cubbage et al. (2010) and Cubbage et al. (2014).

Although timberland investments in the United States have attracted many research interests in recent years, many facets of timberland—a special type of real estate—have not been fully explored yet. An example is the linkage between lumber prices and TIMO returns. In the US South, lumber prices have been high in the past few years with the recovery of the housing market, whereas sawtimber prices have been stagnating due to the supply overhang. The implied higher profit margin of wood products manufacturing has triggered many greenfield as well as brownfield investments in this region. However, booming manufacturing has not led to higher returns of TIMOs. The exact causes need to be examined in future research, but we suspect that they might be related to wood supply agreements attached to TIMO properties that are in favor of wood users and the potential oligopsony in the wood products manufacturing sector (e.g., Mei and Sun 2008; Silva et al. 2019).

Finally, with the rapid progress in real estate finance in academia and timberland investments in practice, we envision a prolific period of research in timberland economics in the future. In addition to traditional forest economics journals, we expect more agricultural economics or real estate economics journals to be the outlets, especially for studies that compare timberland with other types of real estate. In terms of lines of subsequent research, I highlight the following points.

(1) *Financial performance of private- vs. public-equity timberland investments.* Although some past research has made an initial endeavor in the comparison (Mei and Clutter 2020; Scholtens and Spierdijk 2010; Sun and Zhang 2001), the compositions of those return indices will change along the restructuring wave in the timberland sector. Hence, the financial performance of TIMOs and REITs hereafter remains to be seen. Additionally, more advanced asset pricing models need to be applied to private-equity timberland as the standard capital asset pricing model has a relatively low explanatory power on it, resulting in a potential overestimation of the abnormal return.

(2) *Forest sustainability and conservation.* Given a relative short time period of institutional timberland ownership, the impact of timberland shift on forest sustainability and conservation has not been adequately examined yet (Gunnoe and Gellert 2011). Zhang et al. (2012) and Sun et al. (2015) found that TIMOs and REITs manifested sustainability in terms of growth-to-removals and reforestation. Gutierrez Garzon et al. (2020) and Gutierrez Garzon et al. (2021) investigated the role of forest certification and management plan on sustainability via survey and content analysis. Similar methods can be applied to institutional timberland as more data become available.

(3) *Forest carbon.* Despite substantial carbon offsets from domestic forestry projects, few organizations in the United States managed forestland for carbon values (Thompson and Hansen 2012). Conservation easements on working forests can be a solution to regulating institutional timberland owners toward providing both timber and non-timber ecosystem services, including carbon from their forests in the long run (Reeves et al. 2020). More research is needed on the optimal design of such contracts. Meanwhile, utilizing wood pellets to replace fossil fuels in power generation deserves more attention (Dwivedi et al. 2019; Kline et al. 2021; Mei and Wetzstein 2017), and the economics of forest carbon offsets needs to be better understood (van Kooten and Johnston 2016).

(4) *Acquisition and disposition strategies of TIMOs and REITs.* Provided TIMOs and REITs have different cash needs, their investment timing on timberland tends to vary. As we see more transactions of cutover lands sold from REITs to TIMOs and mature stands sold back from TIMOs to REITs, a systematic analysis of the acquisition and disposition strategies of TIMOs and REITs is warranted. Accordingly, the contribution of the three drivers to the total timberland returns is likely to differ between TIMOs and REITs (Mei et al. 2013), and a detailed comparison of cash and appreciation returns between the two parties will also be meaningful.

(5) *Agency problem in timberland business.* As with any other businesses, there is a conflict of interest between timberland owners and managers. Management fees and transaction costs can be prohibitive to timberland investors with recent lackluster stumpage prices and timberland returns (Hiegel et al. 2020). Will direct ownership or special partnerships between REITs and investors, both of which have been booming recently, at least bypass part of the agency problem? If yes, to what extent? There are more questions to be asked than answered.

Bibliography

Cubbage, F., S. Koesbandana, P. Mac Donagh, R. Rubilar, G. Balmelli, V.M. Olmos, R. De La Torre, M. Murara, V.A. Hoeflich, H. Kotze, R. Gonzalez, O. Carrero, G. Frey, T. Adams, J. Turner, R. Lord, J. Huang, C. MacIntyre, K. McGinley, R. Abt, and R. Phillips. 2010. Global timber investments, wood costs, regulation, and risk. *Biomass Bioenergy* 34(12):1667–1678.

Cubbage, F., P. Mac Donagh, G. Balmelli, V.M. Olmos, A. Bussoni, R. Rubilar, R. De La Torre, R. Lord, J. Huang, V.A. Hoeflich, M. Murara, B. Kanieski, P. Hall, R. Yao, P. Adams, H. Kotze, E. Monges, C.H. Perez, J. Wikle, R. Abt, R. Gonzalez, and O. Carrero. 2014. Global timber investments and trends, 2005–2011. *N. Z. J. Forest. Sci.* 44:12.

Dwivedi, P., M. Khanna, and M. Fuller. 2019. Is wood pellet-based electricity less carbon-intensive than coal-based electricity? It depends on perspectives, baselines, feedstocks, and forest management practices. *Environ. Res. Lett* 14(2):024006.

Gunnoe, A., and P.K. Gellert. 2011. Financialization, shareholder value, and the transformation of timberland ownership in the US. *Crit. Sociol.* 37(3):265–284.

Gutierrez Garzon, A.R., P. Bettinger, J. Abrams, J.P. Siry, and B. Mei. 2021. Forest sustainability in state forest management plans: A content analysis. *J. Sustain. For.* 41(1):92-113.

Gutierrez Garzon, A.R., P. Bettinger, J. Siry, B. Mei, and J. Abrams. 2020. The terms foresters and planners in the United States use to infer sustainability in forest management plans: A survey analysis. *Sustainability* 12(1):17.

Hiegel, A., J. Siry, P. Bettinger, and B. Mei. 2020. Timberland transaction costs and due diligence: A literature review and assessment of research needs. *Int. For. Rev.* 22(2):199–210.

Kline, K.L., V.H. Dale, E. Rose, and B. Tonn. 2021. Effects of production of woody pellets in the southeastern United States on the sustainable development goals. *Sustainability* 13(2):821.

Korhonen, J., Y. Zhang, and A. Toppinen. 2016. Examining timberland ownership and control strategies in the global forest sector. *For. Policy Econ.* 70:39–46.

Mei, B., and M.L. Clutter. 2020. Return and information transmission of public and private timberland markets in the United States. *For. Policy Econ.* 113:102092.

Mei, B., M.L. Clutter, and T.G. Harris. 2013. Timberland return drivers and timberland returns and risks: A simulation approach. *South. J. Appl. For.* 37(1):18–25.

Mei, B., and C. Sun. 2008. Assessing time-varying oligopoly and oligopsony power in the U.S. paper industry. *J. Agri. Appl. Econ.* 40(3):927–939.

Mei, B., and M. Wetzstein. 2017. Burning wood pellets for US electricity generation? A regime switching analysis. *Energy Econ.* 65:434–441.

Reeves, T., B. Mei, J. Siry, P. Bettinger, and S. Ferreira. 2020. Towards a characterization of working forest conservation easements in Georgia, USA. *Forests* 11(6):635.

Scholtens, B., and L. Spierdijk. 2010. Does money grow on trees? The diversification properties of U.S. timberland investments. *Land Econ.* 86(3):514–529.

Silva, B.K., F.W. Cubbage, R. Gonzalez, and R.C. Abt. 2019. Assessing market power in the U.S. pulp and paper industry. *For. Policy Econ.* 102:138–150.

Sun, C., and D. Zhang. 2001. Assessing the financial performance of forestry-related investment vehicles: Capital asset pricing model vs arbitrage pricing theory. *Am. J. Agri. Econ.* 83(3):617–628.

Sun, X., D. Zhang, and B.J. Butler. 2015. Timberland ownerships and reforestation in the southern United States. *For. Sci.* 61(2):336–343.

Thompson, D.W., and E.N. Hansen. 2012. Institutional pressures and an evolving forest carbon market. *Bus. Strateg. Environ.* 21(6):351–369.

van Kooten, G.C., and C.M.T. Johnston. 2016. The economics of forest carbon offsets. *Annual Rev. Resour. Econ.* 8(1):227–246.

Zhang, D., B.J. Butler, and R.V. Nagubadi. 2012. Institutional timberland ownership in the US South: Magnitude, location, dynamics, and management. *J. For.* 110(7):355–361.

INDEX

Printed in the United States
by Baker & Taylor Publisher Services